PROGRAMMING LANGUAGES—
"DESIGN AND CONSTRUCTS"

PROGRAMMING LANGUAGES—"DESIGN AND CONSTRUCTS"

[For B.E./B.Tech. (Computer Science/Information Technology), B.C.A., M.C.A., M.Sc. (Computer Science)]

By

SHARAD CHAUHAN

Assistant Professor and H.O.D.
E-Max Institute of Engg. and Technology,
Vill-Badholi, Ambala (Haryana)

UNIVERSITY SCIENCE PRESS

(An Imprint of Laxmi Publications Pvt. Ltd.)

BANGALORE • CHENNAI • COCHIN • GUWAHATI • HYDERABAD
JALANDHAR • KOLKATA • LUCKNOW • MUMBAI • RANCHI
NEW DELHI • BOSTON, USA

Published by :
UNIVERSITY SCIENCE PRESS
(An Imprint of Laxmi Publications Pvt. Ltd.)
113, Golden House, Daryaganj,
New Delhi-110002

Phone : 011-43 53 25 00
Fax : 011-43 53 25 28

www.laxmipublications.com
info@laxmipublications.com

First Edition : 2013

OFFICES

✆ **Bangalore**	080-26 75 69 30	✆ **Chennai**	044-24 34 47 26
✆ **Cochin**	0484-237 70 04, 405 13 03	✆ **Guwahati**	0361-251 36 69, 251 38 81
✆ **Hyderabad**	040-24 65 23 33	✆ **Jalandhar**	0181-222 12 72
✆ **Kolkata**	033-22 27 43 84	✆ **Lucknow**	0522-220 99 16
✆ **Mumbai**	022-24 91 54 15, 24 92 78 69	✆ **Ranchi**	0651-220 44 64

UPL–9667–225–PROG LANG DESIGN CONST–CHA

Typeset at : ABRO Enterprises, Delhi.

C—

Printed at : Repro Knowledgecast Limited, Thane

CONTENTS

PREFACE

It gives me immense pleasure in presenting the first edition of the book **Programming Languages—"Design and Constructs"** to the esteemed readers. The necessity for programming languages in Computer Science curriculum arises because of its key paradigms used in developing modern programming languages. The book covers all the topics related to subject 'Programming Languages' taught in all Engineering Institutions. It also covers all the problems appeared in university examinations in past few years.

This book contains ten chapters. These chapters contain the reasonable amount of exercises, examples with solutions. Since examples are part of the text; they are clearly explained without leaving any ambiguity in the reader's mind. The contents of the book include introduction to programming languages, elementary and structured data objects, syntax and semantics, sequence control, concurrency control, data control, subprogram sequence control, storage management related issues and overview of different programming languages like imperative, procedural, non-procedural, functional and logical programming languages.

The objective of this book is to present the subject and concepts in a clear and more interesting manner. My intention is to cover all topics in the book related to subject. The book is based on the experience gained in teaching a course on the subject. I am sure that this book will help a student to understand each topic without any difficulty. I would welcome the indulgence of my readers in intimating me about any error or shortcoming noticed by them in the book. The valuable suggestions from the readers are invited for further improvement of the book.

—Author

ACKNOWLEDGEMENT

It is difficult to acknowledge adequately the help and encouragement I have received during completion and publication of this work. First, I must express my gratitute to Sh. Om Prakash Aggarwal, Chairman, E-Max group of Institutes, Sh. P.R. Bansal, Vice Chairman, E-Max group of Institutes and all the Directors of E-Max group of Institutes, Badholi, Ambala, for their confidence building encouragement and kind suggestions in writing this book. I should also express my grateful thanks to my colleagues and friends with whom I had occasions to discuss the details of this book.

I owe my idebtedness to my family for their perpetual love and concern, great support, encouragement and prayers while I was writing this book. The main source of inspiration behind this book are my parents, my wife and my little daughter 'PARI'. I express my appreciation to them for their assistance and constant encouragement without which the venture would have failed.

In the end I would like to thank Laxmi Publications who encouraged me for development of such a project in a most desired way.

—Author

Chapter 1 INTRODUCTION

In the early 1950s, symbolic notations started to appear. Grace Hopper led a group at Univac to develop the A-0 language, and John Backus developed speedcoding for the IBM 701. Both were designed to compile simple arithmetic expressions into executable machine language. The real break through occurred in 1957 due to arrival of FORTRAN in 1957. FORTRAN data were oriented around numerical calculations.

The formula $b^2 - 4ac$ was written in FORTRAN as the expression

B ** 2 – 4.0 * A * C.

FORTRAN takes its name from Formula Translation; readable formulas were translated into machine instructions for the IBM 704. FORTRAN was extremely successful and was the dominant language through the 1970s. Because of the suceess of FORTRAN, hundreds of programming languages have since been designed and implemented.

Under the leadership of Peter Naur, the committee developed the International Algorithmic Language (IAL). Although ALGorithmic Language (ALGOL) was proposed. A revision occurred in 1960, and ALGOL 60 comes. In 1963, IBM developed NPL (New Programming Language) at its Hursley Laboratory in England. After some complaints by the English National Physical Laboratory, the name was changed to MPPL (Multi-Purpose Programming Language) which was then shortened to just PL/I. In 1960, COBOL (Common Business Oriented Language) will be designed.

1.1. CONCEPT OF PROGRAMMING LANGUAGES

Prorgramming Languages are notations or symbols. They are used for specifying, organizing and reasoning about computations. The designers of Programming Languages have two goals :

- Making computing convenient for people.
- Making efficient use of computing machines.

The first goal takes the priority, without convenience, efficiency is irrelevant.

A Programming Language have following definitions:

1. It is a tool for instructing machines.
2. It is a tool for controlling computerized devices.
3. A notation for algorithms.
4. A way of expressing relationships between concepts.
5. A tool for high level designs.

The study of programming languages is valuable for a number of important reasons. It increase our capacity to use different constructs in writing programs, enables us to choose languages for projects more intelligently and makes learning new languages easier.

1.2. WHY WE STUDY PROGRAMMING LANGUAGES

It is natural for students to wonder how they will benefit from the study of Programming Language concepts. The following is what we believe to be a compelling list of potential benefits of studying language concepts.

1. Improved Background for Choosing Appropriate Languages

A knowledge of a variety of languages may allow the choice of just the right language for a particular project. Because many programmers have had little formal education in computer science, they have learned programming on their own or through in house training programs. Such programs often teach one or two languages. When given a choice of language for a new project, continue to use the language with which they are most familiar, even if it is poorly suited to the new project. If they know the basic seat uses of each language then the programmer have broader choice of alternatives.

2. Increased Ability to Learn New Language

Through a deep understanding of the underlying structure of natural languages, often can learn a new foreign language more quickly and easily than struggling novices. The process of learning a new Programming Lanugage can be lengthy and difficult, especially for someone who is comfortable with only one or two languages. Once a thorough understanding of the fundamental concepts of languages is acquired, it becomes for easier to see how these concepts are incorporated into design of the language being learned.

3. Easy to Design a New Language

It is difficult for a programmer who have little knowledge of concepts of language to design a new programming language. However, most professional programmers occasionally do design languages. For example, most software systems require the user to interact in some way, even if only to enter data and commands. Many new languages are based on C or Pascal as implementation models. This aspect of program design is often simplified if the programmes is familiar with a variety of constructs and implementation method from ordinary programming languages.

4. Better Understanding of the Significance of Implementation

By learning the concepts of programming languages, it is both interesting and necessary to touch on the implementation issues that affect those concepts. By understanding of implementation issues leads to an understanding of why languages are designed the way they are. Many kinds of programs bugs can only be found and fixed by a programmer who knows some related implementation details.

5. To Improve your Ability to Develop Effective Algorithms

By studying programming languages, it will improve ability to develop effective algorithms. Many languages provide features, that when used properly, are of benefit to the programmer but, when used improperly, may waste large amount of computer time. For example, recussion—a handy programming feature that, when properly used, allow the direct implementation of elegant and efficient algorithms. When used improperly, it may cause an astronomical increase in execution time. New technology, such as the Internet and worldwide web, change the nature of programming. How best to develop techniques applicable in these new environments depends on an understanding of languages.

6. Overall Advancement of Computing

Finally, there is a global view of computing that can justify the study of Programming Language Concepts. Although, it is usually possible to determine why a particular programming language become popular, it is not always clear, at least in retrospect that the most popular langauges are the best available.

For example, many people believe it would have been better if AlGOL 60 had displaced FORTRAN in the early 1960, because it was more elegant and had much better control statements that FORTRAN, among other reasons.

In general, if those who choose languages are better informed, perhaps better languages would more quickly squeeze out poorer ones.

1.3. A BRIEF HISTORY OF PROGRAMMING LANGUAGES

Programming languages designs and implementation methods have evolved continuously since the earliest high level languages appeared in the 1950s. Of the 12 languages described in some detail, the first version of FORTRAN and LISP were designed during the 1950s; Ada, C, Pascal, Prolog, and smalltalk data from the 1970s; C++, ML, Perl and Postscript data from the 1980s; and Java dates from the 1990s. In the 1960s and 1970s, new languages were often developed as part of major software development projects.

We briefly summarise language development during the early days of computing, generally from the mid-1950s to the early 1970s.

FORTRAN OVERVIEW

In 1957, Backus managed a team to develop FORTRAN or FORMULA TRANSLATOR. FORTRAN data were oriented around numerical calculations, but the goal was a full-fledged programming language including control structures, conditionals and input and output statements.

FORTRAN was extremely successful and was the dominant language through the 1970s. FORTRAN was revised as FORTRAN II in 1958 and FORTRAN IV a few years later. Finally, in 1966, FORTRAN IV becomes a standard under the name FORTRAN 66 and has been upgraded twice since, to FORTRAN 77 and FORTRAN 90.

The environment in which FORTRAN was developed was as follows:

1. Computers were still small, slow and relatively unreliable.
2. The primary use of computers was for scientific computations.
3. Because of the high cost of computers compared to the cost of programmers, speed of the general object code was the primary goal of the first FORTRAN compilers.
4. There are no existing efficient ways to program computers.

ALGOL 60

ALGOL 60 has a great influence on subsequent programming language. ALGOL had very different goals:

- ALGOL notation should be close to standard mathematics.
- ALGOL should be useful for the description of algorithms.
- Programs in ALGOL should be compilable into machine language.
- ALGOL should not be bound to a single computer architecture.

The most important new developments are:

1. The concept of block structure was introduced. This allowed the programmer to localize parts of programs by introducing new data environments, or scopes.
2. Procedures were allowed to be recursive. Note that although this recursion is new for the imperative languages, LISP had already provided recursive functions in 1959.
3. Two different means of passing parameters to subprograms were allowed : Pass by value and pass by name.
4. Stack-dynamic arrays were allowed. A stack-dynamic array is one for which the subscript range or ranges are specified by variables, so that the size of the array is set at the time storage in allocated to the array, which happens when the declaration is reached during execution.

   One of the most important contribution to computer science that is associated with ALGOL 60, BNF, was also a factor in its lack of acceptace.

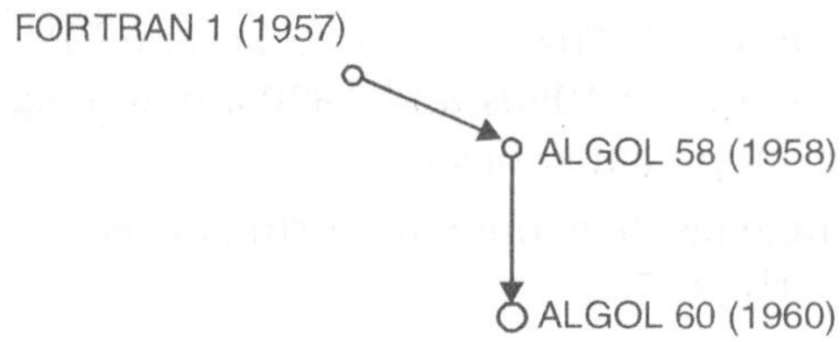

Fig. 1.1 Geneology of ALGOL 60.

PL/I

PL/I represents the first large scale attempt to design a language that could be used for a broad spectrum of application areas. PL/I merged the numerical attributes of FORTRAN with the business programming feature of COBOL. PL/I was the first programming language to have the following facilities:

1. Programs were allowed to create concurrently executing tasks. Although this was a good idea, it was poorly developed in PL/I.
2. Pointers were included as a data type.
3. It was possible to detect and handle 23 different types of exceptions, or runtime errors.
4. Procedures were allowed to be used recursively, but the capability could be disabled, allowing more efficient code for non-recursive procedures.
5. Cross-sections of array could be referenced. For example, the third row of a matrix could be referenced as if it was a vector.

COBOL

In 1959, the U.S. department of Defense sponsored a meeting to develop common business language, which would be business-oriented language that used English as much as possible for its notation. The specifications, published in 1960, were the design for COBOL.

The COBOL language originated a number of novel concepts, some of which eventually appeared in other languages. For example, the DEFINE verb of COBOL 60 was the first high level language construct for macros. Overall, the data division is the strong part of COBOL is design, whereas the procedure division is relatively weak. Every variable is defined in detail in the data division, including the no. of decimal digits and location of the implied decimal point. The poor performance of the early compilers simply made it for too expensive to use. Eventually, of course, people learned more about designing compilers, and computers became much faster. Together, these factors have made COBOL a great success, inside and outside DOD (Department of Defence).

Functional Programming (LISP)

The major break through occurred when John McCarthy of MIT designed List Processing (LISP) for the IBM 704. LISP was designed as a list processing functional language.

Pure LISP has only two kinds of data structures atoms and list. Atoms are either symbols, which have the form of identifiers, or numeric literals. The concepts of storing symbolic information in linked list is natural.

Lists are specified by delimiting their elements with parentheses. Simple lists, in which elements are restricted to atoms, have the form of the example,

(ABCD)

LISP totally dominated AI applications for a quarter of a centuary. It is still the most widely used language for AI. In addition to its success in AI, LISP pioneered functional programming, which has proven to be a lively area of research in programming languages.

Prolog

Prolog is logical programming language. It uses the logical notations to communicate computational processes to a computer. In 1970s, Alain Colmeraner and Philliee Roussel in the AI group at the university of Aix-Marseille, developed the fundamental design of Prolog. Prolog programs consists of collection of statements. Prolog has only a few kind of statement but they can be complex. One common use of Prolog is as a kind of intelligent database.

There is a relatively small group of computer scientists who believe that logic programming provides the best hope for escape from the imperative languages.

Smalltalk

It is object oriented programming language includes data abstraction as one of its three fundamental characteristics, the other two being inheritance and dynamic binding. The concept that led to the development of smalltalk originated in the Ph.D. dissertation work of Alan Kay in the late 1960s at the university of Utah.

Smalltalk has done a great deal to promote two separate aspects of computing. The windowing systems that are new the dominant method of user interfaces to software systems grew out of smalltalk. Today, the most significant software design methodolgies and programming languages are object oriented.

Java

Java like many programming languages, was designed for application for which there appeared to be no satisfactory existing language. The Java design team was headed by James Gosling, who had previously designed the Unix Emacs editor and News Windowing System.

Java is based on C++ but was specifically designed to be smaller, simpler and more reliable. Java has both type and classes. Unlike C and C++, Java includes type coercions (implicit type conversions).

1.4. LANGUAGE PARADIGMS

A paradigm can be thought of as a collection of abstract features that categorize a group of languages which are accepted and used by a group of professionals.

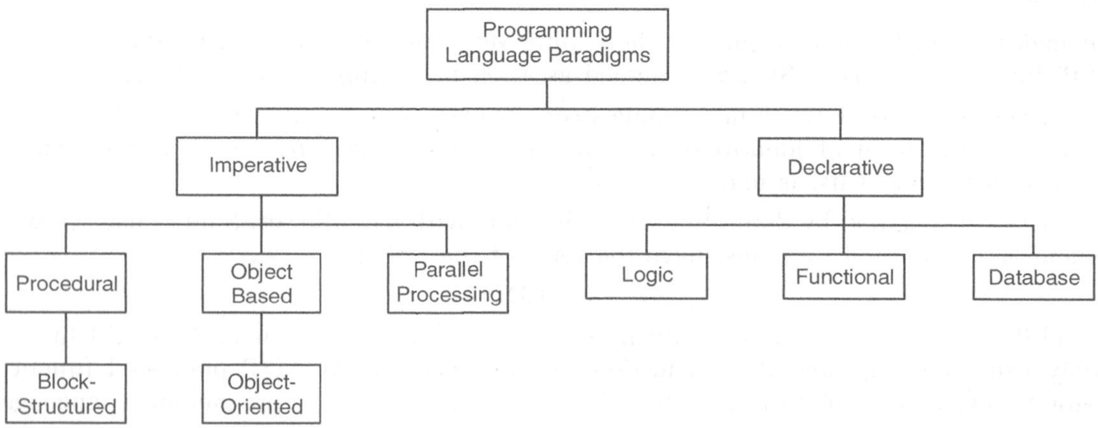

Fig. 1.2 A hierarchy of Programming Language Paradigms.

There are often minor syntactic variations that simply reflect the wishes of one language designers, which have little concrete effect upon the programs written in those languages. We need to look deeper to understand how languages are constructed.

1. Imperative Languages

Imperative or procedural languages are command-driven or statement-oriented languages that is, a computation is viewed as a sequence of actions. FORTRAN, C, Pascal are general purpose imperative languges. A program consists of a sequence of statements, the execution of each statement causes the computer to change the value of one or more locations in its memory, that is, to enter a new state. The syntax of such languages generally has the form

$$\text{Statement}_1;$$
$$\text{Statement}_2;$$
....

FORTRAN was convenient enough and efficient enough that it quickly became the language of choice for scientific programming.

Pascal was designed as a teaching language. Although there were some syntactic differences, Algol 60 remained enough of a subset that wirth [1971] hoped "conversion of ALGOL 60 programs to pascal can be considered as a negligible effort of transcription".

C was created in 1972 by Dennis Ritchie as an implementation language for software associated with the unix operating system. 'C provides a rich set of operators, a proper syntax, and efficient access to the machine. It is a general purpose programming language that is available on a wide range of machines.

2. Block-structured Language

FORTRAN, the first language with programs blocks, partitions the state into blocks representing subroutines and common data. FORTRAN blocks can be thought of as a flat-file, where each block follows its predecessors. Because of this flat structure, FORTRAN is no longer considered to be a block structured language.

The term block structure, now refers to nested scopes. That is blocks may be nested within other blocks, and may contain their own variables. In block structured languages, the procedure is the principal building block of programs.

3. Object-based Languages

The object based languages are those that supports classes of objects and inheritance of attributes of a parent object by its children. An object is a group of procedures that share a state. Since data is also part of a state, data and all the procedures or functions that apply to it can be captured in a single object. Examples are Ada, where objects are called packages; smalltalk, where objects are called (Rightfully) objects. In C++, a collection of objects is grouped into a class. C++ was designed to bring the benefits of objects to imperative programming in C. C++ retains the efficiency of C.

4. Parallel Processing

Concurrent programming has been divided into two broad categories, loosely or tightly coupled systems. The term distributed usually refers to languages for loosely coupled systems that support a group of programmers working on a particular program simultaneously and they communicating through message passing over a communication channels. In a loosely coupled distributed system, a language need not support simultaneous memory sharing.

A tightly coupled system allows more than one running process to access the same memory location. A language associated with the system must synchronize the sharing of memory so that only one process writes to a shared variable at a time, and so that a process can wait until certain conditions are fulfilled before continuing to executes.

Concurrent programming is associated with more than one CPU operating simultaneously in parallel, with or without data sharing. Multiple CPUs are not essential for this paradigm. Recently, work has been done on languages that give the distinction between the loosely and tightly coupled paradigms.

5. Declarative Languages

A declarative language is one in which a program specifies a relation or function. When programming in the declarative style, we make no assignments to program variables. The interpreter or compiler for the particular language manages memory for us. These languages are "higher level" than imperative languages, in that programmer operates more remotely from the CPU itself.

The three declarative paradigms are taken from mathematics : Logic, the theory of functions, and the relational calculus.

- **Logic programming.** Logic programming is based on a subset of the predicate calculus, including statements written in forms known as Horn Clauses. The predicate calculus provides axioms and rules so one can deduce new facts from other known facts. A Horn Clause allows only one new fact to be deduced in any single statements. PROLOG is the exemplar for logic programming languages. Prolog uses a specialized form of logical reasoning for queries. Prolog programs have the brevity and expressiveness of logic.
- **Functional programming.** Purely functional languages operate only through functions. A function returns a single value, given a list of parameters. No global assignments, called side effects, are permitted. Functions themselves are first class values which can be passed to other functions and returned as functional values. Thus functional programming provides the ability for a program to modify itself.

  The basic concept of functional languages originated with LISP, a language designed in 1958 for applications in artificial intelligence. The LISP language is designed Primarily for symbolic data processing. It has been used for symbolic calculations in differential and integral calculus, electrical circuit theory, mathematical logic and other fields of artificial intelligence.
- **The database languages.** The properties that distinguish languages to deal with databases are persistence and the management of change. Database entities do not disappear after a program terminates, but live on indefinitely as originally structured. The data may change and so too may the relationship between data entities or objects.

  A database management system includes a Data Definition Language (DDL) for describing a new collection of facts or data, and a Data Manipulation Language (DML) for interacting with existing databases. Database languages can be embedded in other programming languages for greater flexibility.

1.5. CHARACTERISTICS OF A GOOD PROGRAMMING LANGUAGE

Every programming language have many characteristics that make it successful in comparison with may other languages. Several programming languages have been designed, implemented for several years. Every language have some characteristics that make it better for another programming language. There are various language evaluation criteria and the characteristics to judge a particular language. Some of the characteristics that influence the most important of these criteria are discussed in the following sections.

1. Easy to Read

The most important consideration for judging a language is the ease with which program can be read and understood. A syntax that is particularly cryptic often make a program easy to write but difficult to read when the program must be modified later. Readability must be considered in the context of the program domain. A language should have the property in which constructs that mean different things look different that is semantic meaning should be clear in language syntax.

2. Simplicity of the Language

Simplicity of a language affects the readability of language. readability problems occur whenever, the program's author has learned a different subset from that subset with which the reader is familiar. The form and meaning of most assembly language. statements are models of simplicity. If the language is simple means it is syntatically easy to write a program then it is easy to understand the program to any one. The language should provide a clear and simple set of concepts that can be used to develop algorithms.

3. Orthogonality of the Language

The term orthogonality refers to the reatively small set of attributes or constructs that can be combined with a relatively small number of ways to build the control and data structures of the language and all the combinations should be meaningful. If they are not meaningful then there is no use to design constructs. When the language is orthogonal then it is easy to write programs with fewer exceptions. Orthogonality is closely related to simplicity. By orthogonality we can reduce the exception and by reducing the exception a higher degree of regularity in the design will be meet.

A lack of orthogonality in a high-level language can reduce the simplicity. For example, in C we have two structured data types, arrays and structures (struct), struct can be returned from functions but arrays can not. Too much orthogonality can also create problems.

So we believe that functional languages offer a good combination of simplicity and orthogonality.

4. Syntactic Consideration

A language needs a syntax that, when properly used allows the program structure to effective for the algorithms. The syntax of a language has effect the readability of language. If a program is syntatically correct them it is easy to understand the meaning of the program. The language provide a appropriate data structure, operations on that data structure and a natural syntax for the problem to be solved. Semantics, or meaning, should follow directly from syntax, or form.

5. Reliability of the Language

A program is reliable if its specification part is according to the conditions. There are many techniques for verifying that a program is correct and performs according to the requirement. A program is verfied by formal verification method and informal verification method. Type checking is simply use to test type errors in a program either at compile time or at run time. These are knowns as compile time type checking and run time type checking. Failure of type check is due to countless program errors in a program. Exception handling is also used to handle run time exceptions. Simplicity of semantic and syntactic structure is a primary aspect that tends to simply program verification.

6. Support for Abstraction

Language should support the abstraction. Abstraction means defined the specification and operations in a way that allow many of the details to be ignored. In abstraction specification of data and operations on the data is separated from the implementation of the data and operations. The language should allow data structures, data types and operations to be defined and maintained as self-contained abstraction.

7. Cost

The ultimate total cost of a programming language is a function of many of its characteristics.

- **Cost of training programmers.** This is a function of the simplicity and orthogonality of the language and the experience of the programmer.
- **Cost of writing programs.** This is a function of the writability of the language, which depends on the purpose to the particular application. Both training and writing programs cost can be reduced by good programming environment.
- **Cost of compiling and executing programs.** This will depend upon the performance of compiler and the language design. A language that require many run-time checks has fast code execution optimization is the name given to the collection of methods that compilers may use to decrease the size and/or increase the execution speed of the code they produce.
- **Cost of the language implementation systems.** A language whose implementation system is either expensive or runs only on expensive hardware will have a much smaller chance of ever becoming widely used.
- **Cost of testing and maintainance.** This includes the cost to test whether a program is correct or free of errors. There are various testing tools available in the market to test the programs. The largest cost involved in any program is the cost of maintainance. It includes both corrections and modifications to add new capabilities. Adding new things and making changes in the existing system takes a high cost. In many years research shows that maintainance cost is higher than the cost of initial design, coding and testing of the programs.

1.6. PROGRAMMING ENVIRONMENT

A programming environment is the environment in which new programs are developed and tested. It is the collection of tools that are needed to create the programs and overall development of the software. The mainly used tools in a programming language are editors, verifiers, printers, debuggers. It also consists of integrated tools, which are accessed by a uniform user interface. Every programming language have a set of tools for software development.

Unix provide a portable time sharing operating system. It provides a wide array of powerful support tools for software production and maintenance in a variety of languages.

Borland C++ is a programming environment that runs on IBM-PC micro computer systems and compatible clones. It provides our integrated compiler, editor, debugger and file system, they all are accessed through a graphical interface.

Languages also consists of a support environment that consists of services called the environment framework to manage the development of program. This framework supplier services such as a data repository, graphical user interface, security and communication services.

Another concept related to environment is the concept of job control. If we want to execute a program, we move the mouse to the appropriate picture or icon on the screen and click the mouse. The appropriate program starts to execute. Before the window based system we would type the name of the program to run. This allow the user to be in direct control of determining what steps to perform. If the compilation fails, the user could involve an editor to modify the program and if the compilation succeeds, the user could involve a loader and execute the program.

It is clear that most software development will make use of powerful programming environment in future. This will increase the software productivity and quality of software.

Programming environments have become important part of software development system, in which the language is just one of the components.

1.7. PROGRAMMING LANGUAGE TRANSLATORS, COMPILERS AND INTERPRETER

Translator

A translator denotes any language processor that accepts programs in some source language (which may be high or low level) as input and produces functionally equivalent programs in another object language (which may also be high or low level) as output.

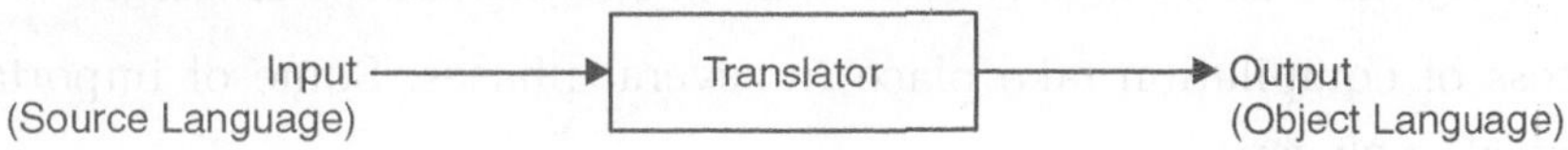

Fig. 1.3 Translation of Source into Object Language.

The translation of a source program into object program is said to occur at translation time. Once translation is complete, the target code is run at a later time, called run time.

Exampe 1.1. Suppose that a target language has instruction of the form

$$X = Y * Z.$$

This instruction multiply y and z and assign the result to X. In other words, the multiplication of y and z becomes the value of X.

The FORTRAN Expression

$$C = a + b$$

translates into a sequence of assembly instructions.

$$R_1 := a$$
$$R_2 := b$$
$$R_3 := R_1 + R_2$$
$$C := R_3$$

when run, these instructions assign C the value of the FORTRAN expression.

A Translator have following names:

(*a*) Assember
(*b*) Compiler
(*c*) Loader
(*d*) Macro
(*e*) Interpreter

(*a*) Assembler

An assembler is a translator whose object language is also, some variety of machine language but whose source language, is an assembly language. Assembly language consist of symbols. In assembly language most of the part is symbolic representation.

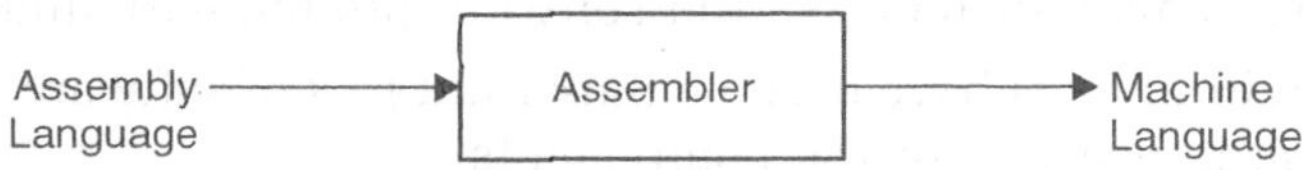

Fig. 1.4 Translation of Assembly Language into m/c Language.

(*b*) Compiler

A compiler is a translator whose source language is a high level language (Like C, C++ etc) and whose object language is close to the machine language of an actual computer.

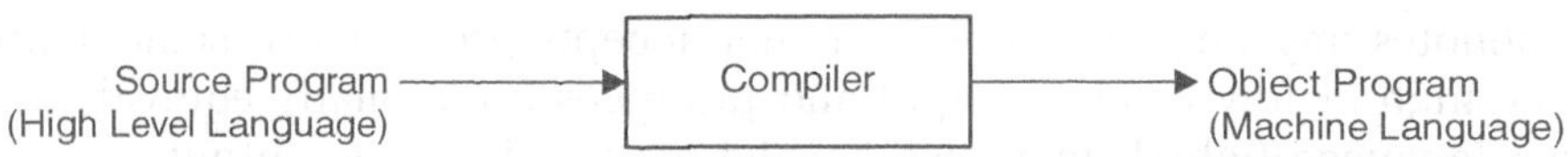

Fig. 1.5 Translation of High Level Language into Machine Language.

The process of compilation take place in several phases. Some of important are:

(*i*) Lexical analyzer
(*ii*) Syntax analyzer
(*iii*) Intermediate code generator
(*iv*) Optimization
(*v*) Symbol table
(*vi*) Code generator.

(c) Loader

A loader or link editor is a translator whose object language is actual machine code and whose source language is almost identical; it usually consists of machine language programs in relocatable form together with tables of data where the relocatable code must be modified to become truly executable.

(*d*) Macro or Preprocessor

A macro or preprocessor is a translator whose source language is an extended form of some high level language such as C++, Java and whose object language is the standard form of the same language. Most C compilers include such a preprocessor for first translating C macro references into standard C source statements.

(*e*) Interpreter

Another extreme of implementation methods, programs are interpreted by another program called an interpreter. An interpreter takes a program and its input at the same time. It scans the program, implementing operations as it encounters them and doing input/output as needed.

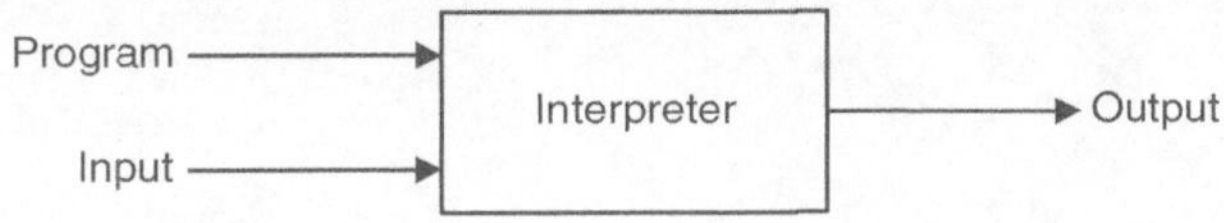

Fig. 1.6 An Interpreter Takes both a Program and its Input and Produces Output.

Interpreter evaluates an expression by examining its structure. Interpretation is a difficult process on programs written in a complicated language, because the meaning of each expression and statement must be determined directly from the source program at run time.

1.8. DIFFERENCE BETWEEN COMPILER AND INTERPRETER

The differences between compiler and interpreter are given below:

Compiler	*Interpreter*
1. It only translate the program.	1. It translates and execute the program.
2. They are faster as they translate the whole program at once.	2. They are slower as they have to translate whole program line by line.
3. Require more memory for execution.	3. Require less memory for execution.
4. It is more efficient.	4. It is less efficient than compiler.
5. It is less flexible.	5. It is more flexible than compiler.
6. Difficult to write compile program.	6. Easy to write.
7. C, C++ uses compiler.	7. Java uses interpreter.

Some Important Terms

- Programming languages are notations or symbols which are used for specifying, organizing and reasoning about computation.

- Main reasons to study programming languages are:
  - (a) To improve background for choosing appropriate language.
  - (b) To increase ability to learn new language.
  - (c) Easy to design a new language.
  - (d) Better understanding of the significance of implementation.
  - (e) To improve ability to develop new algorithms.
  - (f) Advancement of computing.
- Summary of langauge development during the early days of computing.
  - (a) FORTRAN OVERVIEW
  - (b) ALGOL 60
  - (c) PL/I
  - (d) COBOL
  - (e) LISP
  - (f) Prolog
  - (g) Smalltalk
  - (h) Java.
- A language paradigms can be thought of as a collection of abstract features that categorize a group of langauges.
- Imperative or procedural languages are command driven or statement-oriented languages.
- Block structured languages have programs blocks. These blocks representing subroutines and common data.
- Object based languages are those that supports classes of objects.
- A object is a group of procedures that share a state.
- Concurrent programming is associated with more than one CPU operating simultaneously in parallel.
- Loosely coupled system are those which do not share memory among them.
- Tightly coupled system are those which share memory among them.
- A declarative language is one in which a program specifies a relation or function.
- Data Definition Language (DDL) for describing a new collection of facts or data.
- Data Manipulation Language (DML) for interacting with existing data bases.
- Characteristics of a good programming languages:
  - (a) Easy to read
  - (b) Simplicity
  - (c) Orthogonality
  - (d) Syntactic consideration
  - (e) Reliability
  - (f) Support for abstraction
  - (g) Ease of program verification.

- A programming environment is the environment in which new programs are developed and tested.
- A translator denotes any language processor that accepts programs in some source language as input and produce functionally equivalent programs in another object language as output.
- An assembler is a translator whose object language is also some variety of machine language but whose source language is an assembly language.
- A compiler is a translator whose source language is a high level language and whose object language is close to the machine language.
- A loader or link editor is a translator whose object language is actual machine code and whose source language is almost identical to machine language.
- A macro or preprocessor is a translator whose source language is an extended form of some high level language and whose object language is a standard form of the same language.
- An interpreter takes a program and its input at the same time and produce the output.

Review Questions

1. Define the concept of Programming Languages.
2. What are the reasons for studying different kinds of programming languages?
3. Explain briefly the history of programming languages.
4. Define language paradigm. Explain the hierarchy of programming language paradigm.
5. What are the characteristics of good programming language?
6. Write short note on programming environment.
7. Define the term translator. What are different types of translators?
8. Write short notes on:
   (*a*) Imperative languages.
   (*b*) Block structured languages.
   (*c*) Object based languages.
   (*d*) Declarative languages.
   (*e*) Data base languages.
9. Explain logic programming and functional programming.
10. Differentiate between compiler and interpreter.

❑❑❑

Chapter 2 ELEMENTARY DATA TYPE

Elementary or Primitive data type includes integer, real, character, Boolean, enumeration and pointers. In this chapter, we introduce the concept of data type, data object and various characteristics of elementary data type. Then, we discuss the specification and implementation of elementary data objects. We also discuss the various terms related to data objects like scope of data objects, blocks, lifetime of objects etc. Then, we discuss binding of variables to values. This includes static and dynamic binding. We discuss the issue of type checking and type conversion. In the end, we will discuss the specification and implementation of various elementary data objects.

2.1. DATA OBJECT AND DATA VALUE

Data object is a runtime collection of one or more pieces of data in a digital computer. During execution many data objects of different types are created and after execution they are destroyed.

A data object is of two types:

(*a*) **System defined data objects.** These data objects are created automatically as needed during program execution and programmer have no interfere.

(*b*) **Programmer defined data object.** Programmer defined data objects are created by programmer. Programmer also manipulates through statements in the program. Programmer defined data objects are constants, arrays, variables etc.

Data object have many attributes. One of them is data type. The attributes determine the number and type of values that the data object may have and organization of the values. A data value might be a single number, character or a pointer to another data object. A data vlaue is generally represents in the form of bits in the virtual computer storage. A data object is generally represented as a storage in the computer memory. Data object is a place where the data value is stored. Data value is represented by a pattern of bits.

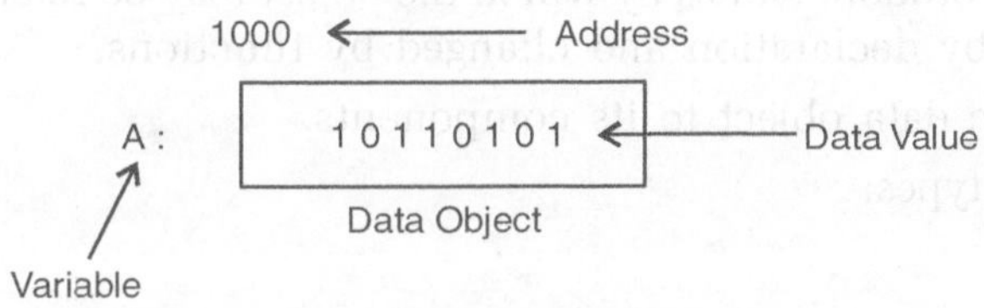

Fig. 2.1. Simple Representation of Data Object, Data Value and Address where the Data Value is Stored.

2.2. THE ROLE OF DATA TYPE

Data type of a variable determines the range of values the variable can have and the set of operations that are defined for values of the type.

For example: The type INTEGER have a value range of –32768 to 32767 and arithmetic operations for addition, subtraction, division, multiplication, along with some library functions for operations. Every programming language deals with some commonly known data types like class of arrays, integers or files and operations for manipulating them.

- **Specification of a data type includes:**

  (*a*) The basic attributes that distinguish one data object to another.

  (*b*) The value that the data object of that type contains.

  (*c*) The operations that performs on data objects of that type.

- **Implementation of a data type includes:**

  (*a*) The memory representation of the data objects of the data type in the storage during execution.

  (*b*) Algorithms are designed to perform operations on the data objects. By using algorithms or procedure we can implement the data objects.

2.3. BINDING

Binding refers to the linking between an attribute and an entity or between an Operation and Symbols. A data object participates in various binding during its life time. The attributes of a data object is invariant but the binding may change. The time at which binding takes place is known as binding time. The various type of bindings are of the forms:

(1) Binding between data object and a set of values that data object may take.

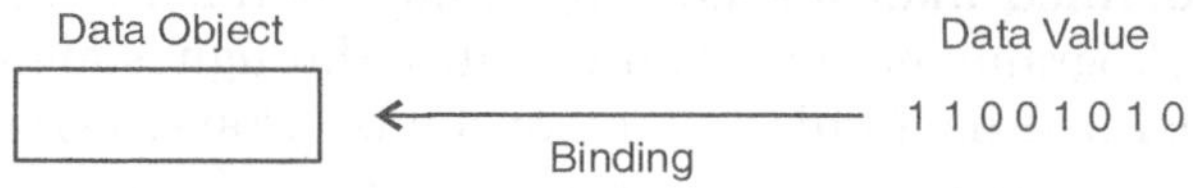

Fig. 2.2. Binding of Data Object and Data Value.

(2) Binding between Storage location in memory and the data object.

(3) Binding resulting from an assignment operation.

$$X = X + 10;$$

(4) Binding to one or more names by which the object may be referenced during execution. This is setup by declaration and changed by functions.

(5) Binding of one data object to its components.

Binding is of two types:

2.3.1. Static Binding

Static binding is done at compile time. Variables are declared of two types an explicit declaration in program that specifies the variable name and its types and an implicit declaration in which variables are declared through default conventions. Both declaration creates static binding. Static binding is fixed during the execution of program. The value of Data object declared is fixed during Static binding. All errors, such as type mismatch, declaration syntax errors are comes out during compile time. Static binding includes declaration of values to the variables, passing actual values to formal values etc.

2.3.2. Dynamic Binding

In dynamic binding the binding is done at runtime. Dynamic binding is not fixed during program execution. In dynamic binding, the type is not specified by a declaration statement. The type is assigned value by a assignment statement and when the assignment statement executes then the binding take place. The type of the value, variable or expression is bounded during execution.

For example: In C++ an expression of the form new char [size] can be evaluated at any time. It uses the current value of size at runtime and allocate an array of size elements, with lower bound O and upper bound size–I.

Example 2.1:

```
int temp;
..................
temp = temp + 1;
```

In this assignment statement some of binding are:

1. **Set of possible type for temp.** Variable temp. has a data type associated with it, such as real, integer or Boolean. The Set of allowable types for temp is often bound at language design time.
2. **Type of temp.** The particular data type associated with variable temp is often bound at compile time through an explicit declaration in the program.
3. **Set of possible values for variable temp.** If temp has data type integer, then its value at any point during execution is one of a set of bit sequences representing real numbers. This values are bound at compiler design time.
4. **Value of variable temp.** A particular value is bound to variable temp. This value is determined at execution time through assignment of a value to temp. The assignment temp = temp + 1 changes the binding of temp, replacing its old value by a new value that is more than one.
5. **Internal representation of the Literal 1.** The interger 1 has a representation as a constant and a representation at execution time, commonly as a sequence of bits. The choice of particular sequence of bits to represent 1 at execution time is usually made at language implementation time.
6. **Meaning of the operator symbol '+'.** The choice of symbol '+' to represent the addition operation is made at language definition time. The symbol '+' is representing real addition, integer addition, complex addition depending on the text. The decision whether '+' represent one of these forms may be taken at compile time.

2.4. SCOPE AND LIFETIME OF A VARIABLE

The lifetime of a variable is the time during which the variable is bound to a specific memory location. So the lifetime of a variable starts when it is bound to a specific value and ends when it is free or unbound to that value.

The important term that effect on the understanding of a variable is scope. The scope of a program variable is the range of statements in which the variable is visible *i.e.,* in how many statement the variable is visible.

The scope rule of a variable determines how references to variables declared outside the subprograms or block that are associated with their declaration. The scope rule determine how a particular occurrence of a name is associated with the variable.

The scope and lifetime of a variable are closely related to each other. Consider the example that a variable is declared in a Pascal procedure. The scope of variable starts from the declaration of variable to the end reserved word of procedure. The lifetime starts when procedure begins and ending when the procedure reaches to the end. The scope and lifetime are closely related but scope is textual concept whereas lifetime is a temporal concept.

Example 2.2: Consider the example in C functions:

```
void display( )
{
    // Statement part
}
```

```
void calculate( )
{
    int temp;
    ...........
    display ( );
}
```

The scope of variable temp is completely within the function calculate. It does not go to the body of the function display. But lifetime of temp extends over the time during which display executes.

2.5 BLOCKS

A block consists of a set of declarations for names such as variable declaration, constant definition and type definitions, followed by a set of statements in which those names may be referenced. Storage allocates to variables, constants and statement part when we enter in the block and deallocates when we exit from the block. Block definitions varies from language to language.

In pascal the representation of block is shown below:

Program Main;
- Local declaration for main

Procedure P_1;
- Local declaration for P_1

begin
- Statements for P_1

end {P_1};

end {Main}

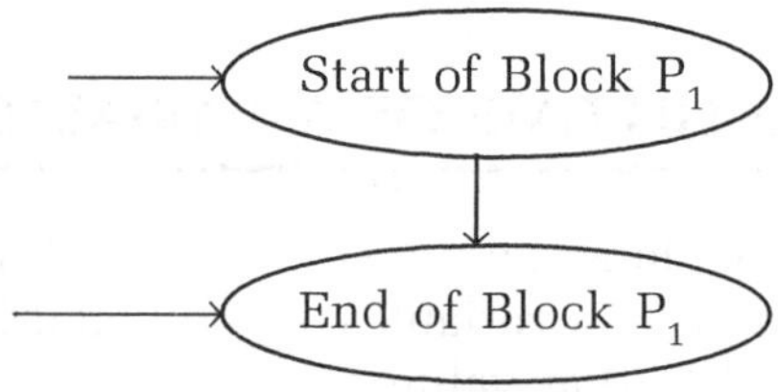

Example 2.3: Representation of Block in Pascal

In C blocks are created like

```
If (A < B)
{
    ...........
    Statement Part;
    ...........
}
```

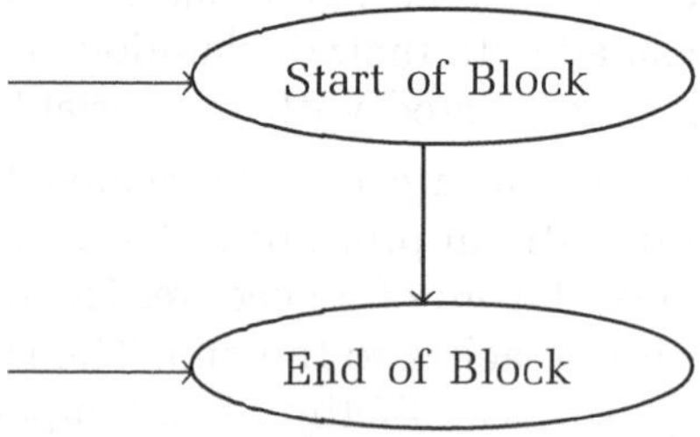

Example 2.4: Representation of block in 'C'

The scopes created by blocks are treated exactly like those created by subprograms. Nesting of blocks is also possible in which definition of one block contains the definition of other blocks. In nesting of block one block begins within the definition of another block and also ends in the definition of another block.

2.6. VARIABLES AND CONSTANTS

A variable is an elementary data object with a name whose value can be modify by assignment operation. The binding of data object to value may change during its lifetime. A variable is defined by programmer in a program. A variable can have a set of attributes, such as name, address, value, type, lifetime, scope etc. A variable have a name that is defined by programmes. It have a address where it can be store.

A value is assigned to a variable. Type means which type of value it contains.

Simple declaration of variable in 'C' language is

int *a*;

here *a* is variable of type integer.

When we use statement

a = 25;

then a values 25 is assigned to *a*.

Here, declaration specifies that *a* is an elementary data object of type integer. This data object is created on entry of subprograms and destroyed on exit. During lifetime the variable is bound with a name '*a*'. The initial value of *a* is 25. Which can be changed during execution of programs.

A constant is a variable that is bound to a value during its lifetime. The value of that variable cannot be changed by assignment or by any input statement. For example, by using the name Pi instead of the constant 3.1415.

In 'C' language constant is declared as

const int A = 25;

Here A is integer constant. Its values *i.e.*, 25 is fixed throughout the program and cannot be changed during execution. The value of constant is bonded to the value 25 during the execution of programs.

2.7. SPECIFICATION AND IMPLEMENTATION OF ELEMENTARY DATA TYPE

Elementary Data Type: Data types that are not defined in terms of other type are called Elementary Data type. A data object that contains a single value is called elementary data object. A collection of elementary data object or class of elementary data object is called elementary data type. It is also known as primitive data types or built in type. There are various elementary data types such as Integers, Floats, Boolean, character etc.

2.7.1. Specification of Elementary Data Types

Specification of elementary data types consists of three main things:

(*a*) **Attributes.** Basic attributes of any data object is used to distinguish it to another object. Every data object have certain attributes that are used to distinguish it to another data object. The main attributes are its name and its type. These are invariant throughout its life time. Attributes are stored is descriptor *i.e.*, part of the data object. Decriptor is collection of memory cells that store variable attributes.

(*b*) **Values.** Elementary data object have contains values throughout the program. A particular type of values is assigned to the elementary data object. The set of values defined by an elementary data type is an ordered set.

For example. In 'C' four classes of integer types are used *i.e.,* int, short, long and char. C permits the programmer to choose among these hardware defined implementation.

(*c*) **Operation:** There are two types of operations that are performed on elementary data type:

(*i*) **Primitive operations.** These operations are built in. These operations are defined at the language implementation time.

(*ii*) **Programmer defined operations.** These operations are defined by programmer. Programmer defined operation are used subprograms or method declarations.

2.7.2. Examples of Primitive Operations

(*a*) Integer addition is an operation that takes two integer data objects as input and produce an integer data object as a result.

integer = integer + integer.

$a = b + c;$

(*b*) Equality of two integer values can be checked and result is produced by a Boolean value.

(integer = integer) → Boolean

In 'C'
```
If (a = = b)
then return 1;
Else return 0;
```

2.7.3. Examples of Programmer Defined Operations

Consider the operation of swapping two integer values using temporary integer variable.

```
void swap (int and x, int and y)
{
    int temp;
        temp = x;
           x = y;
           y = temp;
}
```

When this subprogram or function is called.

The two integer values can be swapped or interchanged.

This is user defined or programmer defined operation.

An operation that has two arguments and produces a single value is termed as binary operation. If it has one argument and one result, it is a unary operation.

- **Subtypes.** A subtype is a part of larger class. We can say that it is subtype of layer class. Larger class is a supertype of this data type. 'C' language defines the types of int, long, short and char as subtypes of integer data type.

Consider the example of Pascal, we may create sub-ranges of integer as

type small integer = 1..... 5;

being a sub-type of integer with range

1, 2, 3 . . . 5.

A subrange type is a coutiguous subsequence of an ordinal type, subrange type enhance readability by making it clear to readers that variables of subtypes can store only certain ranges of values.

Implementation of Elementary Data types. Implementations of Elementary Data type means how the elementary data types are stored in the memory. Implementation consists of storage representation for data object and value of that type and a set of procedures that define the operation in terms of storage representation.

Storage of built in data type or primitive data type is influenced by the underlying computer that execute the program. Storage is depend upon the underlying hardware. The representation of integer or real values is depend upon the hardware.

Attributes of data object may be stored in a descriptor as part of the data object at run time. The representation of a data object is independent of its location in memory. Each operation defined for elementary data object may be implemented as:

(*a*) **Hardware operations.** These operations are completely depend on hardware for example addition and subtraction of integers are implemented using the arithmetic operation built into the hardware.

(*b*) **As an Inline function.** Inline function works as Macro's. When a subprogram is called then the whole function is placed where it is called. It is different from simple call-returns subprogram. When a function is called then whole body of function is placed where it is called.

(*c*) **Function or procedure Subprogram.** The user defined operations such as factorial of a number, square root operation is not directly implemented as a hardware operation. So functions are built to calculate factorial or square root of a number. When function is called for a number. It computes the square root or factorial of the number.

These are the specification and implementations part of elementary data types.

2.8. DECLARATIONS

Declaration is program statement that is used to declare the data objects. Declaration includes name of data objects and its type. Declaration is provided by the programmer in the programs. Programmes specifies the name and type of data that is needed in the program. Declaration is also explicit and implicit. It depends upon the languages whether it provide implicit or explicit declaration.

Consider the example of 'C' Language:

Example 2.5

```
# include<stdio.h>
void main( )
{
    Char name[ 10 ];
    int Rollno;
```

} ⟶ Implicit Declaration of variables

```
        ...............
        // Statement part
        ..............
}
```

In this example name is declared as a character variable whose maximum length is ten. and Rollno. is declared as a variable of type integer.

Some variables are declared implicitly or default declaration. For example, in a FORTRAN subprogram, a simple variable INDEX may be used without explicit declaration. FORTRAN compiler consider it integer by default because its name begins with one of the letters I–N.

User defined operations are declared in the form of subprograms. In 'C' language subprogram is of the form of functions and declared as

void swap (int and *x*, int and *y*);

This function declaration specifies that swap is subprogram name and it takes two argument of type integers and performs operation on these integer values that is swap operation and its return type is void means it do not returns any value.

Why Declaration are required

Declaration is required in every programs to define data objects. Declaration have following important purposes:

(*a*) **Best storage representation.** If the declaration of variables *i.e.,* data type and attributes are defined at compile time then storage management provide best storage for that. If variables are declared in starting of the subprogram then a block of storage is provided at start which is consequent memory locations. When lifetime of variables goes out the memory is free to reuse.

(*b*) **Performing operations.** If Declaration is provided at start line in 'C' language. Then operation performed on that variables is determined at compile time. **For example.**

Z = X * Y;

If X, Y and Z are of type integer and it is declared at the start of the subprogram then it has been determine at compile time that multiplication is perform on X and Y and result is assign to Z. Declaration also provide that type checking is performed at compile time or run time (*i.e.,* static or dynamic type checking).

2.9. TYPE CHECKING

Type checking is process of ensuring that the operands of an operator are of proper type or not. *i.e.,* operands are legal for the operator or is converted into proper type according to rule.

For example:

$$D = b * b - 4 * a * c$$

In this operation compiler determines that whether each operation multiplication, substraction and assignment receives arguments or operands of proper type. If '*' is defined to perform multiplication of two integer values and *a* and *c* are of different types rather than integer then an error will generate. That error is 'type mismatch'. So type checking is done to generate type errors. Type checking is done at compile time or at runtime.

Types of Type Checking

There are two types of type checking:

1. Static Type Checking.
2. Dynamic Type Checking.

1. **Static Type Checking.** Static type checking is done at compile time or during translation of a program. In the declaration of variables the most of the information in provided. It includes name of Data objects and its type. The type of the data object is fixed during program execution. If operation is performed on Data object such as

$$C = A * B$$

then it is assumed that the type of data object name A, B, C is same on each execution of the expression.

For each operation, the number, order and data type of its arguments and results means its prototype. It also consist type of constant data object.

2. **Dynamic Type Checking.** Dynamic type checking is done at run time or during execution of the program. Dynamic type checking is implement by storing a type tag with each data object that tells the data type of the object. For example, integer data object includes a integer value and integer type tag. The operation is performed only if the argument are of proper type otherwise error will generate. In dynamic type checking the type of data object with a variable name is changed as needed during execution of programs. Type information is stored at execution time of the program. Due to lack of support from hardware dynamic type checking is implemented by softwares. Dynamic type checking have more flexibility in program design because no declaration are needed because a type tag is associated with each data object.

Difference between Static Type and Dynamic Type Checking

Static Type Checking	***Dynamic Type Checking***
1. Type checking is done at Compile time.	1. Type checking is done at Runtime.
2. Storage cost is low because type information is not required at runtime.	2. Storage cost is high because type tags for data objects must be stored at runtime.
3. Easy to debug because type checking checks data type at compile time.	3. Difficult to debug because type checking checks data type at runtime.
4. It reduce the flexibility of programmer.	4. It does not reduce the flexibility of programmer.
5. C, C++ uses static as well as dynamic type checking.	5. Perl, Prolog, APL only uses dynamic type checking.

2.10. STRONG TYPING

We define a programming language to be strongly typed if type errors are always detected. This requires that the types of all operands can be determined, either at compile time or at runtime. A strongly typed language is one in which each name in a program in the language has a single type associated with it, and that type is known at compile time. This means all types are statically bound.

The weakness of this definition is that it ignores the possibility that, although a variable is type may be known, the storage location to which it is bound may store values of different types at different times.

FORTRAN is not strongly typed. Pascal is nearly strongly typed, but it fails in its design of variant record. ADA is nearly strongly type. C and C++ are not strongly typed language because both allow function for which parameters are not type checked. ML is strongly typed but in a slightly different sense than that of the imperative language. Java is strongly typed.

2.11 TYPE CONVERSION AND COERCION

Type conversion is an operation that convert data object of one type to the data object of another type. The signature of a type conversion operation is

conversion op: $type_1 \rightarrow type_2$

Here type conversion convert $type_1$ to $type_2$.

In during type checking, if a mismatch occurs between the actual type of an argument and the expected type for that operation, then either

1. The type mismatch may be flaged as an error and action will be taken against him.
2. A coercion is applied to change the type of the actual argument to the correct type.

Type conversion is of two types:

1. **Explicit type conversion.** In many programming language built in function are used that explicitly convert one type to another. Pascal use function round to convert a real number to an integer value. We can explicitly cast an expression to coerce it to correct type also

   For example. In Ada, we can have

   AVG = Float (Sum)/Float (count)

   Where AVG is floating–point type and Sum and Count can be any numeric type.

   In C–based language, explicit type conversions are called casts. The syntax of a cast is not that of a function call; rather, the desired type is placed in parentheses just before the expression to be converted, as shown in (int) angle.
2. **Implicit type conversion.** Implicit type conversion are also known as a coercion. It is applied to change the type of the actual argument to the correct type. Coercions involved automatically in certain cases of type mismatch. For example, consider the following C program:

```
void main( )
{
    int a, b;
    float d;
    ...............
```

```
    a=b*d;
    .............
}
```

Example 2.6

In this expression $a = b * d$ is mixed mode type expression in which multiplication of a integer variable (*b*) and a float variable (*d*) is performed. In this integer value is converted into float value. Compiler would not detect this an error. It would simply coerce the value of the other operand *b*, to float. If mixed-mode expression were not legal in C, this keying error would have been detected by the compiler as a type error.

2.12 ASSIGNMENT AND INITIALIZATION

Assignment is the basic operation for changing the binding of a value to data object. This change, however, is a side effect of the operation. It provides the mechanism by which the user can dynamically change the bindings of values to variables. The general syntax of simple assignment is:

<target; variable> <assignment–operator> <expression>.

C, C++, FORTRAN and Java use the equal sign for the assignment operator.

For example in C:

A = B + C;

In this addition of B and C is assigned to variable A.

Assignment statement are of multiple types:

Simple assignments. In which values are stored into single location. For example:

A = B + C;

Multiple targets. It allows asssignment of the expression value to more than one location. For example, in PL/I the statement

Sum, Total = 0.

Compound Assignment operator. It is a shorthand method of specifying a commonly needed form of assignment. The form of assignment that can be abbreviated with this technique has the destination variable also appearing as the first operand in the expression on the right side, as in

$a = a + b.$

Consider the assignment: A:= A.

In this different interpretation given to both references of the variable *A*. The right most *A* refers to the value contained in the named data object. Such references are often called the right hand side (of the assignment operator) value or *r*–value of a data object. Similarly, the left most A refers to the location of the data object that will contain the new value. Such references are called the left hand side (of the assignment operator) value or *L*–value. We can then define an assignment operation as:

(*a*) Compute the L–value of the first operand expression.

(*b*) Compute the *r*–value of the second operand expression.

(*c*) Assign the computed *r*–value to the computed *L*–value data object.

(*d*) Return the computed *r*–value as the result of the operation.

Initialization. An Uninitialized variable, or generally, an uninitialized data object, is a data object that has been created but not get assigned a value. (*i.e.*, L–value with no *r*–value) creation of a data object ordinarily involves only allocation of a block of storage. Uninitialized variable are a serious kind of programming error for professional programmers as well as beginners.

The random bit pattern contained in the value storage area of an uninitialized data object ordinarily cannot be distinguished from a valid value because the valid value also appears as a bit pattern.

Because of the effect of uninitialized variables on program reliability, immediate initialization of variable values on creation is considered good program practice.

For example in C:

```
int A = 10;
```

In Ada. Each variable declaration may also include an initial value for the variable using the same syntax used for ordinary assignment.

For example:

```
A: array (1...3) of int: = (10, 20, 30);
```

Create an Array A and assign each element an initial value explicitly in the declaration.

2.13. NUMERIC DATA TYPES

Numeric data type are found in every programming languages. Many early programming language had only numeric primitive types. Integer and Real number types are the most common because they are often directly supported in the computer hardware.

2.13.1 Integers

The most common primitive numeric data type is integer. Many computers now support several sizes of integers, and these capabilities are reflected in some programming language. For example, Ada follows implementation of three integer sizes. SHORT INTEGER, INTEGER and LONG INTEGER.

Specification Part. The set of integer value defined for the type forms an ordered subset, within some finite bounds, of the infinite set of integers studied in mathematics. The range values is then defined to be from – maxint to maxint. C language has four different integer specifications int, long, short and char.

Operations on Integers

(*i*) **Arithmetic Operation.** Arithmetic operation is of two types:

(*a*) Unary operation

(*b*) Binary operation

(*a*) **Unary operation.** Unary operation have the syntax

Unary OP: integer → integer

Where Unary OP may be negation (–) or identity (+).

For example in C:

A = – A;

A = A++; etc.

(*b*) **Binary operation.** Binary operation contains two operands to perform operation the syntax of Binary operation is

Binary op: integer of integer → integer where op be addition (+), substraction (–), multiplication (×), division (/), remainder (mod) or a similar operation.

For example:

C = A * B;

B = X + Y; etc.

(*ii*) **Relational Operation.** Relational operations have the syntax

Relop: integer op integer → Boolean when op is equal, not equal, less than, greater than, less than as equal, and greater than or equal. It returns Boolean value means true or false.

(*iii*) **Assignment.** Assignment operation may be used to assign the value of one data object to another. Syntax for assignment between integer data object may be

assignment: integer op integer → integer where op is assignment operator (=).

For example:

A = B;

Here A and B data object contains integer values.

Implementation. An integer value is represented in a computer by a string of bits, with one of the bits, typically the left most, representing the sign. There are three ways to store integer in memory.

1. **Storage with no descriptor.** In this type of storage no runtime descriptor is required only the value is stored. It is used where the language provide declaration and Static type checking for integer data objects.

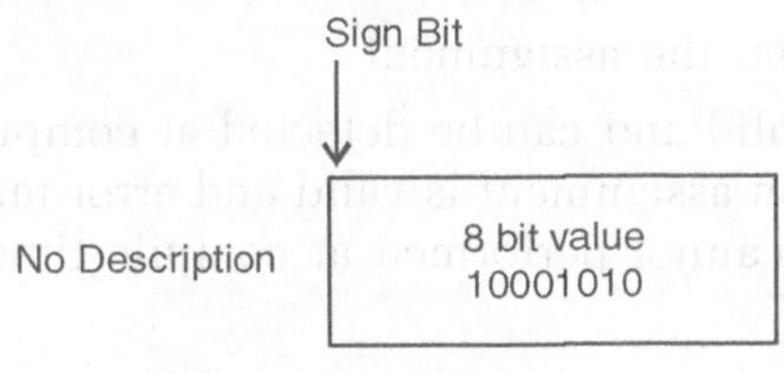

Fig. 2.3

2. **Storage of descriptor in separated word.** In this type of storage a descriptor is used which stores a separate word to store description A separate memory is used to store descriptor.

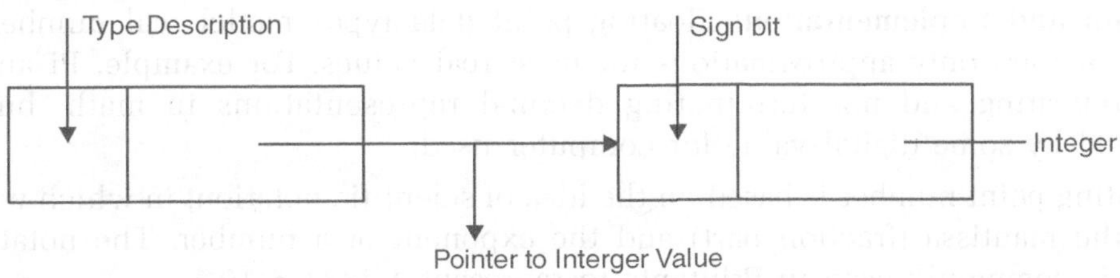

Fig. 2.4

It is used in LISP. It has disadvantage of taking double storage for single integer value.

3. **Store descriptor in same word.** In this type of storage same word or location is used to store the descriptor and Integer value. In this, descriptor is stored along with the value.

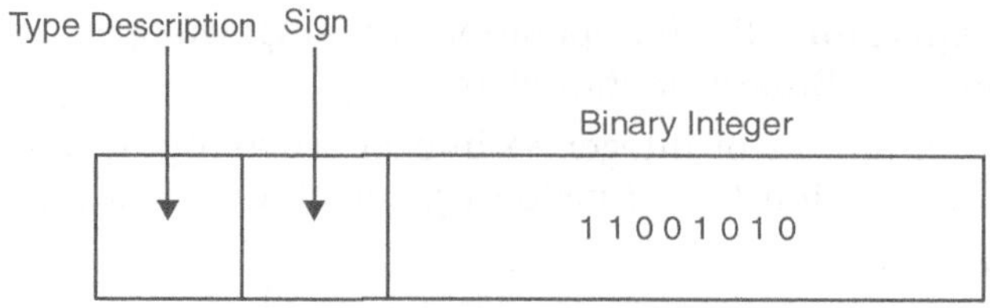

Fig. 2.5

2.13.2 Subrange Type

A subrange type is a contiguous subsequence of an ordinal type. It consist of sequence of value within some restricted range. **For example.**

(1) 10.....20 is a subrange of integer type

A: integer rage 10.......20.

It is the format used in Ada.

(2) In pascal declaration of integers 1 to 10 is given as

A: 1......10 of integers.

Implementation of Subrange type. It has two important effect on implementations:

1. It has small range of value. A subrange value can be stored in fewer bits than a general integer value. For example, an integer in the Subrange 1...10 requires only four bits of storage for its representation. Whereas a full integer value requires 16, 32 or more on typical machine.
2. By declaring a variable as subrange type allows more effective type checking to be performed on the values assigned to that variable. For example, if variable ABC is

   ABC: 1 to 10, then the assignment

   ABC: = 0; is invalid and can be detected at compile time. If ABC is declared to be of integer type, then assignment is valid and error must be checked at testing time. Some time checking cannot performed at compile time, for example,

   ABC: = ABC + 1;

   for this runtime checking is needed to determine whether the new value assigned to ABC is within declared bounds.

2.13.3 Floating-point Real Numbers

Specification and Implementation: Floating point data types model real numbers, but the representations are only approximations for most real values. For example, Pi and sqart (2) have non-repeating and non-terminating decimal representations in math, but must be approximated by some digital value for computer used.

A floating point number is based on the idea of scientific notation, in which we represent both the mantissa (fraction part) and the exponent of a number. The notation 1.2834 E – 4 is commonly used in Printants to represent 1.2834 $*$ 10^{-4}.

The floating point real number is represented as

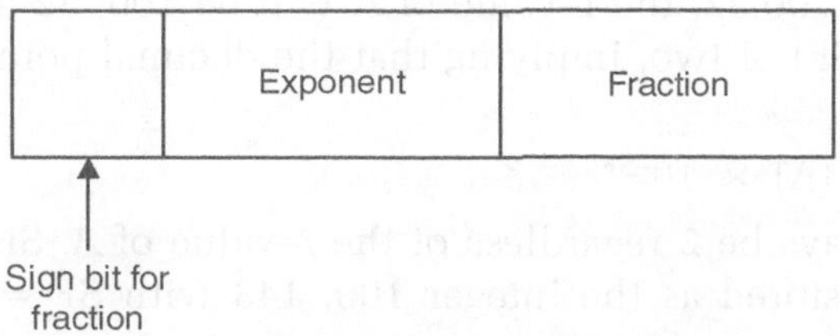

Fig. 2.6. Floating Point Representation.

Storage representation for floating-point real type are based on an underlying hardware representation in which a storage location is divided into mantissa and exponent. IEEE Standard 754 [IEEE 1985] has become the accepted definition for floating point format in many implementation.

A double-precision form of floating point number is often available, in which an additional memory word is used to store and extended mantissa. Both single and double precision are generally supported by hardware arithmetic operations for addition, subtraction, multiplication and division. Most languages provide no control over the precision of these reals. Some languages like PL/I and Ada make provision for doing so.

2.13.4 Fixed Point Real Numbers

Specification. The fixed point number representation specifies both a fixed number of digits and the position of the decimal point. They are much like integers then, except for the radix (decimal or binary) point. They are available in language like COBOL and PL/I. A simple declaration in PL/I is:

Declare Tax Fixed Decimal (8, 2);

Here the variable Tax can be represent a decimal number in the range from – 999999.99 to 999999.99.

In COBOL, the declaration is given as a PICTURE Clause—for example,

X PICTURE 9999 V 99.

Which declare X as a fixed point variable with four digits before the decimal and two digits after.

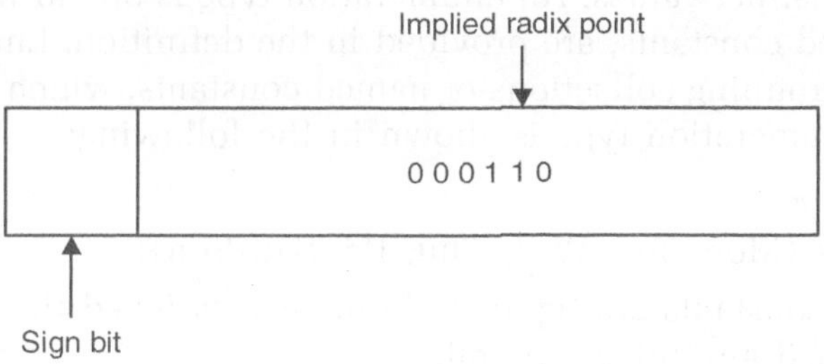

Fig. 2.7. Representation of Fixed Point Real Number.

Implementation. A fixed point type may be directly supported by the hardware or it may be simulated by software. For example, in PL/I, fixed data are of type FIXED DECIMAL.

We can write

DECLARE A FIXED DECIMAL (10,2),

B FIXED DECIMAL (10, 3);

Signifying A is 10 digits with two decimal places: B is 10 digits with three decimal places. If A has the value 100.32, the r–value of A will be 100, 32 and the object A will have an attribute scale factor (SF) of two, implying that the decimal point is two places to the left. That is in

Value (A) = r value (A) × 10^{-SF}

Scale factor will always be 2 regardless of the r–value of A. Similarly, if B has the value 100. 143, then it will be stored as the integer 100, 143 with SF = 3.

2.13.5 Complex Numbers

A complex number consists of a pair of numbers representing the number's real and imaginary parts. A complex-number data type may be easily provided by representing each data object as a block of two storage locations containing a pair of real values. Operation on complex numbers may be software simulated because they are unlikely to be hardware implemented.

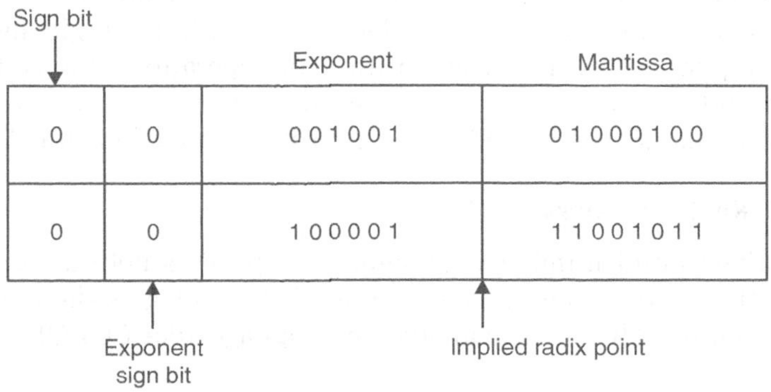

Pair of reals in consecutive locations

Fig. 2.8. Representation of Complex Numbers.

2.14. ENUMERATIONS

Specification

It is an ordered list of distinct values. An enumeration type is one in which all of the possible values, which are named constants, are provided in the definition. Enumeration type provide a way of defining and grouping collections of named constants, which are called enumeration constants. A typical enumeration type is shown in the following:

'C' example.

```
enum days {Mon, Tue, Wed, Thu, Fri, Sat, Sun};
```

The enumeration constants are typically implicitly assigned the values, 0, 1, 2......., but can be explicitly assigned any integer literal.

In above example the value of Mon = 0, Tue = 1, Wed = 2, ..., Sun = 6.

The Boolean type is essentially a predefined enumeration type: boolean = (false, true) where false = 0, true = 1

C and Pascal were the first widely used languages to include an enumeration data type.

In C ++ we could have

enum colors {red, blue, green, yellow, black}:

The red = 0, blue = 1, green = 2, yellow = 3 and black contains value 4.

Implementation. The storage representation for a data object of an enumeration type is represented as a sequence by one of integers 0, 1, 2,..... Because only a small set of value is involved and values can never be negative. For example, if a class contains any four possible values, represented at runtime as 0 = red, 1 = blue, 2 = green and 3 = yellow. Because only two bits are required to represent these four possible values in memory, a variable of type class needs to be allocated only two bits of storage. We can also overside the default + values and set any values desired for enumeration values, for example,

enum class {red = 10, blue = 20, green = 30, yellow = 40}

This is the implementation part of enumerations.

2.15. BOOLEANS

Booleans type are simplest of all types and is common in most general purpose languages. The two values true and false can be ordered so that false < true, but such comparisons would be unusual.

Specifications. The Boolean data type consists of data objects having one of two values– true or false. They were introduced in ALGOL 60 and have been included in most general–purpose language designed since 1960.

In Pascal and Ada, the Boolean data type is considered. Simply a language–defined enumeration, viz.,

type Boolean = (false, true);

which both defines the names true and false for the values of the type.

The most common operations on Boolean type include assignment as well as the logical operations.

Boolean and Boolean → Boolean (Conjunction)

Boolean or Boolean → Boolean (Inclusive disjunction)

not Boolean → Boolean (negation or complement)

Implementation. It would seem natural to implent Boolean Values as single bits, using 0 for false and 1 for true. Since many machines cannot address single bits, a byte or word may be allocated. In C, integer values are used, with false as 0 and true as any non-zero value.

Because a large amount of storage may be used by either of these representations, provision is often made in a language for collections of bits. Java has an explicit Boolean type, but C does not. In C, integer is used. True is any non-zero value and false is 0. This can potentially cause some problems.

For example,

```
int flag;
flag = 7.
```

It will set flag to 7 or 111 in binary, which would represent a true value.

2.16. CHARACTERS

Most data represented in computers in the form of numeric codings. The most commonly used coding is ASCII (American Standard Code for Information Interchange), which uses the values 0 to 127 to code 128 different characters.

Specification. A Character data type provides data object that have a single character as their value. The set of possible character value is usually taken to be a language–defined enumeration corresponding to the standard character sets supported by the underlying hardware and operating system. The ordering of the character in this character set is called the collating sequence for the character set. In some language, the char type may be used to represent objects other than single characters. In C, char can save space in place of short integers. The collating sequence is important because it determines the alphabetical ordering given to character strings by the relational operations. Operations performed on character data includes relational operations, assignment and sometimes to check whether a character value is one of the special classes letter, digit or special character.

Implementation. Implementation of character data values is directly supported by the underlying hardware and operating system because of their use in input–output. Sometime language definition specify to use a particular character set that is not supported by hardware. Although the same characters may be represented in both characters sets, its storage represention and its collating sequences, may be differ. The language implementation may have to provide appropriate conversions to the alternative character-set representation or provide special implementation of the relational operations that take account of differences in the collating sequence.

Some Important Terms

- A data object is a runtime collection of one or more pieces of data in a digital computer.
- System defined data object are created automatically during program execution.
- Programmer defined data object are created by programmer.
- A data value might be a single number, character or a pointer to another data object.
- Data type of a variable determine which type of values the variable can have.
- Basic elements of specification are attributes, values and operations.
- Basic elements of implementation are representation and implementation of operations.
- Binding refers to the linking between are attribute and an entity or between an operation and symbols.
- Static binding is done at compile time.
- Dynamic binding is done at run time.
- Lifetime of a variable is the time during which a variable is bound to a specific memory location.
- The scope of variable starts from the declaration of variable to the end of procedure in which it is declared.
- A blocks consists of a set of declaration for names such as variable declaration, constant definition and type definitions.

- A variable is an elementary data object with a name whose value can be modify by assignment operations.
- A constant is a variable that is bound to a value during its life time.
- Elementary data object contains a single value.
- Operations that are performed on elementary data type are:
  (*a*) Primitive operations.
  (*b*) Programmer defined operations.
- A subtype is a part of larger class or we can say that it is sub-type of larger class.
- Operations that are performed on Data Objects are.
  (*a*) Hardware operation.
  (*b*) As an inline function.
  (*c*) Function or procedure subprograms
- Declaration of a program statement is used to declare the data objects.
- Type checking is a process of ensuring that the operands of an operator are of proper type or not.
- Static type checking is done at compile time or during translation time.
- Dynamic type checking is done at runtime or execution time.
- A language is said to be strongly typed if type errors are always detected at compile time.
- Type conversion is an operation that convert data object of one type to the data object of another type.
- Type conversion can be of two types:
  – Explicit type conversion
  – Implicit type conversion.
- Assignment is the basic operation for changing the binding of a variable to a data object.
- A subrange type is contiguous subsequence of an ordinal type.

Review Questions

1. What do you mean by data object and Data values?
2. Differentiate between system defined and programmer defined data objects.
3. Explain the role of data type in programming language.
4. What do you mean by binding? Differentiate between static and dynamic binding.
5. Explain scope and life time of a variable. How these two terms are related to each other?
6. Write short notes on:
   (*a*) Blocks
   (*b*) Variables and constants
   (*c*) Implicit and explicit type conversion
   (*d*) Data objects and data types.
7. Explain the specification and implementation of elementary data type.

8. Define the term type checking. Also explain the static and dynamic type checking.
9. What do you mean by Type conversion? Also explain Implicit and Explicit type conversion.
10. Write short notes on.
    (*a*) Declaration
    (*b*) Strong typing
    (*c*) Subrange type
    (*d*) Assignment and initialization.
11. Explain the concept of numeric data type in detail.
12. Differentiate between static and Dynamic type checking.

❑❑❑

Chapter 3 SYNTAX AND SEMANTICS

The study of programming languages, like the study of natural languages, can be divided into examinations of syntax and semantics. The main purpose of a language is to express meaning by means of sound. Programming language implementor obviously must be able to determine how the expressions, statements of a language are formed. The validity of a sentence is based on their syntax and semantics.

3.1. SYNTAX AND SEMANTICS

Syntax

Syntax of a programming language is the form of its expressions, statements and program units. The syntax of a programming language is what the program looks like. For specifying rules for a programming language means to tell how statements, declarations and other constructs of language are written.

Different languages have different syntax for the same thing. For example, Syntax of Declaration of array in Pascal and *'C'* languages are different.

In Pascal we declare.

A : array [0 - - 5] of integer;

On the other hand in 'C' we declare as

int A [6];

Both create similar data objects at run time but their syntax is very different.

The Syntax of a programming language is the set of rules to determine whether a sentence is well formed or not. For example in 'C' the syntax of if statement is

if (<expr>) <statement>

Syntax rules specifies whether a sentence is legal or not. Example, the syntax of a sample C++ program is illustrated in program in Fig. 3.1

```
# include<iostream.h>
void main( )
{
//statement part
}
```

Fig. 3.1. A Simple C+ + Program.

Semantics

The semantics of a programming language is the meaning given to various syntactic constructs. In case of programming language semantics should follow directing from syntax. Therefore, semantics of a language describe the relation between syntax and computation. The semantics of a statement means whether it is true or not.

For example: if (<expr>) (statement)

The semantics of this statement means current value of the expression is true or not. Describing syntax is easier than describing semantics, partly because a concise and universally accepted notation is available for syntax description, but none has yet been developed for semantics. If two sentences are syntactically correct then it does not means they are semantically correct. It could also possible that the meaning of two syntactically correct statements having different syntax have the same semantics (meaning).

3.2. THE GENERAL PROBLEM OF DESCRIBING SYNTAX

A language whether natural or artificial contains the set of strings of characters from some alphabet. A sentence consists of strings of a language.

The lowest level of description of programming language syntax include its identifiers, literals, operators, keywords and other special characters. These units are known as Lexemes. The lexical rules include three terms:

(*a*) **Input Alphabet.** It contains all input symbols that are used to make a valid sentences *e.g.*, the alphabet for machine language is $\Sigma = \{0, 1\}$

(*b*) **Alphabet* (Σ*).** It is defined as the set of all possible strings or words that can be derived from a given alphabet or it can be derived from another alphabet, *e.g.*, if $\Sigma = \{0, 1\}$ the $\Sigma^* = \{\Sigma, 0, 1, 00, 01, 10, 11, ...\}$

(c) **Language.** It is defined as a set of strings or words from alphabet satisfying a given criteria.

A token is a category of its lexemes. For example, an identifier is a token that can lexemes or instance such as total, sum, etc.

Consider the following 'C' statements:

Index = 5 + C * 10;

The lexemes and token of this statement are:

Lexemes	Tokens
Index	identifiers
=	Rel_operator
5	int_literal
+	plus_operator
C	identifier
*	multiply-operator
10	literal
;	semicolon

Lexical rules are implemented Recognizers.

Another rules for describing syntax are syntactic rules. They are implemented using language generators.

Example:

a/b*

The lexical rules transform it into

id/id*

where *id* represent identifier.

The syntactic rules reflect that it is incorrect syntactically because the presence of two binary operator consecutively is a meanigless construct. For each binary operator requires two operands which are not present here. Syntactic rules also impose a tree like hierarchical structure on the meaningful syntactically correct.

3.2.1. Language Recognizers and Language Generators

Languages can be formally defined in two different ways:

(a) **Language Recognizers.** Consider a language L defined over an alphabet Σ of characters. To define L using the recognition method, we would need to construct a mechanism R, called a recognition device that is capable of reading strings of characters from the alphabet Σ. R would need to be designed so that it indicated that a given input string was or was not in L. It would either accept or reject the given string. Recognition devices, however, are not used to enumerate all of the sentences of a language.

For example, consider a language L defined over alphabet $\Sigma = \{a, b\}$ as:

$L = \{x | x \varepsilon \{a, b\}$ and accepts strings $abb\}$

The language Recognition device R is

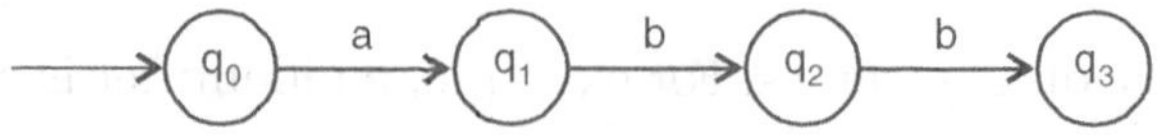

Fig. 3.2. A Language Recognition Device R

This language Recognition device are known as finite automata.

(*b*) **Language generators.** A language generator is a device that can be used to generate the sentences of a language. A generator seems to be a device of limited usefulness as a language descriptor. Generators can more easily read and understand them. A language generation method constructs a language generator G and capable of generating a string of language by a process called derivation. For example, consider a language L over alphabet

$$\Sigma = \{a, b\}$$

$$L = \{a^n, b^n \mid n \geq 1\}$$

$$G = \begin{Bmatrix} S & \rightarrow & asb \\ S & \rightarrow & ab \\ S & \rightarrow & \varepsilon \end{Bmatrix}$$

$$W = aaa\ bbb$$

Derivation:

$$\begin{aligned} S &\Rightarrow asb \\ &\Rightarrow aasbb \\ &\Rightarrow aaabbb \end{aligned}$$

i.e., $S \Rightarrow aaabbb$

It means we have derived *aaabbb* starting from start symbol S using the rules of language generator G in finite number of steps.

3.3. FORMAL METHODS OF DESCRIBING SYNTAX

The formal definition of the syntax of a programming language is usually called a grammar. A grammar consists of a set of rules that specify the sequence of characters that form allowable programs in the language being defined. The various formal methods for describing of syntax are:

(*i*) Context free grammars

(*ii*) BNF grammars

(*iii*) Extended BNF

(*iv*) Syntax Graphs

(*v*) Finite state automata

(*vi*) Regular Grammars and regular expressions.

3.3.1. Context Free Grammars (CFG)

It is a notation used to specify the syntax of language. Context free Grammars are used to design parsers. The context free grammar was developed by linguist Norm Chomsky for the definition of natural language syntax. Grammars are rewriting rules and may be used for both recognition and generation of programs.

A context free Grammar (*G*) can be defined as:

It is a 4-tuple (V, Σ, P, S)

where

(*i*) V is a set of Non-Terminals or variables.

(*ii*) Σ is set of terminals

(*iii*) P is set of productions or set of rules.

(*iv*) S is start symbol.

G is context free is every production (*P*) is of form $A \to \alpha$, where $A \Sigma U$ and $\alpha \Sigma (V U \Sigma)^*$.

Example 3.1. *Write down Grammar for language*

$$L = \{a^n | n \geq 1\}$$

Sol. Let $G = (V, \Sigma, P, S)$

where $V = \{S\}$

$$\Sigma = \{a\}$$

$$P = \begin{Bmatrix} S & \to & as \\ S & \to & a \end{Bmatrix}$$

These productions generate the language a^n

i.e.,

$$S \Rightarrow a$$

$$S \Rightarrow as \Rightarrow aa \text{ or } a^2$$

$$S \Rightarrow as \Rightarrow aas \Rightarrow aaa \text{ or } a^3$$

$$\vdots$$

$$S \Rightarrow as \Rightarrow aas \Rightarrow aaas \Rightarrow ..... \Rightarrow a^n$$

The terminals symbols are basically tokens used in a language.

Example 3.2. *Find out language generated by a Grammar*

$$G = (\{s\}, \{a, b\})$$

$$P = \begin{Bmatrix} s & \to & asb \\ s & \to & ab \\ s & \to & \wedge \end{Bmatrix}$$

Sol.

$$S \Rightarrow a\ s\ b$$

$$\Rightarrow a\ a\ s\ b\ b$$

$$\Rightarrow a\ a\ a\ s\ b\ b\ b$$

$$\cdots\cdots\cdots\cdots$$

$$\Rightarrow a^{n-1}\ s\ b^{n-1}$$

$$\Rightarrow a^{n-1}\ a\ b\ b^{n-1}$$

$$\Rightarrow a^n\ b^n$$

$\therefore$ Language $L = \{a^n\ b^n | n \geq 1\}$

Example 3.3. *Write a context free Grammar for Palindrome language.*

$L = \{W\ C\ W^R | W\ \Sigma\ \{a, b\}^*\}$ having middle symbol C. Here R means reverse of string.

Sol. Language represents a Palindrome with a middle symbol '*C*'.

∴ Grammar $G = (V, \Sigma, P, S)$ will have productions.

$$S \rightarrow a\ s\ a$$
$$S \rightarrow b\ s\ b$$
$$S \rightarrow c$$

Example:

To generate Palindrome $a\ b\ c\ b\ a$, derivation is

$$S \Rightarrow a\ s\ a$$
$$\Rightarrow a\ b\ s\ b\ a$$
$$\Rightarrow a\ b\ c\ b\ a$$

3.3.2. BNF Grammars

The Backus-Naur-Form (BNF) was developed in the late 1950s by the linguists John Backus and Peter-Naur for the syntactic description of ALGOL. BNF is a very natural notation for describing syntax. It is popular method of describing programming language syntax. BNF is meta language *i.e.*, a language used to describe another language. A BNF grammar *G* is defined as

$$G = (V, \Sigma, P, S)$$

where V = Set of abstraction in a BNF grammar. The abstractions are often called variables or non-terminals.

Σ = Set of terminal symbols.

P = A set of productions or rules.

S = A special non-terminal called the start symbol.

The various parameters used are described as:

(1) **Abstractions.** BNF uses abstractions for syntactic structures. The non-terminals or variables are enclosed between < and >.

Example: The *C* assignment statement is represented by the abstraction <assign>. The actual definition of <assign> may be given by

<assign> → <var> = <expression>

(2) **Rules or productions.** The productions or rules in BNF have the general from $A \rightarrow \alpha$.

The symbol on the left side of → are called the left hand side (LHS) and the text to the right of the arrow is the definition of right hand side (RHS).

Example: Consider a production

<assign> → <var> = <expression>

The rules specifies that the abstraction <assign> is defined as an instant of the abstraction <var> followed by lexeme =, followed by an instance of the abstraction <expression>.

3.3.2.1. Derivations

Derivation means replacing a given string's non terminal by right hand side of production rule. The sequence of terminals from the starting symbol is called derivation.

We can derive terminal strings, beginning with start symbol, by repeatedly replacing a variable by some production. The language of CFG is set of terminal symbols we can derive so. This language is called context free language.

Derivation are denoted by ⇒.

Types of Derivation:

(*a*) **Leftmost Derivation.** A derivation $A \overset{*}{\Rightarrow} w$ is called leftmost derivation if we apply production only to the leftmost variable at every step. Here, $*$ means 0, 1, 2, ... n number of derivations.

(*b*) **Rightmost Derivation.** A derivation $A \overset{*}{\Rightarrow} w$ is a rightmost derivation if we apply production to the rightmost variable at every step. It is also called canonical Derivation.

Example 3.4. *Let G be a CFG with productions.*

$$S \to A\,A$$
$$A \to a\,B$$
$$B \to b$$
$$B \to \Sigma$$

Find (1) Leftmost (2) Rightmost derivation for string *abab*.

Sol. (1) **Leftmost Derivation:**

$$S \overset{lm}{\Longrightarrow} A\,A$$
$$\overset{lm}{\Longrightarrow} a\,B\,A$$
$$\overset{lm}{\Longrightarrow} a\,b\,A$$
$$\overset{lm}{\Longrightarrow} a\,b\,a\,B$$
$$\overset{lm}{\Longrightarrow} a\,b\,a\,b$$

(2) **Rightmost Derivation:**

$$S \overset{rm}{\Longrightarrow} A\,A$$
$$\overset{rm}{\Longrightarrow} A\,a\,B$$
$$\overset{rm}{\Longrightarrow} A\,a\,b$$
$$\overset{rm}{\Longrightarrow} a\,B\,a\,b$$
$$\overset{rm}{\Longrightarrow} a\,b\,a\,b$$

3.3.2.2. Parse trees (Derivation trees)

A Parse Tree for a *CFG* $G = (V, \Sigma, P, S)$ is a tree satisfying following conditions:

1. Root has label S.
2. Every vertex has label which can be a variable (V), terminal (Σ) or Σ.
3. If $A \rightarrow C_1\ C_2\ .....\ C_n$ is a production, then $C_1, C_2, ...\ C_n$ are children of node labelled A.
4. Leaf nodes are terminals (Σ) and Interior nodes are variables (V).

Yield. Yield of Derivation Tree is the concatenation of the labels of the leaves in left to right ordering.

Example 3.5. *Consider the following Grammar*

$$<S> \Rightarrow a <A> <S> \mid a$$

$$<A> \Rightarrow <S>\ b <A> \mid <S> <S> \mid ba$$

Show that $S \overset{*}{\Rightarrow} aa\ bb\ aa$ *and construct Parse tree whose yield is aabbaa.*

Sol.

$$\begin{aligned} <S> &\overset{lm}{\Longrightarrow} a <A> S \\ &\Rightarrow a <S>\ b <A> <S> \\ &\Rightarrow aa\ b <A> <S> \\ &\Rightarrow aa\ bb\ a <S> \\ &\Rightarrow aa\ bb\ aa \end{aligned}$$

$$\therefore \quad S \overset{*}{\Rightarrow} aa\ bb\ aa$$

Derivation tree or Parse tree

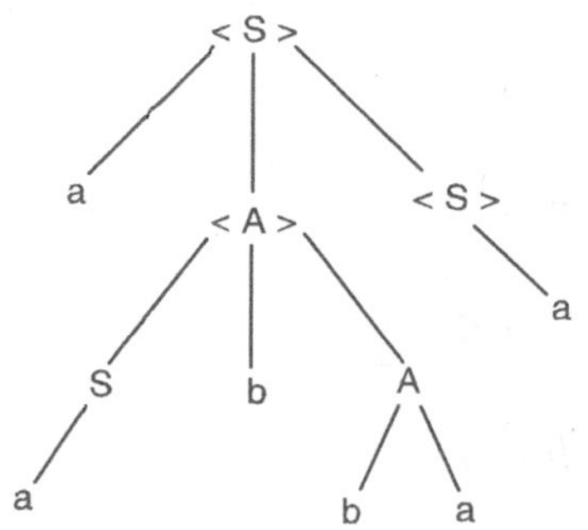

Fig. 3.3. A Parse Tree.

Yield = Left to Right ordering of leaves = *aa bb aa*

Example 3.6. *Consider the following grammar*

$$<S> \rightarrow b <B> \mid a <A>$$

$$<A> \rightarrow b \mid b <S> \mid a <A> <A>$$

$$<B> \rightarrow a \mid a <S> \mid b <B> <B>$$

Find (a) Leftmost (b) Rightmost derivation for string b a a ba ba. Also find derivation or Parse tree.

Sol. (*a*) **Left most Derivation**

S ⇒ *b* <*B*>
⇒ *bb* <*B*> <*B*>
⇒ *bb a* <*B*>
⇒ *bb aa* <*S*>
⇒ *bb aa b* <*B*>
⇒ *bb aa b a* <*S*>
⇒ *bb aa b a b* <*B*>
⇒ *bb aa ba ba*

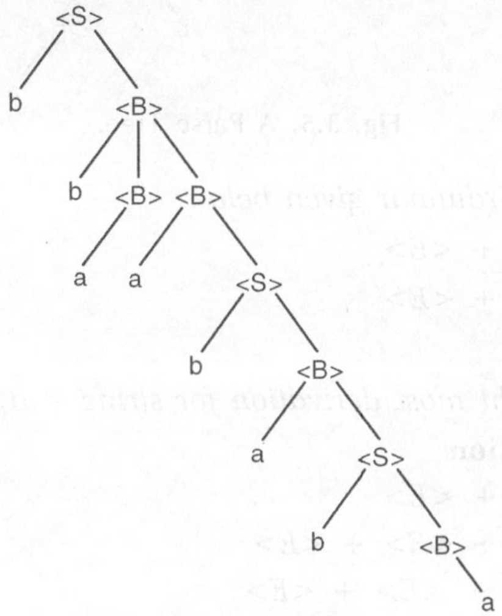

Fig. 3.4. A Parse Tree.

(*b*) **Right most Derivation**

S ⇒ *b* <*B*>
⇒ *bb* <*B*> <*B*>
⇒ *bb* <*B*> *a* <**S**>
⇒ *bb* <*B*> *a b* <*B*>
⇒ *bb* <*B*> *a b a* <*S*>
⇒ *bb* <*B*> *a b a b* <*B*>
⇒ *bb* <*B*> *abab a*
⇒ *bb aa b a b a*

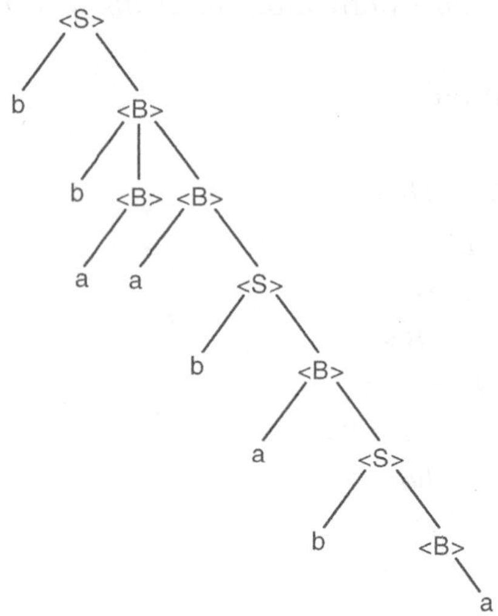

Fig. 3.5. A Parse Tree.

Example 3.7. *Consider Grammar given below:*

$$<E> \rightarrow <E> + <E>$$
$$\mid \; <E> + <E>$$
$$\mid \; <id>$$

Find (1) Leftmost (2) Right most derivation for string $<id> + <id> + <id>$

Sol. (1) **Leftmost Derivation**

$$<E> \Rightarrow <E> + <E>$$
$$\Rightarrow <E> + <E> + <E>$$
$$\Rightarrow <id> + <E> + <E>$$
$$\Rightarrow <id> + <id> + <E>$$
$$\Rightarrow <id> + <id> + id$$

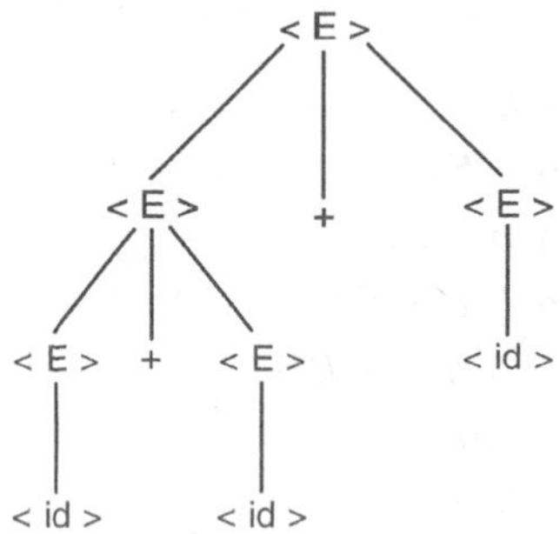

Fig. 3.6. A Parse Tree.

(2) **Rightmost Derivation**

$$<E> \Rightarrow <E> + <E>$$
$$\Rightarrow <E> + <E> + <E>$$
$$\Rightarrow <E> + <E> + <id>$$
$$\Rightarrow <E> + <id> + <id>$$
$$\Rightarrow <id> + <id> + <id>$$

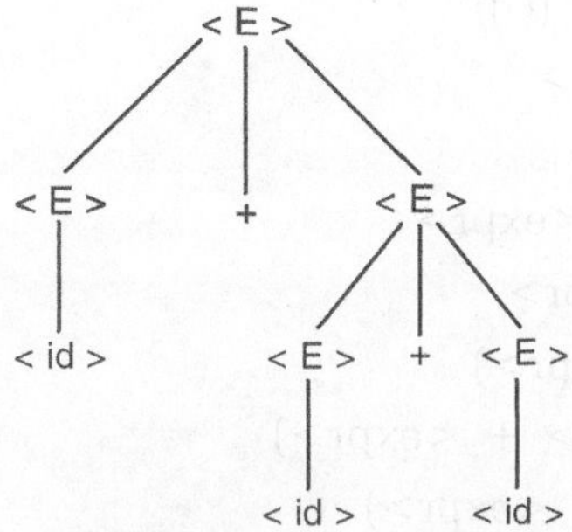

Fig. 3.7. A Parse Tree.

Example 3.8. *Consider the grammar for simple assignment statement*

<assign> → <id> = <expr>

<id> → A |B| C

<expr> → <id> + <expr>

*| <id> * <expr>*

|(<expr>)| <id>

Show a Parse tree and left most derivation for the following.

(a) A = B * (C + A)

(b) A = B * (A + (C))

Sol. (*a*) A = B * (C + A) is given as

<assign> ⇒ <id> = <expr>

⇒ A = <expr>

⇒ A = <id> * <expr>

⇒ A = B * (<expr>)

⇒ A = B * (<id> + <expr>)

⇒ A = B * (C + <id>)

⇒ A = B * (C + A)

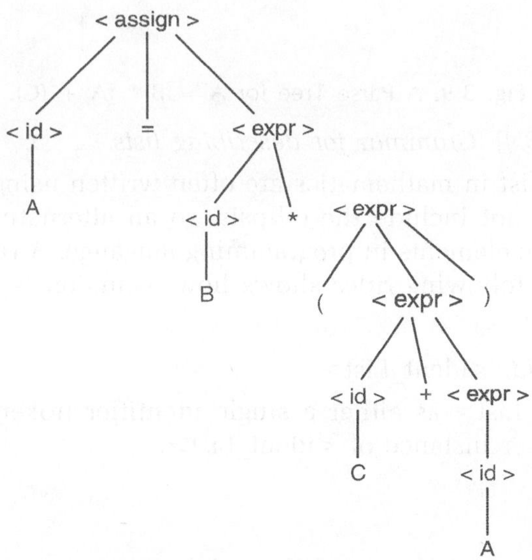

Fig. 3.8. A Parse Tree.

(*b*) *A* = *B* * (*A* + (*C*))

<assign> → <*id*> = <expr>

⇒ *A* = <expr>

⇒ *A* = <*id*> * <expr>

⇒ *A* = *B* * <expr>

⇒ *A* = *B* * (<expr>)

⇒ *A* = *B* * (<*id*> + <expr>)

⇒ *A* = *B* * (*A* + <expr>)

⇒ *A* = *B* * (*A* + (<expr>)

⇒ *A* = *B* * (*A* + (<*id*>))

⇒ *A* = *B* * (*A* + (*C*))

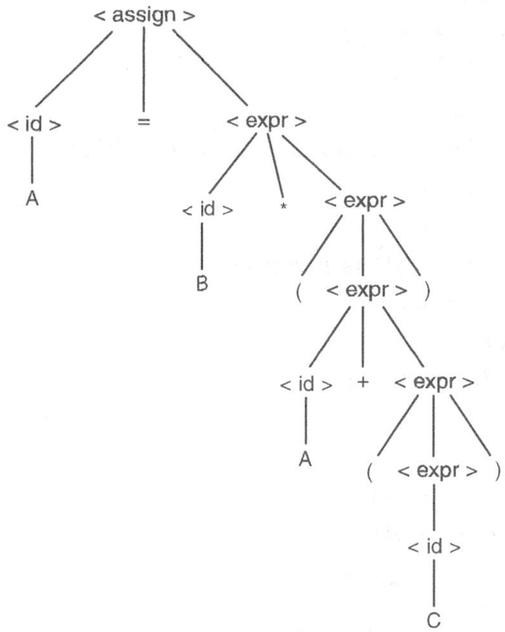

Fig. 3.9. A Parse Tree for A = B * (A + (C).

Example 3.9. *Write BNF Grammar for describing lists.*

Sol. Variable-length list in mathematics are often written using an ellipsis (...); 1, 2, ... is an example. BNF does not include the ellipsis, so an alternative method is required for describing lists of syntactic elements in programming langauge. A rules is recursive is its LHS appears in its R.H.S. The following rules shows how recursion is used to describe lists:

<ident_List> → *id*

|*id*, <ident_List>

This defines <ident_List> as either a single identifier (token) or token followed by a comma followed by another instance of <ident_List>.

Example 3.10. *Write a small language defined by following grammar.*

<Program> → begin < Stmt_List> end
<Stmt_List> → <Stmt>
| <Stmt>; <stmt_list>
<Stmt> → <var> = <expression>
<var> → A |B| C
<expression> → <var> + <var>
*| <var> * <var>*
| <var>

Sol. The language defined by above grammar has only one statement form: assignment. This programs consist of special word begin and end. In between them there is a List of statements followed by semicolon. The expression is either a single variable or two variables separated by either a + or * operator. The variables name will be *A*, *B* and *C*.

3.3.2.3. Ambiguity

A CFG or BNF Grammar *G* is said to be ambiguous if there exists more than one derivation tree for a given string.

Or

A Grammar that produces more than one left most derivation (or Right most Derivation) for the same sentence is called ambiguous Grammar.

Example: Following sentence in English.

"In Books selected information is given."

It gives two different meaning as:

- In Books, "selected information is given."
- In Books selected, "Information is given."

So, the above sentence can said as an ambiguous one in language of English.

The syntactic ambiguity of language structures is a problem because compilers often base the semantics of those structures on their syntactic form. If for a language there is more than one parse tree, the meaning of the structure cannot be determined uniquely.

Operator Precedence Rules. According to operator precedence rule, An operator in an arithmetic expression have the higher precedence than the other operators. Consider the following grammar

<assignment> → <*id*> = <expression>
<*id*> → *A* |*B*| *C*
<expression> → <expression> + <expression>
| <expression> ∗ <expression>
| <expression> / <*id*>

Consider a string

$$A = B + A * C$$

The two distinct parse tree will be:

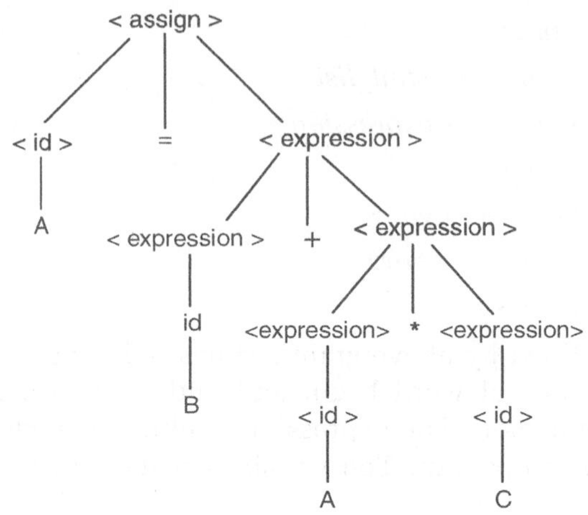

(a)

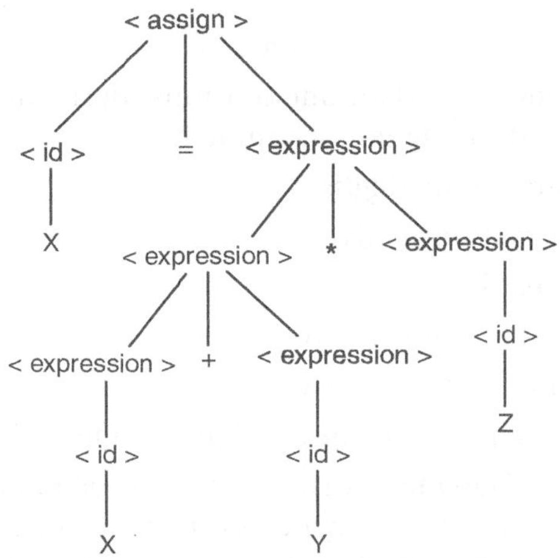

(b)

Fig. 3.10. Two Distinct Parse Trees for the Same Sentence.

$A = B + A * C$

In the above example the two distinct Parse trees for the same expression. The first tree '+' operator have a higher precedence than '*' and in the second tree '*' operator has a higher precedence than '+' operator. The first tree considers the expression of the form $B + (A * C)$ and the second tree considers the expression of the form $(B + A) * C$. According to operator precedence Rule '*' has higher precedence than '+'. So according to operator precedence rule first tree will be a correct one and a valid Parse tree.

Associativity of operators:

Consider a string $X = x + y + z$

The leftmost derivation for these string is of two forms

(*i*) <assign> → <*id*> = <expression>

⇒ *X* = <expression>

⇒ *X* = <expression> + <expression>

⇒ *X* = <*id*> + <expression>

⇒ *X* = *X* + <expression>

⇒ *X* = *X* + <expression> + <expression>

⇒ *X* = *X* + <*id*> + <expression>

⇒ *X* = *X* + *Y* + <expression>

⇒ *X* = *X* + *Y* + <*id*>

⇒ *X* = *X* + *Y* + *Z*

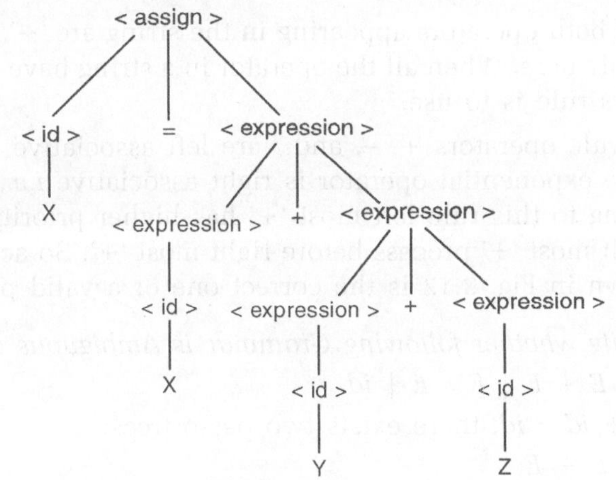

Fig. 3.11. A Parse Tree of X = X + Y + Z.

(*ii*) <assign> → <*id*> = <expression>

⇒ *X* = <expression>

⇒ *X* = <expression> + <expression>

⇒ *X* = <expression) + <expression> + <expression>

⇒ *X* = <*id*> + <expression> + <expression>

⇒ *X* = *X* + <expression> + <expression>

⇒ *X* = *X* + <*id*> + <expression>

⇒ *X* = *X* + *Y* + <expression>

⇒ *X* = *X* + *Y* + <*id*>

⇒ *X* = *X* + *Y* + *Z*

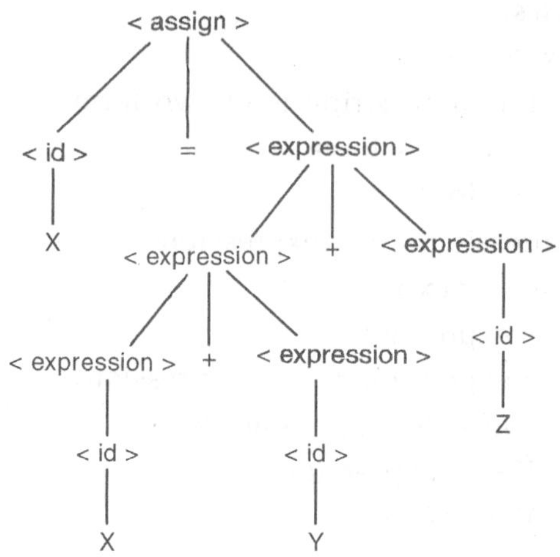

Fig. 3.12. A Distinct Parse Tree from the String X = X + Y + Z.

In the above string both operators appearing in the string are '+'. So the rule of operator precedence does not apply here. When all the operator in a string have same precedence. Then associativity of operators rule is to use.

According to this rule operators +, –, and / are left associative *i.e.,* starts froms left to right for evaluation. The exponential operator is right associative *i.e.,* evaluation starts from right to left. So according to this rule left most '+' has higher priority than right '+'. In the second parse tree the left most '+' process before right most '+'. So according to associativity rule the parse tree shown in Fig. 3.12 is the correct one or a valid parse tree.

Example 3.11. *Verify whether following Grammar is Ambiguous or not*

$$E \rightarrow E + E \mid E * E \mid id.$$

Sol. For string *id + id * id*, there exists two parse trees.

(*i*) $E \Rightarrow E + E$

$\Rightarrow id + E$

$\Rightarrow id + E * E$

$\Rightarrow id + id * E$

$\Rightarrow id + id * id$

$\Rightarrow$

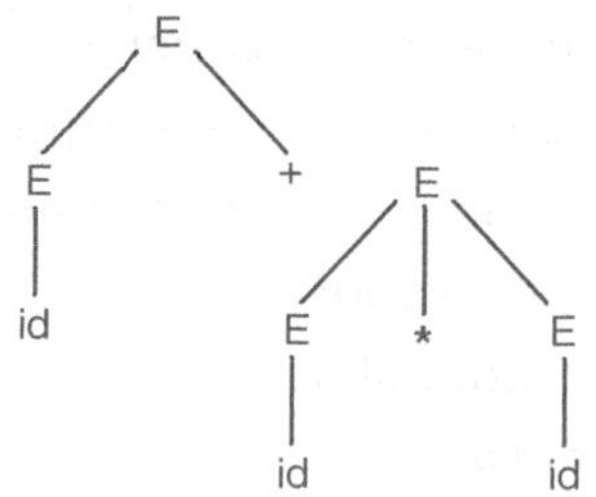

lm

(*ii*) $E \Rightarrow E * E$

$\Rightarrow E + E * E$

$\Rightarrow id + E * E$

$\Rightarrow id + id * E$

$\Rightarrow id + id * id$

$\Rightarrow$

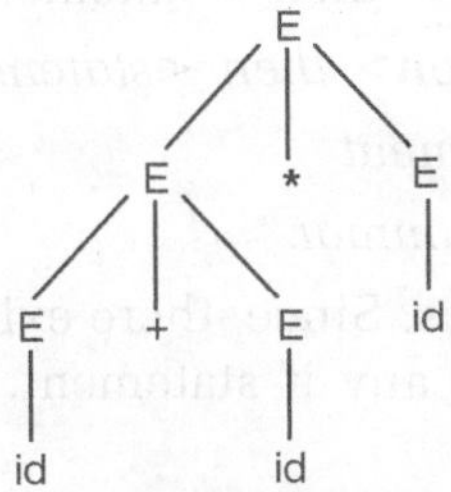

So, same string is generated using two different leftmost derivations. Each having a different parse tree.

∴ Two different parse trees exist for string $id + id * id$

∴ Grammar is Ambiguous.

3.3.2.4. Conversion of ambiguous to unambiguous grammar

The productions containing more than one occurrence of a given non-terminal on its right hand side are ambiguous productions.

Example: $E \rightarrow \mathbf{E} * \mathbf{E}$

It contains two E's on R.H.S.

We can convert these type of Ambiguous productions to unambiguous production by introducing a new Non-terminal to move rightmost of these non-terminal farther down the Parse Tree.

Example 3.12. *Consider the Grammar*

$E \rightarrow E + E \mid E * E \mid (E) \mid id$

Convert this ambiguous Grammar into Unambiguous Grammar.

Sol.

Step 1: Introduction a non-terminal T (term) which cannot be further addition of two terms:

$E \rightarrow E + T \mid T$

$T \rightarrow E * E \mid (E) \mid id$

Step 2: As, we have production $E \rightarrow T$. Substitute E with T to get

$T \rightarrow T * T$

Introduce another non-terminal F (factor) which cannot be further factorized or cannot be multiplication of two numbers.

Substitute T with F to get,

$T \rightarrow T * F \mid F$

$F \rightarrow (E) \mid id$

∴ Unambiguous Grammar will be

$E \rightarrow E + T \mid T$

$T \rightarrow T * F \mid F$

$F \rightarrow (E) \mid id$

Example 3.13 : *Prove that following grammar is Ambiguous for the string "if C then if C_2 then S_1 else S_2".*

<statement> → if <condition> then <statement>

| if <condition> then <statement> else <statement>

| other statement

Convert it into Unambiguous grammar.

Sol. Given grammar is Ambiguous. Since, there exists two Parse trees for the same string. Because else condition can belong to any if statement.

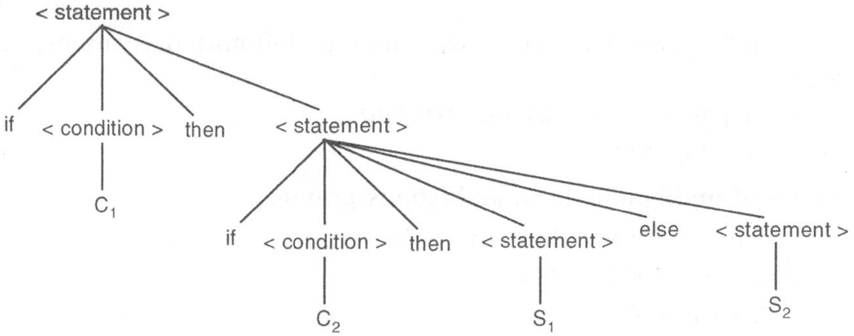

Fig. 3.13. One Parse Tree for if then Else Statement.

In above Parse Tree, else belong to second if

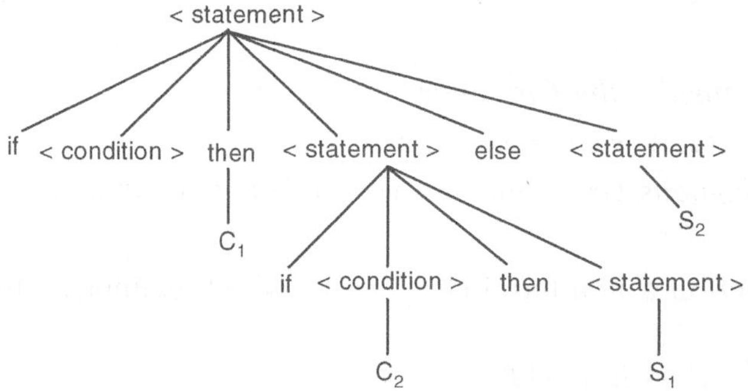

Fig. 3.14. Another Parse Tree for if then Else Statement.

In above Parse Tree, else belongs to first if.

Conversion to Unambiguous Grammar. The Unambiguous Grammar will be:

<statement> → <match_statement>|<unmatch statement>

<match_statement> → is <condition> then <match_statement> else <match_statement>

| other_statement

<unmatch statement> → if <condition> then <statement>

| if <condition> then <match_statement>

else <unmatch statement>

3.3.3 Extended BNF (EBNF)

There are few minor inconveniences in BNF. So BNF is extended in several ways. Most extended versions of BNF are called Extended BNF or simply EBNF. Three extensions are commonly included in the various versions of EBNF.

1. The first denotes an optional part of an RHS, which is delimited by brackets.

   For example: consider the 'C' language selection statement.

   Its BNF representation is

   <select> → if (<expression>) <statement>;

   | if (<expression>) <statement> else <statement>;

   Its corresponding EBNF will be

   <select> → if (<expression>) <statement> [else <statement>];

   Without the use of the brackets, the syntactic description of this statement would require two rules.

2. The second extension is the use of braces in an RHS to indicate that the enclosed part can be repeated indefinitely, or left out altogether. This extension allows lists to be built with a simple rule, instead of using recursion and two rules.

   For example: Consider the list of identifiers.

   BNF : <identifier-List> → <identifier>

   <identifier>, <identifier-List>

   Its corresponding EBNF will be

   EBNF : <identifier_List> → <identifier> {, <identifier>}

   The part enclosed within braces can be iterated any number of times.

3. The third common extension deals with multiple-choice options, when a single element must be chosen from a group, the option are placed in parentheses and separated by the (OR operator|) For example, the following rules describes a Pascal for statement.

   BNF will be

   <For statement> → For <var> : = <expression> to <expression> do <statement>

   It correspanding EBNF will be

   <For statement> → for <var> : = <expression> (to|down to) <expression> do <statement>

   It would require two BNF rules to describe this structure.

Example 3.14. *Convert the following BNF Grammar to EBNF version.*

BNF: *<expression> → <expression> + <term>*

| <expression> – <term>

| <term>

*<term> → <term> * <fact>*

| <term> / <fact>

| <fact>

Sol. The corresponding EBNF for the above BNF will be

<expression> → <term> {(+|-) <term>}

<term> → <factor> {(*|/) <factor>}

3.3.4. Syntax Graphs

A graph is a collection of nodes, some of which are connected by lines called edges. A directed graph is one in which the edges are directional that is, they have arrowheads on one end to indicate a direction. A Parse tree is a restricted form of directed graph.

A syntax graph is a graphical way to express extended BNF rules. Each rule is represented by a path from the input on the left to the output on the right. Any valid path from input to output represents a string generated by that rule.

Syntax graphs use different kinds of nodes to represent the terminal and non-terminal symbols of the right side of a grammar's rules. Rectangle nodes contain the name of syntactic units (non-terminals). Circles or ellipses contain terminal symbols. Syntax chart for assignment statement will be

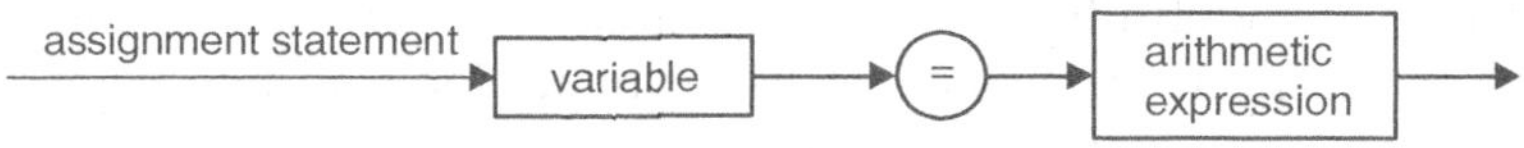

Fig. 3.15. Syntax Graph for Assignment Statement.

Syntax graph or syntax chart for the If then else statement will be

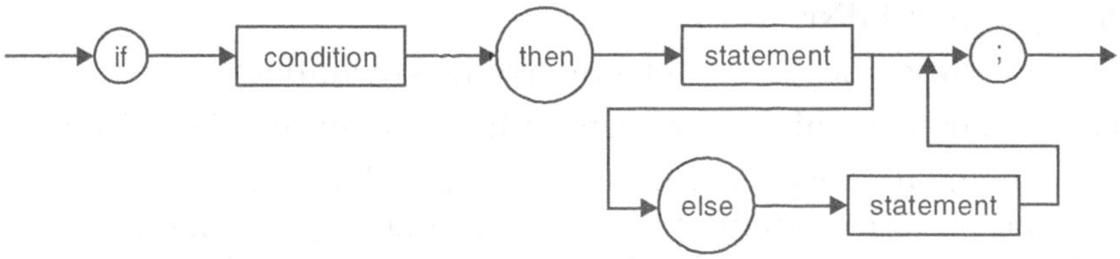

Fig. 3.16. Syntax Graph for if then Else Statement.

3.3.5. Finite State Automata

In Finite Automata, Finite means finite number of states and Automata means, the Automatic Machine which works without any interference of human being. Finite Automata checks whether a string is token or not. The example of tokens are identifiers, constants, operators, keywords, literal, etc.

Finite Automata can be represented by 5 tuples

$(Q, \Sigma, \delta, qs, F)$

(*a*) Q is finite non-empty set of states.

(*b*) Σ is finite set of input symbols.

(*c*) δ is transition function.

(*d*) $q_0 \in Q$ is initial state.

(*e*) $F \subseteq Q$ is the set of final states.

Example 3.15. *Design Finite Automata which accepts string "abb".*

Sol.

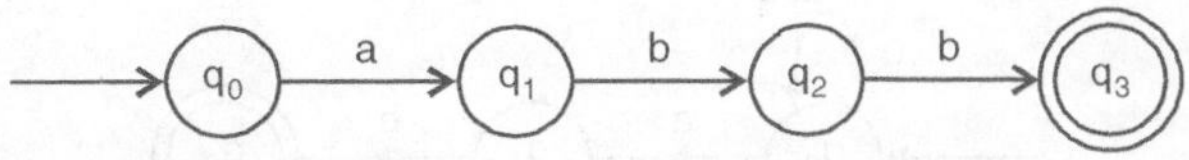

States : $Q = \{q_0, q_1, q_2, q_3\}$

Input symbols : $\Sigma = \{a, b\}$

Transition Fraction δ : $\{\delta\ (q_0, \alpha) = q_1, \delta\ (q_1, b) = q_2, \delta\ (q_2, b) = q_3\}$

initial state : q_0

Final state (*F*) : $\{q_z\}$

Types of Finite Automata

(*a*) **Deterministic Finite Automata (DFA):** "Deterministic" means on each input there is one and only one state to which the automata can have transition from its current state.

DFA is a 5-tuple $(Q, \Sigma, \delta, q_0, F)$ where

(*a*) Q is finite non empty set of states

(*b*) Σ is finite set of input-symbols

(*c*) δ is a transition function to move from current state to next state

$\therefore\ \delta : Q \times \in \rightarrow Q$

(*d*) $q_o \in Q$ is initial state

(*e*) $F \subseteq Q$ is set of final states.

Example: Consider a string ending with *ab* as shown in Fig. 3.17.

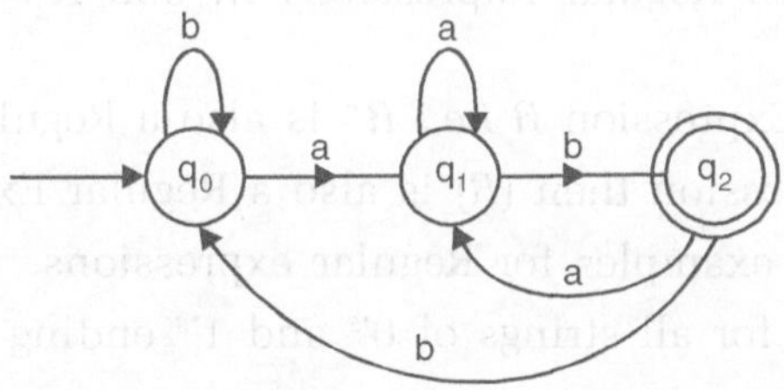

Fig. 3.17. A DFA for all Strings Ending with ab.

(*b*) **Non-Deterministic Finite Automata (NFA):** "Non-Deterministic" means there can be several possible transitions. So, output is non-deterministic for a given input.

NFA is a 5-tuple $(Q, \Sigma, \delta, q_0, F)$ where

(*a*) Q is finite non-empty set of states.

(*b*) Σ is finite set of input symbols.

(*c*) δ is transition function to move from current state to next state.

$\delta : Q\ X\ \Sigma \rightarrow 2^Q$

(*d*) $q_o \in Q$ is initial state.

(*e*) $F \subseteq Q$ is set of Final states.

Example: Consider a NFA ending with *ab* as shown in Fig. 3.18.

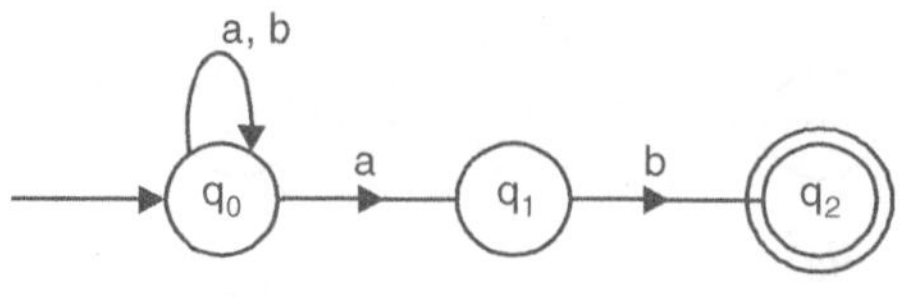

Fig. 3.18. A NFA for all Strings Ending with ab

3.3.6. Regular Grammars and Regular Expressions

Regular grammars. Regular grammars are special cases of BNF grammars. Regular grammars have rules of the form:

<non-terminal> : = <terminal> <Non-terminal> | <terminal>

A grammar that generate binary strings ending in 1 is given by:

$$A \to OA \mid 1A \mid 1$$

The first two alternatives are used to generate any binary string and the third is used to end the generation with a final 1.

Regular Expressions. Regular Expressions define the language accepted by finite automata (Transition Diagram). Regular Expressions are defined over an alphabet Σ. Regular expressions are used to specify tokens.

Rules of Regular Expressions

1. $\in$ is a Regular expression.
2. Union of two Regular Expressions R_1 and R_2. *i.e.,* $R_1 + R_2$ or $R_1 | R_2$ is also a Regular Expression.
3. Concatenation of two Regular Expressions R_1 and R_2. *i.e.,* $R_1\ R_2$ is also a Regular Expression.
4. Closure of Regular Expression R *i.e.,* R^* is also a Regular Expression.
5. If R is Regular Expression then (R) is also a Regular Expression.

Consider the following examples for Regular expressions.

1. Regular expressions for all strings of $0^{\prime s}$ and $1^{\prime s}$ ending with 11 will be

   $R = (0 + 1)^*\ 11$
2. Regular Expression for constant will be

   Constant = digit digit*
3. Regular expression for all strings of $0^{\prime s}$ and $1^{\prime s}$ beginning with 0 and Ending with 1.

   $R = 0\ (0 + 1)^*\ 1$
4. Regular expressions for strings of length zero or one.

   $R = \in\ |a|\ b$

3.4. ATTRIBUTE GRAMMARS

An attribute grammar is an extension of a context free grammar. The extension allows certain language rule to be described, such as compatibility. An attribute grammar is a device used to describe more of the structure of a programming language than is possible with a CFG.

There are some difficulties in BNF. The first one is the implementation of compatibility rules and second the rule that all variables must be declared before they are referenced cannot be specified using BNF.

These two problems exemplify the category of language rules called static sementics rules. The static sematics of a language is only indirectly related to the meaning of programs during execution.

Basic Concepts. Attribute grammars are grammars to which have been added attributes, attribute computation functions and predicate functions.

1. **Attributes.** Attributes are associated with grammar symbols that are similar to variables in the sense that they can have values assigned to them.

Each grammar symbols *X*, is a set of associated attributes *A*(*X*).

The set *A*(*X*) consists of two disjoints sets *S*(*X*) and *I*(*X*) called synthesized and inherited attributes.

(*a*) **Synthesized Attributes.** A synthesized attributes are used to pass semantic information up a parse tree. A synthesized attribute relates the LHS non-terminal to the values of the RHS non-terminal.

(*b*) **Inherited Attributes.** An inherited attributes pass semantic information down a tree. An inherited attributes relates values in a tree with non-terminal values higher up in the tree.

2. **Attribute Computation Functions.** They are sometime called semantic function that are associated with grammar rule to specify how attribute values are computed.

(*a*) **For synthesized attribute.** For a grammar rule $X_0 \rightarrow X_1$ ..... X_n, the synthesized attributes of X_0 are computed with a semantic function.

$S(X_0) = f(A(x_1), \ldots A(x_n))$

The value of a synthesized attribute on a parse tree node depends only on the values of the attributes on that node's children node.

(*b*) **For inherited attributes.** Inherited attributes of symbols X_j are computed with the semantic function of the form $I(X_j) = f(A(x_0), \ldots\ldots A(x_n))$.

So the value of an inherited attribute on a parse tree node depends on the attribute value of that node's parent node.

3. **Predicate functions.** It states some of the syntax and static semantic rules of the language are associated with grammar rules.

A predicate function has a form of a Boolean expression on the attribute set $\{A(x_0), \ldots A(x_n)\}$.

If derivation is allowed with an attribute grammar *i.e.*, every predicate associated with every non-terminal is true and if a violation show in the syntax or semantic rules of the language then a false predicate function value results.

If all the attribute values in a parse tree have been computed the tree is said to be fully attributed.

Intrinsic attributes are syntnesized attributes of leaf nodes whose values are determined outside the parse tree.

Example of Attribute Grammar:

Consider the following grammar

<assignment> → <variable> : = <expression>

<expression> → <variable> + <variable>

| <variable>

<variable> → *X* |*Y*| *Z*

The attributes for the non-terminals in the example attribute grammar are described as:

1. **Actual type.** A synthesized attribute associated with the non-terminals <variable> and <expression> that is used to store actual types, int or real.
2. **Expected type.** An inherited attribute associated with the non-terminal <expression>. It stores the type either real or integer.

An Attribute Grammar for simple Assigment statement

Rule 1. Syntax Rule : <assigment> → <variable> : = <expression>

Semantic rule : <expression>. expected-type ← <variable>. actual-types.

Rule 2. Syntax rule : <expression> → <variable> [2] + <variable> [3]

Semantic rule : <expression>. actual_type ←

if (<variable> [2]. actual-type = int) and

(<variable> [3]. actual-type = int)

then int

else real

end if

Predicate : <expression>. actual_type = <expression>. expected_type.

Rule 3. Syntax rule : <expression> → <variable>

Semantic rule : <expression>. actual-type = <variable>. actual_type.

Predicate : <expression>. actual-type = <expression>. expected_type.

Rule 4. Syntax rule : <variable> → *X* |*Y*| *Z*

Semantic rule : <variable >. actual-type ← look_up (<variable>. string)

Consider the parse tree of sequence

X = *X* + *Y* generated by the grammar

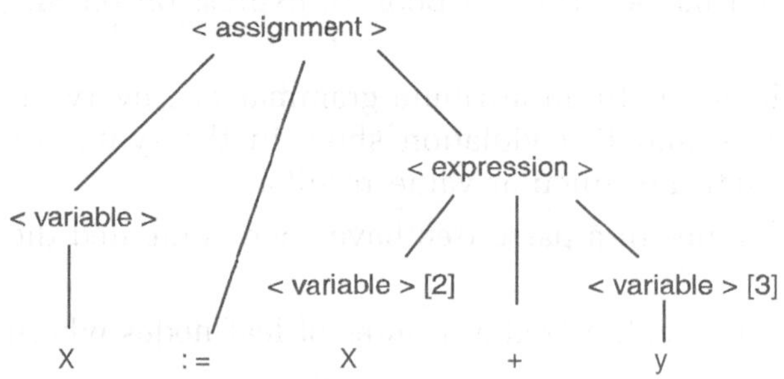

Fig. 3.19. A Parse Tree for *X* : = *X* + *Y*.

Computation of Attribute Values

Attributes are computed in the given order.

1. <variable>. actual-type ← look_up (*X*) [Rule 4]
2. <expression>. expected-type ← <variable>. actual_type [Rule 1]
3. <variable> [2]. actual-type ← look_up [*X*] [Rule 4]
   <variable> [3]. actual-type ← look_up [*Y*] [Rule 4]
4. <expression>. actual-type ← either int or real [Rule 2]
5. <expression>. expected-type = <expression>. actual-type is either True or False (Rule 2)

Evaluation of Attribute Grammar:

Flow of Attribute is shown below:

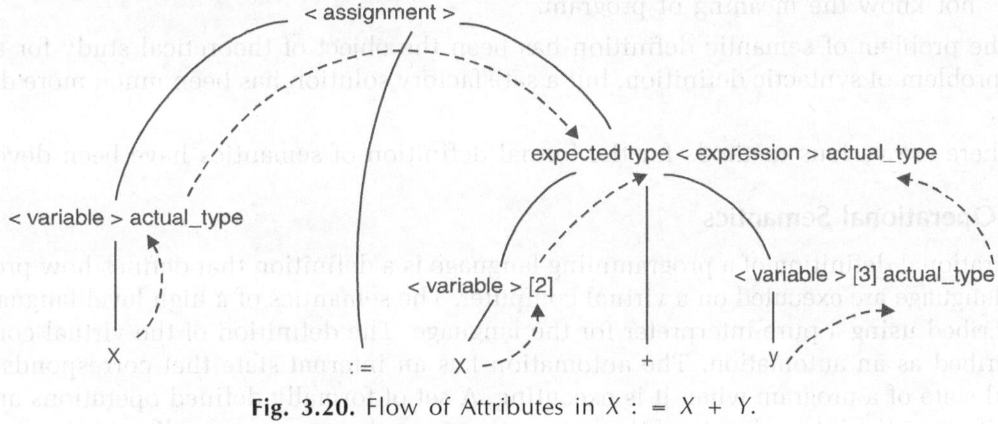

Fig. 3.20. Flow of Attributes in *X* : = *X* + *Y*.

Fully Attribute Parse Tree is given below

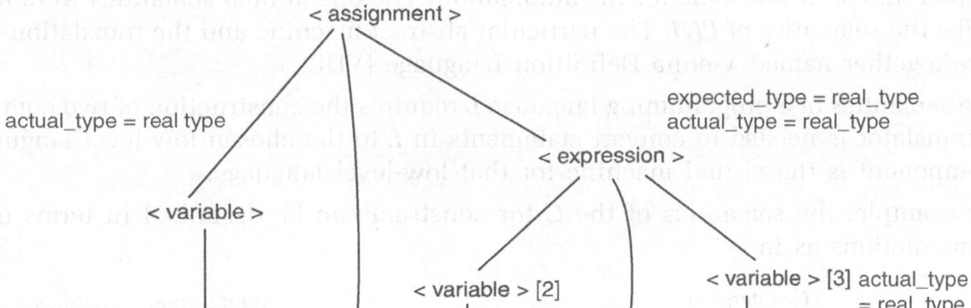

Fig. 3.21. A Fully Attributed Parse Tree for *X* : = *X* + *Y*.

3.5. DYNAMIC SEMANTICS

The semantics (dynamic semantics) is used to describe the meaning of expressions, statements and program units. A programming language must define the meaning of each construct in the language both alone and in conjunction with other language constructs.

There are various reasons why we may be concerned with describing semantics:

1. Programmers must know the meaning of each statement that is executed.
2. Compiler writers also knows the semantics of the language for which thay are writing compilers from English descriptions.
3. The program correctness proofs rely on some formal description of the language semantics.
4. A programmer may misunderstand what a program will do when executed if it does not know the meaning of program.

The problem of semantic definition has been the object of theoretical study for as long as the problem of syntactic definition, but a satisfactory solution has been much more difficult to find.

There are various methods for the formal definition of semantics have been developed.

3.5.1. Operational Semantics

An operational definition of a programming language is a definition that defines how programs in the language are executed on a virtual computer. The semantics of a high level language can be described using a pure interpreter for the language. The definition of the virtual computer is described as an automation. The automation has an internal state that corresponds to the internal state of a program when it is executing. A set of formally defined operations are used to specify how the internal state of the automation may charge corresponding to the execution of one instruction in the program. A second part of the definition specifies how a program text is translated into an initial state for the automation. The operational semantics were first used to describe the semantics of *PL/I*. The particular abstract machine and the translation rules for *PL/I* were together named Vienna Definition Language (VDL).

The semantics of a programming language *L* requires the construction of two components. First, a translator is needed to convert statements in *L* to the chosen low-level language. The other component is the virtual machine for that low-level language.

For example, the semantics of the *C* for construct can be described in terms of a very simple instructions as in

		C-statement		operational semantics
for	(expression 1;	expression 2;	expression 3)	expression 1;
	↓	↓	↓	loop : if expression 2 = 0 go to out
{	Initial	condition	increment	....
	....			expression 3;
}				go to loop
				out; ....

Evaluation. The first and most significant use of formal operational semantics was to describe the semantics of *PL/I*.

Operational semantics provides an effective means of describing semantics for language users and language implementation as long as descriptions are kept simple.

Operational sematics dependes on algorithms not mathematics.

3.5.2. Axiomatic Semantics

This method extends the predicate calculus to include programs. Axiomatic semantics was defined in conjunction with the development of a method to prove the correctness of programs. It defines the meaning of the program explicitly. Axiomatic definitions are defined for each control structure and command. Operational semantics are used to specify the meaning of statement.

(a) Assertions in Axiomatic Semantics

The logical expressions are called predicates or assertions. An assertion immediately preceding a program statement describes the constraints on the program variables at that point in the program. An assertion immediately following a statement describes the new constraints on those variables after execation of the statement.

Assertions of the statement are of two types:

1. **Post-condition.** An assertion immediately following a program statement *S* that do describes new constraints on program variables after the execution of the statement is called a post-condition. Consider the following assignment statement and post condition:

   Sum = 2 * x + 1 {Sum > 1}

   Here {Sum > 1} represents a post-condition.

2. **Pre-condition.** An assertion immediately preceding a program statement *S* that describes the constraints on program variables at that point is called a precondition. One possible precondition for above statement is {x > 10}. *i.e.,* we write

   {x > 10} Sum = 2* x + 1 { Sum > 1}

(b) Weakest Pre-condition

The weakest pre-condition is defined as the least restrictive pre-condition that will guarantee the validity of the associated post-condition. For example, in the semantic notation

Sum = 2* x + 1; {Sum > 1}

All pre-conditions like {x > 10}, {x > 50} and {x > 100} are valid pre-condition but {x >0} is the weakest of all pre-condition in this case.

The weakest pre-condition can be computed from the given post-condition for each statement of a language. The program correctness proofs can be constructed by computing the weakest pre-condition. The weakest pre-condition is computed by a inference rule.

An axiom is a logical statement that is assumed to true and an Inference rule is a method of inferring the truth of one assertion on the basis of the values of other assertions.

(c) Assignment Statements

Consider an assignment statement

$$x = E$$

and Q be its post-condition. Then its pre-condition P is defined by the axiom

$$P = Q_{x \rightarrow E}$$

which means that P is computed as Q with all instances of x replaced by E.

For example,

$$a = b/2 - 1 \{a < 10\}$$

Here $\{a < 10\}$ is post-condition.

The weakest pre-condition is computed by substituting $b/2 - 1$ in the assertion $\{a < 10\}$ as follows

$\{b/2 - 1 < 10\}$

$\{b/2 < 11\}$

$\{b < 22\}$

This the weakest post-condition.

The rule of consequence (Inference rule) states that if S_1, S_2 ..... S_n are true, then the truth of S can be inferred as

$$\frac{S_1, S_2 \ldots S_n}{S}$$

The form of rule of consequences is

$$\frac{\{P\}\, S\, \{Q\}, P' \Rightarrow P, Q \Rightarrow Q'}{\{P'\}\, S\, \{Q'\}}$$

Consider $P = \{x > 3\}$ and $Q' = \{x > 0\}$ and $P' = \{x > 5\}$ we can write as

$$\frac{\{x > 3\}\; x = x - 3\, \{x > 0\}, \{x > 5\} \Rightarrow (x > 3), (x > 0) \Rightarrow \{x > 0\}}{\{x > 5\}\; x = x - 3\, \{x > 0\}}$$

(d) Sequence of Statements

The weakest pre-condition for a sequence of statements cannot be described by an axiom. Let S_1 and S_2 be adjacent program statement. If S_1 and S_2 have the pre-and post-conditions.

$\{P_1\}\ S_1\ \{P_2\}$

$\{P_2\}\ S_2\ \{P_3\}$

The inference rule for such a two-statement sequence is

$$\frac{\{P_1\}\, S_1\, \{P_2\}, \{P_2\}\, S_2\, \{P_3\}}{\{P_1\}\, S_1; S_2\, \{P_3\}}$$

In this $\{P_1\}\ S_1;\ S_2\ \{P_3\}$ describes the axiomatic semantics of the sequence S_1, S_2. If S_1 and S_2 are the assigment statements

$x_1 = E_1$

and $x_2 = E_2$

Then we have

$\{P_3\ x_2 \rightarrow E_2\}\ x_2 = E_2\ \{P_3\}$

$\{P_3\ x_2 \rightarrow E_2\}\ \{x_1 \rightarrow E_1\}\ x_1 = E_1\ \{P_3\ x_2 \rightarrow E_2\}$

where $\{(P_3\ x_2 \rightarrow E_2)\ x_1 \rightarrow E_1\}$

(e) Selection Statement

For selection statements, we consider only selections that include else clauses.

The inference rule is

$$\frac{\{B \text{ and } P\}\ S_1\ \{Q\}, \{(\text{not } B) \text{ and } P\}\ S_2\ \{Q\}}{\{P\} \text{ if } B \text{ than } S_1 \text{ else } S_2\ \{Q\}}$$

Selection statements must be proven for both of their cases.

(f) Logical Pretest Loops

Another essential construct of an imperative programming language is the while loop.

It is more difficult to compute the weakest precondition for a while loop. The inference rule for while loop is

$$\frac{(I \text{ and } B)\ S\ \{I\}}{\{I\} \text{ while } B \text{ do } S \text{ end } \{I \text{ and } (\text{not } B)\}}$$

where I is called loop invariant. It is crucial to find the weakest pre-condition.

The axiomatic description of a while loop is written as

$\{P\}$ while B do S end $\{Q\}$

The complete axiomatic require all of the following to be true in which I is the loop invariant:

$P \Rightarrow I$

$\{I\}\ B\ \{I\}$

$\{I$ and $B\}\ S\ \{I\}$

$(I$ and (not B)) $\Rightarrow Q$

the loop terminates.

The process of weakest pre-condition as a function, *wp*. In general

Wp. (statement, post-condition) = Pre-condition.

(g) Evaluation

For axiomatic method, an axiom or an inferance rule must be defined for each statement type in the language. It is a difficult task.

Axiomatic semantics is a powerful tool for reaseach into program correctness proofs and it provides an excellent framework in which to reason about program. It is useful in describing the meaning of programming languages.

3.5.3. Denotational Semantics

Denotational Semantics is the most widely used method for describing the meaning of programs. It is solidly based on recursive function. It is long and complex method. The concept of denotational semantics is to define for each language entity both a mathematical object and a function that maps instances of that entity on to instances of the mathematical object.

Consider the following example.

The syntax for binary number can be deseribed by the following grammar rules:

<binary> → 0
| 1
| <binary> 0
| <binary> 1

A parse tree for the binary number 101 is shown as

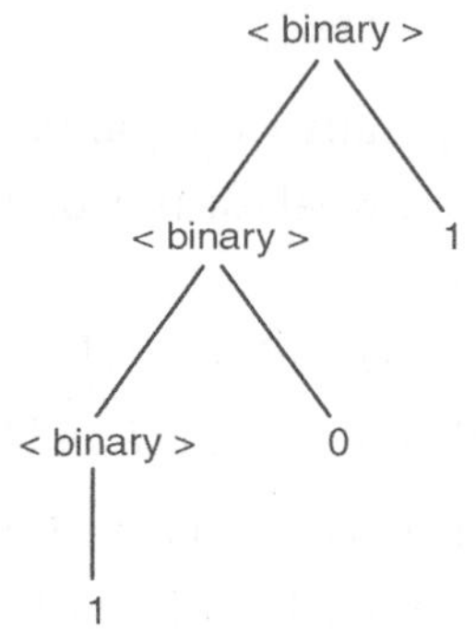

Fig. 3.22. A Parse Tree for a Binary Number 101.

The semantic function *M* bin for mapping the syntactic objects as:

M bin ('0') = 0
M bin ('1') = 1
M bin (<binary> '0') = 2∗ *M* bin (<binary>)
M bin (<binary> '1') = 2∗ *M* bin (<binary>) + 1

Now Parse Tree with denoted object for 101 will be

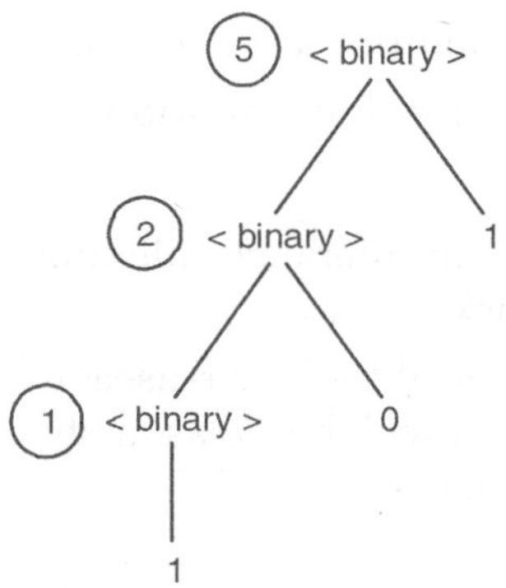

Fig. 3.23. A Parse Tree with Denoted Object for 101.

Similarly for a parse tree with denoted objects for 110 will be

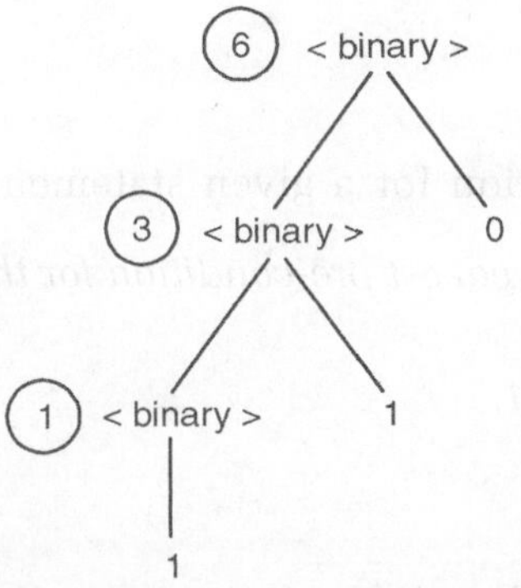

Fig. 3.24. A Parse Tree with Denoted Objects for 110.

We now show the similar example for describing the meaning of syntactic decimal literals.

$$<decimal> \rightarrow 0|1|2|3|4|5|6|7|8|9$$
$$|<decimal>\ (0|1|2|3|4|5|6|7|8|9)$$

The syntactic rules are

$$M_{decimal}\ ('0') = 0$$
$$M_{decimal}\ ('1') = 1$$
$$\vdots$$
$$M_{decimal}\ ('9') = 9$$
$$M_{decimal}\ (<decimal>\ '0') = 10 * M_{decimal}\ (<decimal>)$$
$$M_{decimal}\ (<decimal>\ '1') = 10 * M_{decimal}\ (<decimal>) + 1$$
$$\vdots$$
$$M_{decimal}\ (<decimal>\ '9') = 10 * M_{decimal}\ (<decimal>) + 9$$

Evalvation. Denotational semantics can be used as an aid to language design. The statements for which the denotational semantic description is complex and difficult for designer. Due to complexity these are little use to language users. It not provide guidance to the implementor.

Example 3.16. *Calculate the weakest pre-condition for the following assignments statements.*

1. $x = 2 * y - 3\ \{x > 25\}$
2. $x = x + y - 3\ \{x > 10\}$

Sol. 1. $x = 2 * y - 3\ \{x > 25\}$

The pre-condition is computed as

$$2 * y - 3 > 25$$
$$2 * y > 28$$
$$y > 14$$

Thus the weakest pre-condition is $\{y > 14\}$

2. $x = x + y - 3\ \{x > 10\}$

The weakest pre-condition is computed as

$$x + y - 3 > 10$$
$$x + y > 13$$
$$y > 13 - x$$

Thus the weakest pre-condition for a given statement is $\{y > 13 - x\}$.

Example 3.17. *Consider the weakest pre-condition for the following sequence of assignment and their post-condition.*

*y = 3 * x + 1;*
x = y + 3;
{x < 10}

Sol.
y = 3 * x + 1
x = y + 3;
{x < 10}

The weakest pre-conditon for the last assigment statement is

$$y + 3 < 10$$
$$y < 7$$

This is then used as the post-condition of first

$$3 * x + 1 < 7$$
$$3 * x < 6$$
$$x < 2$$

Example 3.18. *Calculate the weakest pre-condition for the following selection statements and the post-condition.*

if (x > 0)
y = y − 1
else y = y + 1

Sol. Let us consider the post-condition for one selection statement is $\{y > 0\}$.

We can use the axiom for assigment on the then clause

$$y = y - 1 \; \{y > 0\}$$
$$y - 1 > 0$$
$$\Rightarrow \quad y > 1 \qquad ...(1)$$

Similarly we can apply the same axiom to else clause.

$$y = y + 1 \; \{y > 0\}$$
$$y + 1 > 0$$
$$\Rightarrow \quad y > -1 \qquad ...(2)$$

From (1) and (2) we apply the rule of consequence *i.e.*,

$\{y > 1\} \Rightarrow \{y > -1\}$.

Thus the weakest pre-condition will be $\{y > 1\}$.

Some Important Terms

- The validity of a sentence is based on their syntax and semantics.
- Syntax of a programming language is the form of its expressions, statements and program units.
- Semantics of a programming language is the meaning given to various syntactic constructs.
- The programming language can be formaly defined in two distinct ways:
  - Language recognizers
  - Language generators
- Language recognizers is a device capable of reading strings of characters from the alphabet Σ.
- Language generator is a device that can be used to generate the sentences of a language.
- There are various formal methods of describing syntax.
  - Context free grammars
  - BNF grammars
  - Extended BNF
  - Syntax graphs
  - Finite state automata
  - Regular grammars and regular expressions.
- BNF is meta language *i.e.*, a language used to describe another language.
- Derivation means replacing a given string's non-terminal by right-hand side of production rule.
- There are two types of derivation
  - Left-most derivation
  - Right-most derivation
- Yield of Derivation tree is the concatenation of the labels of the leaves in left to right ordering.
- A grammar that produces more than one left most derivation for the same sentence is called Ambiguous Grammar.
- Multiplication (*) operator has higher precedence than addition (+) operator.
- +, – and / are left associative.
- EBNF are the extended version of BNF.
- A syntax graph is a graphical way to express extended BNF rules.
- Finite automata checks whether a string is token or not.
- Finite automata may be
  - Deterministic finite automata
  - Non deterministic finite automata
- 'Deterministic' means on each input there is one and only one state to which the automata can have transition from its current state.
- 'Non-Deterministic' means there can be several possible transitions.

- Regular grammar are special cases of BNF grammars.
- Regular expressions define the language accepted by finite automata.
- An attribute grammar is a device used to describe more of the structure of a programming language.
- Dynamic semantics is used to describe the meaning of expressions, statements and program units.
- An operational definition of a programming language is a definition that defines how programs in the language are executed on a virtual computer.
- Axiomatic semantics was defined in conjunction with the development of a method to prove the correctness of programs.
- An assertion immediately following a program statement *S* is called post-condition.
- An assertion immediately preceding a program statement *S* is called pre-condition.
- The weakest pre-condition is defined as the least restrictive pre-condition that will guarantee the validity of the associated post-condition.
- An axiom is a logical statement that is assumed to true.
- An inference rule is method of inferring the truth of one assertion on the basis of the values of other assertions.
- Denotational semantic is used to define for each language entity both a mathematical object and a function.
- Denotational semantic can be used as an aid to language design.

Review Questions

1. Define the term syntax and semantics of a language.
2. Explain the general problem of describing syntax.
3. Explain language recognizers and language generators.
4. Explain formal methods of describing syntax.
5. Write short notes on:
   (*a*) CFG and BNF
   (*b*) BNF and EBNF
   (*c*) Regular grammar and regular expression.
6. Explain Parse Tree or Derivation Tree. Also explain Left-most and Right-most derivation.
7. Explain the concept of Ambiguity.
8. Explain the terms:
   (*a*) Syntax Graphs
   (*b*) Finite State Automata
   (*c*) Attribute Grammar.
9. Explain the term Dynamic semantic. Also explain various types of Dynamic semantics.
10. Define term Derivation. Also explain Parse Tree or Derivation Tree.
11. Describe the approach of using axiomatic semantics to prove the correctness of a given program.
12. Describe the basic concepts of denotational semantics.
13. What is a grammar? Explain the backus and nor form grammar using suitable examples.
14. Differentiate between context free grammar and regular grammar.

Chapter **4**

STRUCTURED DATA OBJECTS

In chapter 2, we have discussed primitive type or elementary data objects. In application point of view we find that the data is generally structured in some ways. Most imperative languages provide some support for structured types. Users may be able to define their own types, and this can create some meaningful programs. Virtually all languages have included features for creating complex data objects out of the elementary data objects defined by the language designers. Various types can be combined to create aggregate types, composed of elements of other types, such as arrays and records. Most programming language have at least one built in type, although there are typeless languages, where data objects can be coerced automatically from one type to another. Arrays, lists and sets are ways to create homogeneous collection of data objects. Records are a mechanism for creating non-homogeneous collection of data objects.

4.1. STRUCTURED DATA OBJECTS AND DATA TYPES

Primitive data objects contains single elements. But a structured data objects or a data structure contains other data objects as its elements or components. In structured data objects we are taken more complex setting. In structured data objects, contains arrays, records, stacks, lists and sets are considered. Data objects that are made up of other data objects, called its components, is termed as a structured data object or data structure. Component of an array may be a number or it may be character string or another array.

The binding of data structures to values, names and location are important. The specification and implementation of structural data is the main problem. How we can make component data objects of a data structure and its relationship in such a way that selection of a components from the structure is straight forward. Second is storage issues that are not present with primitive data objects.

4.1.1. Specification of Data Structure of Structured Data Objects

The main points for specifying structured data objects are given below:

1. **Type of components.** Type of components includes whether a data structure is homogeneous if all its components are of the same type or it is hetrogeneous if its components are of different types. Arrays, files and sets are examples of homogeneous type while records and lists are the examples of hetrogeneous type.
2. **Total number of components.** A structured data objects contains another structured data objects as its components. The components of structured data object is of either fixed size, if the number of components is invariant during its lifetime or of variable size if the number of components changed dynamically. The operation that are performed on variable size data structure is insertion and deletion of elements. Arrays and records are example of fixed size and stacks, files, tables, lists are example of variable size.
3. **Structure of the components.** The most common used sequence of components is linear sequence of components in which elements are arrayed in sequence. Array, stacks, lists, files, records follow linear sequence of components. The elements arrays are stored in contiguous memory locations. The mainly used organization of components is linear sequence.
4. **Name to be used to select a component.** In structured data object we need a mechanism to identify each component individually. A unique name is given by which it can be identify. For an array, the name of an individual component may be an integer subscript.
5. **Maximum number of components.** The maximum size of the components may be specified by a programmer. For example, the size of stack may be specified in terms of length. It will easy to access the elements in some sort.

4.1.2. Operations on Structured Data Objects

There are various operations that are performed on the structured data objects. The specification of the domain and range of operation on data structure may be given in the same manner as in the case of elementary types. The operations that are performed on data structure are:

1. **Creation and destruction of structued data object.** This operation contains the creation of new data structure and destruction of old data structure.

For example: Array is created in *'C'* like.

int a [10];

this will create an array of type integer and its maximum length is ten.

2. **Insertion of new components.** This operation will insert the new components to the existing data structure.

   For example: We can insert an element in array and we can also insert an element in stack by push operation.

3. **Deletion of existing component.** This operation will delete an element from a data structure. Deletion of elements means it will not contain in the existing data structure.

4. **Selection of a component.** This operation consist of processing of data structures often proceeds by retrieving each component of the structure. There are two types of selection operation to access components of a data structure.

   (*a*) **Sequential selection.** In this we can select a component by sequential operation. We can move in the list sequentially to select a component.

   (*b*) **Random selection.** This operation contains random selection of component. In this we can randomely pick a component in the structured data object.

5. **Operation performed on whole data structure.** In this we can perform the operation on the complete data structure. It contains entire data structure as arguments and produce new data structure as results.

   For example: Addition of two arrays and produce a new array, another example of this is merging of two arrays and produce a new array.

4.1.3. Implementation of Structured Data Objects

Implementation of structured data objects means how the structured data object is stored in memory there are two things regarding storage first how the components of the structure is stored and second the storage of optional descriptor in memory. There are two ways to implements structured data objects:

1. **Sequential storage representation.** In this storage representation the elements are stored in continous memory location. A single block of storage is provided for descriptor and components.

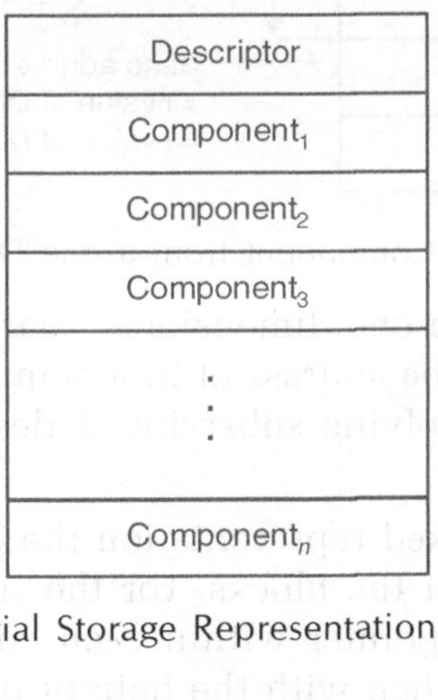

Fig. 4.1. Sequential Storage Representation with Descriptor.

2. **Linked list representation.** In linked list represeartation, the data structure is stored in several non-continous blocks of storage, with linked together though pointers.

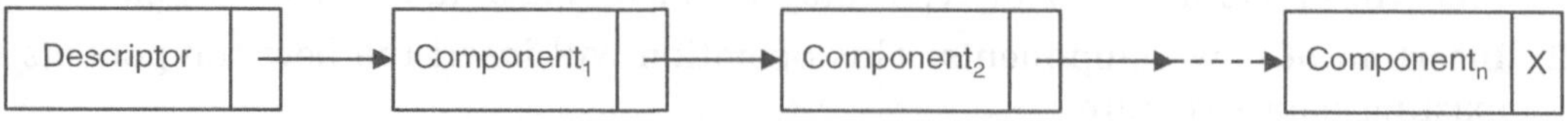

Fig. 4.2. Linked List Representation of Data Structure.

In this figure component 1 is connected to the component 2 by pointers. A pointer from one block to another is called a link. Link contains address of another component. This will help him to find next element in the memory.

4.1.4. Implementation of Operation on Structured Data Objects

In the implementation point of view, the main operation is the component selection operation. How we can select a component *A [I]* from an array. We know there are two ways a sequential selection on a random selections. The two basic types of component selection are implemented differently for sequential and linked storage representation.

1. **Sequential representation.** In sequential representation the components are stored in contigeous memory locations. The random selection of a component include is base-address-plus-offset calculation using an accessing formula. The relative location of the selected component within a sequential block is called its offset. The starting location is known as base address. The accessing formula given the name or subscript of the desired component, specifies how to compute the offset of the component. Selection of the desired component is given by the formula.

Location of desired component = Base address + Offset

One offset = Subscript of the desired component × Component size

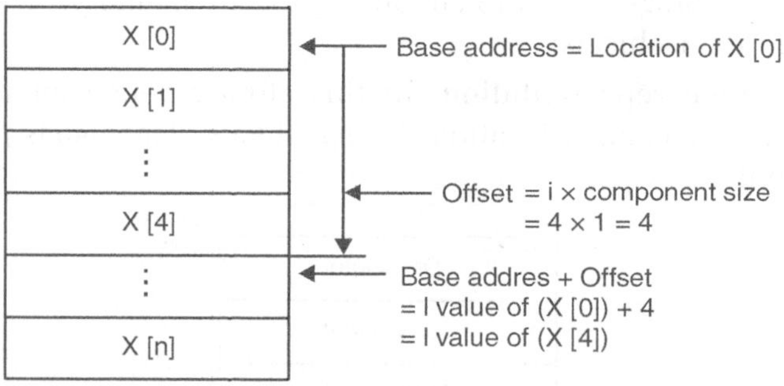

Fig. 4.3. Selection of X [4] Component from a one Dimensional Character Array.

In the Fig. 4.3, the *x* [n] is the one dimensional char array. The size of each component is therefore one. Base address will be address of first component in the array [l value of *x* [0]). Offset will be calculated by multiplying subscript of desired component to the component size.

Linked representation. In linked representation the elements are stored in blocks and a chain of pointer is used to connect the blocks. For the selection of the component we have to know the poisition of the link pointer within each component block. Selection includes selecting the first component and then with the help of pointers we can reach to the desired component. It is easy technique but pointer position within the component block must be known. By following the pointer to the next block we can select a desired components in the linked representation.

4.1.5. Storage Management of Structured Data Objects

When a data object is created, its life-time begins when the binding of the object to a particular storage location is made and its life-time ends when this binding is no more remains. Like in C++ constructors are used to construct object then their life time begins and when their life time ends, destructors member function are called to free the storage location created by the objects.

For the structured data objects, individual components have their own life-times, which are determined by the time at which they created and by the time at which they are deleted from their structure. When a data object is created, an access path to data object must also be created by which we can access the object. During the life-time of a data object, additional access paths to it may be created.

For example: By passing it as an argument to a subprogram. There are two problems regarding the storage management.

(*a*) **Garbage object.** A data object is said to be garbage when its all access path are destroyed but the data object continues to exist. In this case the object is of no use because it cannot be accessed. However its binding to storage location remains same. But its storage is of no use.

(*b*) **Dangling reference.** A dangling reference is problem associated with a data object is that when a data object is destroyed but its access path remains there. The access path leads to the location of a data objects. But life-time of the data object ends because the data object is destroyed.

Dangling references are generally more serious than garbage because they may compromise the integrity of the entire run time structure during program execution. Garbage is less serious, but still troublesome. A data object that is garbage ties up storage that might otherwise be relocated for another purpose. This will effect on the storage management. Because data object that remain there has no use but it contains the storage. It has no use because it cannot be accessed. Dangling reference violates the security of the type checking structure. Dangling reference also destroying the integrity of the storage management system.

4.2. DECLARATION AND TYPE CHECKING OF STRUCTURED DATA OBJECTS

Declaration of structured data objects. Declaration means how the structured data object is created or how we can declare a data object of structured type.

For Example: In '*C*' language we can declare a two dimensional array like this

int a [10] [10];

Attributes of Array *A* are:

(*a*) Data type is an Array.

(*b*) Number of dimensions in two.

(*c*) Number of components is 10 × 10 = 100.

(*d*) Subscripts naming the rows are the integers from 0 to 9 and subscript naming the columns are the integers from 0 to 9.

(*e*) Data type of each component is integer.

This declaration allows a sequential storage representation for *A* and a appropriate accessing formula for selecting any component *A* [*i*] [*j*]. Without declaration, the attributes of *A* would be determined at runtime.

Type checking for structured data objects. Type checking is more complex for structured data objects because component selection operation are taken place.

The main problems are:

(*a*) **Checking the existence of selected component.** For a selection operation the argument must be of right type. If for a selection operation the argument is of proper type but that component does not exist in the data structure.

For example. An array may receive a subscript that is out of bounds for a particular array. This problem is not releated with type checking. It gives an incorrect *L*-value. The operation receiving the result is given an invalid argument. Component selection use an accessing formula to compute the offset of the selected component in the sequention block. Run time checking is required to determine whether the component exists before the formula is used to find its *L*-value.

(*b*) **Checking the type of a selected component.** For selected a component a complex path is formed to the desired component.

For example: *A* [3] [4]. Link → Value

Selects the component via a pointer link to a particular component of row 3 and column 4 of an Array A. Static type checking guarantees that if the component does exist, then it is of the right type. It cannot be assumed that the selected component exists when needed at runtime.

4.3. VECTORS AND ARRAYS

Vector and array are the most common type of data structures. A vector is a data structure composed of a fixed number of components of the same type organized as a simple linear sequence. A vector is also termed as one dimensional array or linear array. An array is a data structure that holds a sequence of element of the same type. A fundamental property of arrays is that *A* [*i*], the ith element of array *A*, can be accessed quickly, for any value of *i* at run time. The index of *i* is often an integer, but it does not need to be. A language designer can allow the index to be any type or value.

Specification of vectors are:

1. Data type of each component are same *i.e.,* all components are of same type.
2. Number of components which is given by subscript range, one for each dimension.
3. Subscript is to be used to select each component, which is given by a range of integers, with first integer designated the first component and second designated by the second component.

For example, consider the following Pascal declaration.

A : Array [1996 . . 2000] of real;

which contains five component each a real number, where components are selected by the subscripts 1996, 1997, 1998, 1999, 2000.

In '*C*' language we declare it as

float a [5];

declares a '*C*' Array of 5 components with subscripts ranges from 0 to 4.

Operations on vectors. The operation on vectors are operations to create and destroy vectors, assignment to component of a vector and operation that perform arithmetic operations on pair of vectors of the same size, such as addition of two vectors. Vectors are of fixed size so insertion and deletion of components are not allowed.

The main operation on vectors is to select a particular component from a vector is called subscripting. The subscripting operation returns the *l*-value or location of the relevent data objects.

Implementation. The components of a vector are homogeneous. It implies that the size and structure of each component is same and fixed size implies the number and position of each component of a vector are invariant throughout its life-time. A sequential storage representation is appropriate and is shown in Fig. 4.4.

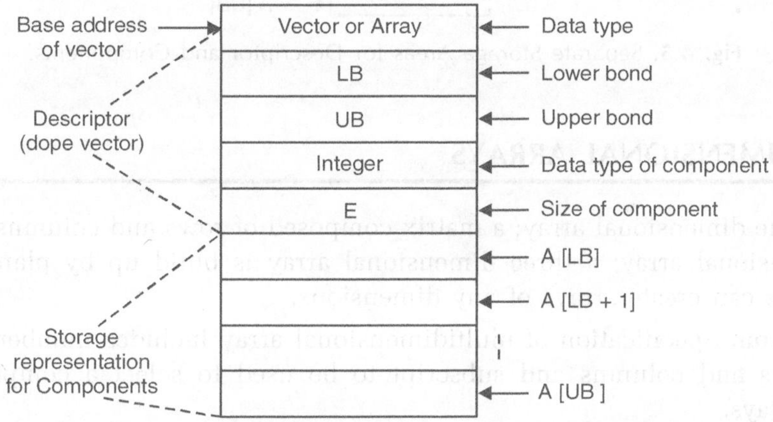

Fig. 4.4. Full Descriptor Representation of Vector A.

Location of desired component = Base address + Offset

and Offset = Subscript of the × Component size derived component

$$l \text{ value } (A[I]) = \alpha + [I - LB] \times E$$

where α = Base Address

LB = Lower Bourt

E = memory locations.

Let us now address the element with subscript 0 of our vector.

$$l \text{ value } (A[0]) = \alpha + (0 - lB) \times E$$

$$= \alpha - LB \times E$$

$$= M$$

M represents the Address that the element 0 of the vector would occupy, if it exists. Since the zeroth element may not be part of the array, this address is called the virtual origin (V_0).

The concept of virtual origin (V_0) gives an accessing formula.

l value $(A(I)) = V_0 + I \times E$

Note that if the subscript *I* is not within the range $LB \leq I \leq UB$,

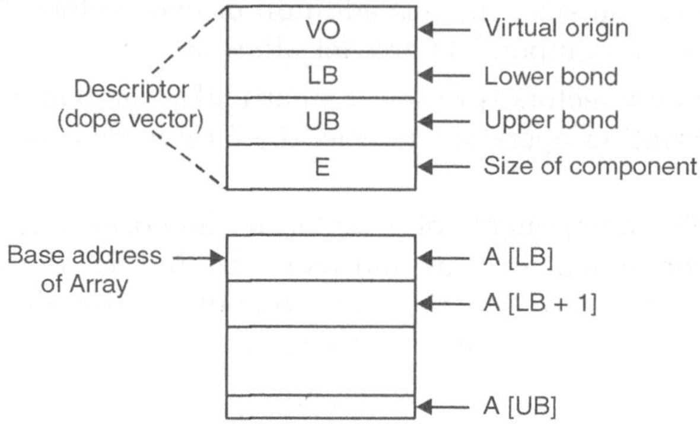

Fig. 4.5. Separate Storage Areas for Descriptor and Components.

4.4. MULTIDIMENSIONAL ARRAYS

A vector is a one dimensional array; a matrix composed of rows and columns of components is a two dimensional array; a three dimensional array is build up by planes of rows and columns. So we can create arrays of any dimensions.

Specification. Specification of multidimensional array includes number of dimensions, number of rows and columns and subscript to be used to select a component in multi-dimensional arrays.

In pascal we declared as

A: array [1 .. 5, –5 ..... 1] of integer;

It means lower bound of row is 1 and upper bound of row is 5. Also the lower bound of column is –5 and upper bond of columns is 1.

Implementation. A matrix can be implemented as a row-major order or column major order. When a matrix is stored in memory all elements of it are stored linearly since computer's memory can only be viewed as consecutive units of memory.

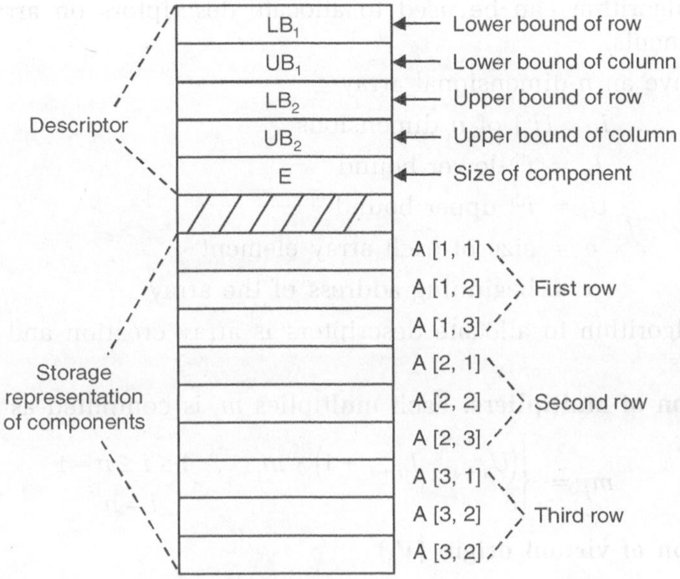

Fig. 4.6. Row Major Representation of a Matrix.

Suppose we have a matrix having declaration

int A [3, 3];

It means, it has three rows and three columns if it is stored as row major order then the representation is shown in Fig. 4.5.

For selecting a component when the matrix A has M rows and N columns we use the following formula.

$$l \text{ value } (A[I, J]) = \alpha + (I - LB_1) \times S + (J - LB_2) \times E$$

where

α – base address

S – length of row $= (UB_2 - LB_2 + 1) \times E$

LB_1 = lower bound of row

LB_2 = lower bound of columns

UB_2 = upper bound of columns.

To find the L-value of $A[I, J]$, first determine the number of rows to skip over, $(I - LB_1)$ Multiply the length of row to get the location of the start of the Ith row and J^{th} component in the row.

$$V_0 = \alpha - LB_1 \times S - LB_2 \times E$$

$$l \text{ value } (A[I, J]) = V_0 + I \times S + J \times E$$

Similar to the vector case,

E = component size

S = size of each row of the matrix

V_0 = virtual origin

Higher dimensionality arrays. The formulas to higher dimension is straight forward. The following general algorithm can be used to allocate descriptors on array creation and for accessing array elements.

Assume we have an n-dimensional array

$A\,[L_1 : V_1, \ldots\ldots L_n : U_n]$ of n dimensions

where L_i = i^{th} lower bound

U_i = i^{th} upper bound

e = size of each array element

α = beginning address of the array

The general algorithm to allocate descriptors is array creation and for accessing array elements is given as

- **Computation of multipliers.** Each multiplies m_i is computed as follows:

$$m_i = \begin{cases} (U_{i+1} - L_{i+1} + 1) \times m_{i+1}, & 1 \le i \le n-1 \\ e & i = n \end{cases}$$

- **Computation of virtual origin (V_0)**

$$V_0 = \alpha - \sum_{i=1}^{n} (l_i \times m_i)$$

The multipliers m_i aid the virtual origin V_0 can be stored in the run time descriptors for the array.

- **Address of array element.** The address of element $A\,[S_1, S_2, \ldots\ldots S_n)$ is given by

$$l \text{ value } (A\,[S_1, S_2, \ldots\ldots S_n]) = V_0 + \sum_{i=1}^{n} (S_i \times m_i).$$

4.5. RECORDS

A record is the collection of data items of hetrogeneous type means records is the collection of components having different types. Records allow variable relevant to an object to be grouped together and treated as a unit.

Specification. Records and vectors have fixed length data items but both differ by

(*a*) Components of records are of different data types while components of vectors are of same data type.

(*b*) Component of records are named with identifiers while components of vectors are indexed with subscripts.

A record type with K field can have the following form:

```
record
    <name1>   :  <type1>;
    <name2>   :  <type2>;
    ...
```

<name$_k$> : <type$_k$>;

end

where, <name *i*> is the name of field *i* and <type *i*> is the type of field *i*.

In 'C' language we can declare a record as

```
Struct student type
{
    int Rollno;
    Char Name;
    int Age;
    float fees;
    student;
}
```

Here studenttype is the name of record having four components Rollno and Age of type integer. Name is of type character and fees is of type float. We can declare the variable of structure. Like shown in above. Student is a variable of type studenttype means student is a object of type studenttype.

For selecting a component we use as:

Student . Rollno;

Student . Age;

Attributes of a record includes the number of components, data type of each component and the selector used to name each component.

The Array element selected by *A* [*i*] can change at run time, depending on the value of *i*, but the record field name is fixed at compile time. Main operation is component selection operation.

Implementation. The storage representation for a record consists of a single sequential block of memory in which the components are stored in sequence (Figure 4.6).

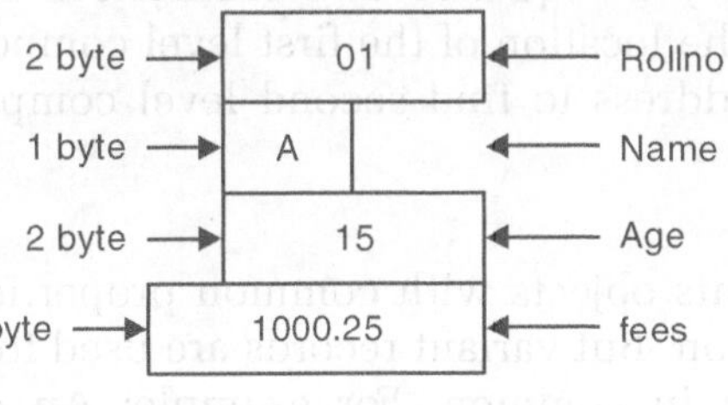

Fig. 4.7. Storage Representation for Struct Employee.

At run time no descriptor is required to indicate data type.

Component selection uses the following access formula for I^{th} component.

$$l \text{ value } (R \cdot I) = \alpha + \sum_{i=1}^{I-1} (\text{size of } R \,.\, i)$$

where α is the base address of the storage block representing *R* and $R \cdot i$ is the ith component. Offset of any component may be computed during translations. The summation is necessary because of the possibly differing size of each component. However the summation may also be computed during translation to give the offset.

4.5.1. Arrays of Records

In some languages, there is provision made for components of the two types to be intermixed with components of elementary types.

For example in 'C' we can declare arrays of records as

```
Struct Employee Type
{
    int ID;
    int Age;
    float Salary;
    Employee [100];
}
```

which declare a vector of 100 components, each of which is an Employee Type record. A component of such a composite data structure is selected by using a sequence of selection operations to select first a component of the vector and then a component of the record as in Employee [2]. *ID*.

A record may also have components that are arrays or other records, leading to records that have hierarchical structure consisting of a top level of components, some of which may be arrays or records.

Implementation. The storage representations developed for simple vectors and records extend without change to vector and records whose components are themselves vectors or records. A vector of records has the same storage representation as a vector of integer or any elementary type, except that the storage block for a record. Similarly, a record whose components are records or vectors retains the same sequential storage representation, but with each component represented by a subblock that may be represents the entire record. Selection of the components requires only a sequence of selection starting from the base address and computing an offset to find the location of the first level component, followed by computation of an offset from the base address to find second level component.

4.5.2. Variant Records

A Record may often represents objects with common properties; all records of the same type have the same field in common. But variant records are used for representing objects that have some but not all properties in common. For example: An employee have some common properties like *ID*, Age, Name, Department but an employee may be paid either hourly or monthly. It may be useful to have a single record type that has several variants.

For example: A record containing employee payroll information may have two variants, one for salaried employees paid by the month and one for employee paid by the hour. The Pascal declaration:

```
type   Pay = (Salary, Hourly)
Var    Employee : Record
       ID : integer;
```

```
            Age : integer;
      Case  Pay : Pay type of
            Salary :  (MonthRate : real;
                      StartDate : integer);
            Hourly :  (HourRate : Real;
                      overtime : integer;
                      Hoursworked : real;)
      end
```

This defines a variant record. The record has component *ID*, Age, Pay. When the value of Pay = Salary, then the record has the components Month Rate and Start Rate, while if the value of Pay = Hourly, then its has the components Hour rate, overtime, Hours worked, etc.

The component pay is called tag or Discriminant because it serves to indicate which variant of the record exists at a given point during program execution.

The selection operation for components of a variant record is the same as that for an ordinary record. For example, Employee, Salary.

A component in variant record may exist at one point during execution and may later disappear during point of execution and later may reappear if the tag changes back to its original value. So there is two possible solutions.

- **Dynamic checking.** The tag component may be checked at runtime before the component is accessed to ensure that the tag value indicate the component exist. If the tag has the proper value, then the component is accessed; if not, then it is a runtime error.
- **No checking.** The language design may also allow variant record definition without an explicit tag component that may be checked at runtime, so that selection of component to be valid whenever executed.

Implementation. Implement of a variant record is easier than using it correctly.

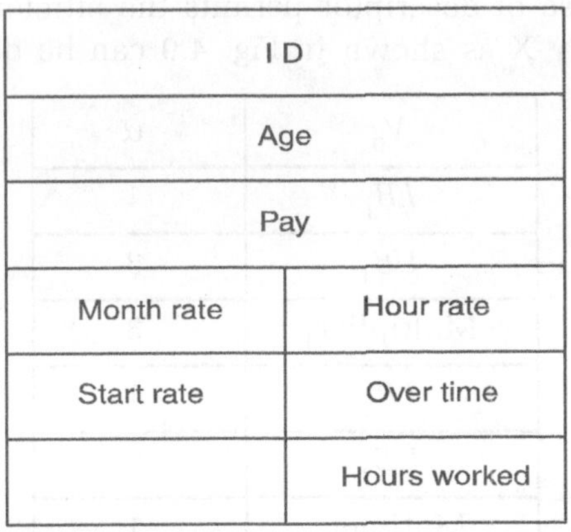

Fig. 4.8. Storage Representation for Variant Records.

During translation, the storage required for the components of each variant is determined and largest possible variant is allocated to the record as shown in Fig. 4.8.

When dynamic checking is done for component selection, then at runtime the base address plus offset calculation is same but first the value of base field is checked to ensure that the proper variant currently exists. But when no checking is done then for selecting a component of a variant record, the offset of the selected component within the storage block is computed during translation and during execution, the offset is added to the base address to determine the location of the component. If that location is currently used as part of a component in the current variant, then unpredictable changes are made in the value of that component.

4.6. SLICES

Specification. A slice is a substructure of an array that is itself an array.

For example: Suppose X is a matrix, then first row of X is a possible slice. A slice may also represent a column slice or multidimensional slice.

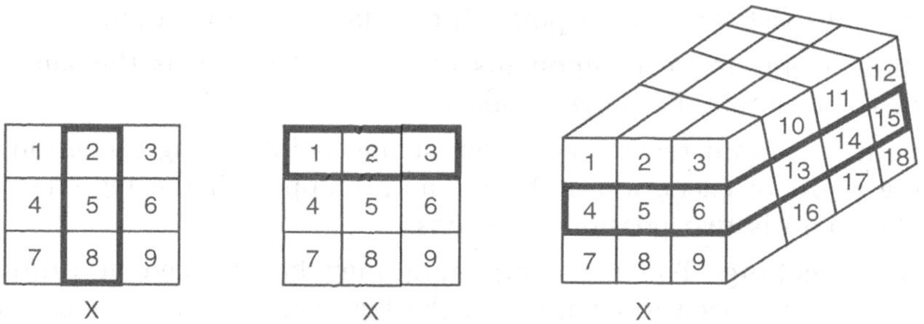

Fig. 4.9. Array Slices.

Figure 4.9 shows some examples of Array slices. *PL/I* was one of the earliest language to implent slices.

FORTRAN 77 also permits the use of slices.

Implementation. The use of descriptor permits the efficient implementation of a slice. For example, the 3 by 3 array X as shown in Fig. 4.9 can be described by the descriptor:

V_0	α
LB_1	1
UB_1	3
Multiplier_1	3
LB_2	1
UB_2	3
Mutipler_2	1

The address of $A\,[I, J]$ is given by the formula l-value $(A\,[I, J]) = \alpha + I \times 3 + J \times 1$

Note that in this case, multiplier 2 which represent the size of data object, is also the distance *b/w* successive elements of the array. In this case, the elements are contiguous. However not need be true.

4.7 CHARACTER STRING TYPES

A character string data type is important in all languages. A character string type is one in which the values consists of sequences of characters. Character string constants are used to label output, and input and output of all kinds of data are often done in terms of strings.

Specification. Character string data types may be identified in three different forms.

1. **Fixed length strings.** A string data object may have a fixed length that is declared in the program. This data object always contains the value of string of this fixed length. The length of string is static. It is also called static length string.
2. **Limited dynamic length strings.** In this type strings having a varying length upto a declared and fixed maximum set by the variable is definition. The Actual value stored in the data object may be a string of shorter length possibly even the empty string of no characters. The length of string value may be of varying length but it truncated when it exceeds the maximum set.
3. **Unlimited dynamic length string.** This type of strings have varying length with no maximum length. These are called unlimited dynamic length string. Java script and Perl allowed this type of string length option. It provides maximum flexibility. In this length may vary dynamically with no maximum value.

Operations Performed on Strings

In *C* and C++ languages if strings are not defined as a primitive type, string data is usually stored in arrays of single characters and referenced as such in language.

C and C++ use char array to store character strings and all operations performed on strings are stored in header file string.h. Most of language use the convention that character strings are terminated with a special character, null, which is represented with zero.

Following are the some operations that are performed on character strings.

1. **String length.** It is used to find out the length of the character string. For example, consider the strlen function used in *C* and C++. It calculates the length of string and returns the integer value.
2. **Concatenation.** Concatenation is the operation of joining two character strings of different length to make a long string. In *C* and C++ we use strcat operation to concatenate two strings. For example, If || is the symbol for the concatenation operation then "AMIT" || "KUMAR" gives "AMIT KUMAR".
3. **Comparison operation.** It is the relation operation (equal, less than, greater than) which lexicographically (alphabatic) compares two given string. *C* and C++ use strcmp function to compare two string. In lexicographically ordering string *A* is considered to be less than string *B* if either the first character of *A* is less than the first character of *B*, if the first character are equal and second character of *A* is less than the second character of *B*, and so on.
4. **Substring selection using subscripts.** In this operation a substring of a character string is selected using positioning subscripts.

   Many languages provide an operation for selecting a substring by giving the position of its first and last character. Consider the substring selection of PROGRAMMING LANGUAGES = STR (10 : 19) which assign the character in position 10 through 19 of string STR to string variable LANGUAGES.

5. **Pattern matching.** Pattern matching is another substring selection operation which takes as one argument a pattern data structure, where the pattern specifies the form of the substring desired. In the second argument to the pattern matching operation is a character string that is to be scanned to find a substring that matches the pattern. **For example.** Consider we want to select the first non blank character of string following the word 'THE'. Perl, Jawa Script and PHP include built in pattern matching operations. Pattern matching capabilities are included in the class libararies as C++, Jawa and *C#*.
6. **Formatting of Input-Output Data.** Character string are also used to format the Input-output data. This feature are used in FORTRAN and *C*.
7. **Static and Dynamic string.** String values may be either static or dynamic. In Perl the string '$ABC' is static and will print the value $ABC, by the statement print '$ABC', whereas string "$ABC" is dynamic and the statement print "$ABC" will cause the string to be evaluated and the value of the variable $ABC in printed.

Implementation. The different character string type is implemented in different forms.

1. **Implementation of static or fixed character string.** In this a descriptor is required at compile time which has three fields. The first field of every descriptor is name of the type. The second field is type length in character. The third field is the address of the first character.

Static string
Length
Address

Fig. 4.10. Compile Time Descriptor for Static String.

For example. Storage of string "Character" is represented as

9	C	H	A
R	A	C	T
E	R		

Fig. 4.11. Strings Stored 4 Characters Per Word Padded with Blanks.

2. **Implementation of limited dynamic string.** Limited dynamic string requires runtime descriptor.

Limited dynamic string
Maximum length
Current length
Address

Fig. 4.12. Runtime Descriptor for Limited Dynamic String.

Runtime descriptor stores the fixed maximum length and the current length as shown in Fig. 4.13.

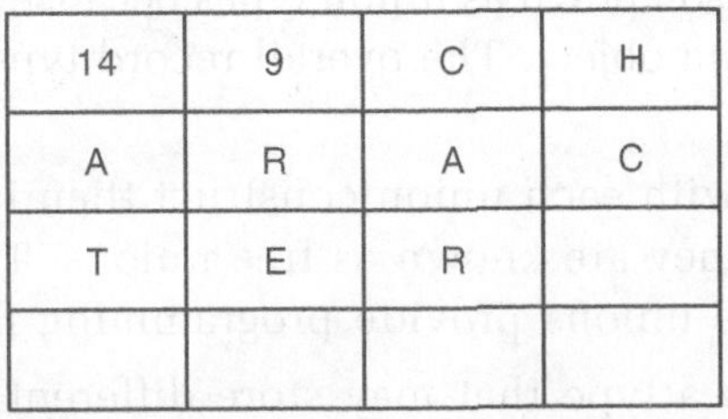

Fig. 4.13. Maximum and Current String Length Stored at Header of String.

Static and limited dynamic length strings require no special dynamic storage allocation. In the case of limited dynamic length strings, sufficient storage for the maximum length is allocated when the string variable is bound to storage, so only a simple allocation process is involved.

3. **Implementation of unlimited dynamic strings.** Dynamic length string requires more complex storage management. For string of unlimited length either a linked storage representation of fixed length data objects may be used or a contiguous array of characters may be used to contain string. This latter method is the technique used in C, which often requires dynamic runtime storage management to allocate such storage.

Unbonded with fixed allocations.

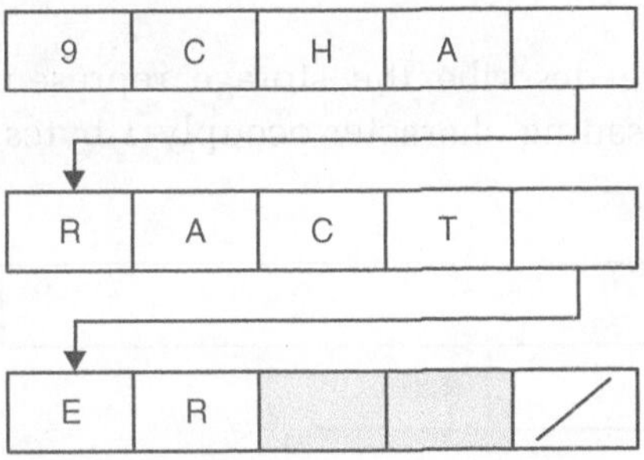

Fig. 4.14. String Stored at 4 Characters per Block and Length at Header of String.

Unbounded with variable allocations

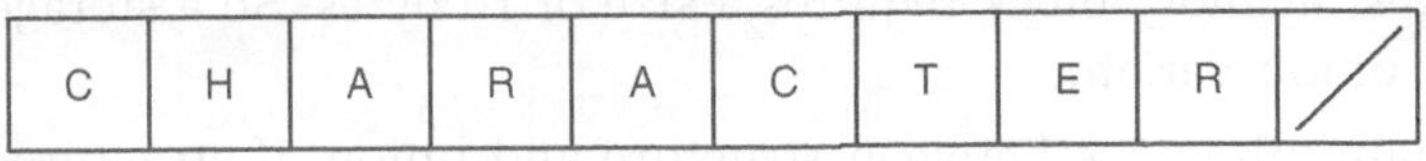

Fig. 4.15. String Stored as Contiguous Array of Character Terminated by Null Character.

4.8. VARIABLE SIZE DATA STRUCTURES

Variable size data structures are those in which number of components of data structure changes dynamically. It includes operations such as insert and delete components from structures. In this type of data structures there is a pointer data type that allows fixed size data objects to be linked together explicitly by the programmer.

4.9. UNION

Record type with variants are also known as union types because each variant may be considered as a separate class of record data object. The overall record type appears as the union of these sets of data objects.

If a tag field is included with each union construct then it is called discriminated union type. If tags are omitted then they are known as free unions. The language FORTRAN, *C* and C++ provide free unions. The unions provide programming flexibility.

Specification. A union is a type that may store different type values at different times during the program execution. Unions are potentially unsafe constructs in many languages. This is the reason why FORTRAN, *C*, C++ are not strongly typed. They do not allow type checking of references to their unions.

Consider the following declaration of union

```
Union
{
    char name [10];
    int Rollno;
    float marks;
    Student;
}
```

Implementation. Now we describe the storage representation for a *C* union variable student as described earlier. Assuing character occuply 1 bytes, an integer 2 bytes and a float 4 bytes in memory.

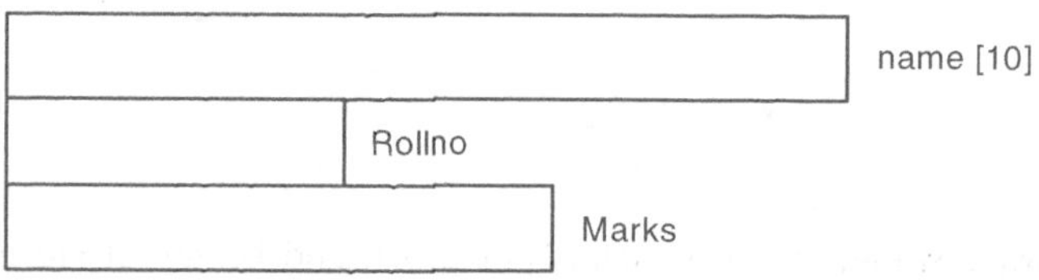

Fig. 4.16. Storage Representation for a Union in C.

Here the longest memory block requires a size of 10 bytes. So a storage block of 10 bytes is allocated to the union variable.

This is the main difference between structure and union. If structure is used instead of union then structure occupy 16 bytes of memory. Structure include sum of all variable (10 for name, 2 for Rollno, 4 for marks) but union use the memory same as the largest member of the structure.

4.10. POINTERS AND PROGRAMMER-CONSTRUCTED DATA OBJECTS

A pointer type is one in which the variables have a range of values that consists of memory addresses and a special value, null. The value null represents not a valid address and is used to indicate that a pointer cannot currently be used to reference any memory cell. A pointer type is a value that provides indirect access to elements of a known type. A creation operation for data objects of fixed size. The creation operation both allocates a block of storage for new data object and returns its *L*-value, which may then be stored as the *r*-value of a pointer data object. The creation operation differs in two ways: (*a*) The data objects created need have names because they are accessed through pointer and (*b*) data objects may be created during execution of a program.

Pointer Types. A pointer type in Pascal has the form

↑<type-name>

The restriction to type name in ↑ <type-name> instead of ↑ <type> can be programmed arround, since a type declaration can be used to give a name to any desired type.

In the following declaration, type link is a pointer to a cell:

type link = ↑ cell

Except in pointer types like ↑ cell, types most be declared before they are used.

Specification. Pointers have been designed for two distinct kinds of uses. First, pointers provide some of the power of indirect addressing, which is heavily used in assembly language. Second, pointers provide a method of dynamic storage management. A pointer can be used to access a location in area where storage is dynamically allocated, which is called keep. A single data object of pointer type may be treated in two ways.

(*a*) **Pointer references data objects of a single type.** The pointers are allowed to reference data object of only single type.

For example int * ρ.

Here * designates the type of ρ as type pointer and type int designates that ρ is of type integer. So it may reference to data object of only integer type. This approach is used in *C*, Pascal and Ada where static type checking is used.

(*b*) **Pointer references data objects of different type.** In this approach pointer data object references data objects of varying types at different times during program execution. This approach is used in languages like small talk where data object are checked at execution time or where dynamic type checking is used.

Operations on pointers

1. **Dynamic Allocation.** This operation allocates storage for object and also create a pointer to the object. In Pascal and Ada, this is accomplished by the procedure call new (ρ). In *C*, the Malloc function is used.

   For example,

   P = malloc (sizeof (int));

   Here *P* is a pointer to objects of type int. The above statement two-word block of storage to be used as an object of type integer and store the address in ρ.

2. **Dereferencing operation.** Dereferencing is the second fundametal operation. A dereferencing operation for pointer values that allows a pointer to be followed to the data object to which it points. Consider a pointer variable Ptr that is bound with the value 7000. Suppose that the memory cell whose address is 7000 has the value 200. A normal reference to Ptr fields 7000 but a dereferenced reference to Ptr field 200.

Problems in pointers

1. **Dangling pointers.** A dangling pointer or dangling reference, is a pointer that contains the address of a heap-dynamic variable that has been deallocated.
2. **Lost Heap-Dynamic variable or Garbage.** Garbage is an allocated heap dynamic variable that is no longer accessible to the user program. They are not useful for their original purpose.

Implementation. A pointer data object is represented as a storage location containing the address of another storage location. The address is base address of the block of storage representing the data object pointed to by the pointer. Two major storage representations are used for pointer values.

1. **Absolute Address.** A pointer value may be represented as the actual memory address of the storage block for the data object. It is efficient technique. But storage management is difficult for this technique.
2. **Relative Address.** A pointer value may be represented as an offset from the base address of some larger heap storage block within which the data object is allocated.

If absolute address is used for pointer values, then data objects creation operation, new, may be allocated storage in memory. The use of relative address as pointers requires the initial allocation of a block of storage within which subsequent allocation of data objects by new takes place.

4.11. SETS

A set is one whose variables can store unordered collection of distinct values. It is differ from list where ordered collection of values may be repeated. The only design issue that is particular to set types is the maximum number of elements in a set base type.

Set Types:

The type

Set of *S*

represents subsets of *S*. For example, consider variable *X* declared by

Var *X* : set of [1..3]

X can denote one of the following sets:

[ ], [1], [2], [3], [1, 2], [1, 3], [2, 3], [1, 2, 3]

Since these are all the subsets of [1, 2, 3], the type set of *S* in Pascal should be called "subset of *S*."

The following example shows the set type and some set type variables.

```
type colors = (red, blue, green, yellow);
     colorset = set of colors;
var set 1, set 2 : color set;
```

constant values can be assigned to the set variables set 1 and set 2, as in

```
set 1 : = [red, blue];
set 2 : = [green, yellow]
```

Basic Operation on Sets

1. **Membership test.** The operation in tests is an element x belongs to a set A. (*i.e.*, $x \in A$).
2. **Insertion and deletion of single values.** Insert data value X in set A provided it is not already a member of X. Delete data value X from A if it is a member of A.
3. **Union, Intersection and difference of sets.** Given two sets A and B, create a set X that contain all members of both A and B with duplicated values deleted is called union operation.

   $X = A \cup B$

   Given two set A and B, create a set X to contain only values that are members of both sets A and B is called intersect operation.

   $X = A \cap B$

   Given two set A and B, create a set X to contain values that are in A but not in B is called difference operation.

   $X = A - B$ $\{x | x \in A \text{ and } x \notin B\}$

Implementation. There are two types of storage representation of sets.

1. **Bit strings in memory.** The bit string storage representation is used where the size of value is small. Suppose there are N elements in the universe. Then a set of element chosen from this universe may then be represented by a bit string of length N.

   For example: Consider a set of ordinal base type ['*A*' -- '*J*'] then variables of this set type can use the first 10 bits of a machine word, with each set bit (1) representing a present element and each clear bit (0) representing an absent element, using this scheme, the set value

   ['*A*', '*C*', '*E*', '*G*', '*J*']

   would be represented as

   1010101001

   The hardware support for bit string operations, if provided, makes manipulation of one bit string representation of sets efficient.
2. **Hash coded representation.** Another approach for a set is based on the technique of hash coding. This method may be used when the set contains large values. It allows the membership test, insertion and deletion of values efficiently. But union, intersection and difference operations of values is done inefficiently. This method required a large allocation of storage. LISP implemetation use this storage representation. In this method rather storing the elements of a set in sequential location within block, however, the elements are scattered randomly through the block.

   When we wish to add a new element a, represented by a bit string B_a, to the set S, represent by the block of storage M_s. We must determine whether a is already member of S and if not, add it to the set. We determine a position for B_a within the block M_s by the application of a hashing function to the bit string B_a. The hash function extracts a hash address I_a from the result. This hash address is used as an index pointing to a position in block M_s.

A collision occurs when two different data item *a* and *b* produces the same hash value I_x.

There are various techniques to handle collision. These are rehashing, sequential scan and bucketing. By these techniques we can handle collisions.

4.12. LISTS

List is a data structure that composed of ordered sequence of data structures. List is a collection of data structures.

Syntax and Specification

The LISP syntax represents a typical list structure:

(Function Name Data_1, Data_2, ... Data_n)

LISP executes by providing function name to arguments Data_1 through Data_n.

List are similar to arrays in that they consist of ordered sequence of object. The first member is called head and the other members are called tails of lists. Lists are of fixed length. They can grow and shrink during program execution. It has rarely homogeneous elements. Language that use lists typically declare such data implicitly without explicit attributes for list members.

Operations. Operations in lists include the ability to construct lists. Following primitives are provided in LISP for component selection.

1. **Content of the address register (CAR).** It returns a pointer to the first list element (head). For example (CAR (*X*, *Y*) = *X*).
2. **Content of the decrement register (CDR).** It returns a pointer to the list with the first element deleted. Example (CDR (*X*, *Y*) = *Y*).
3. **The CONS primitive.** It takes two pointers as operands and allocates a new list element memory word, stores the two pointers in CAR and CDR fields in the words and return a pointer to the new word. For example,

   (CONS (*xyz*) (*mno*) = ((*xyz*) *mno*)

Implementation. Lists are usually stored as a single linked list structures. The link list represent of lists in LISP has three fields as shown.

TYPE	Head field	Tail field

Fig. 4.17. A List Data Structure.

Each node has two pointer and represent an element A node for an atom has its first pointer pointing to some representation of the atom, such as its symbol or numeric value. The internal representation is shown as in Fig. 4.18.

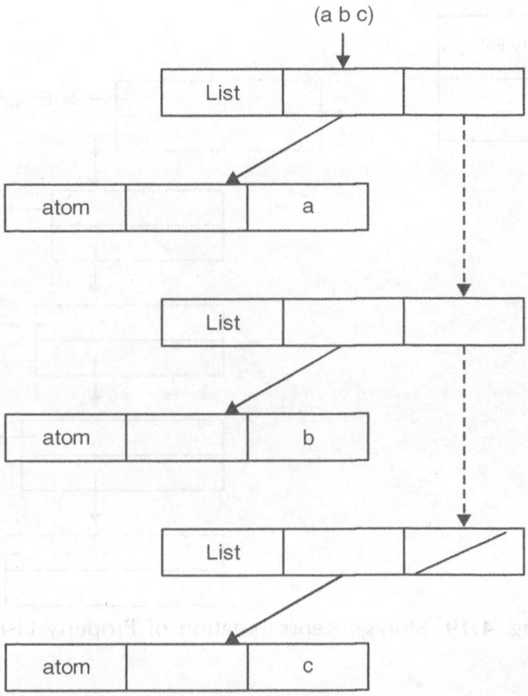

Fig. 4.18. Internal Representation of LISP List (abc).

Lists are primitive data objects in language like *ML*, LISP and Prolog but do not appear in the usual compiled language like *C*, Pascal, or Ada.

Variation on lists. There are different variations of lists.

1. **Stacks and queues.** A stack is a list in which component selection, insertion and deletion are restricted to one end called TOP of stack. It is last in first out (LIFO) means the element last inserted is deleted first.

   A Queque is a list in which component selection and deletion are restricted to one end and insertion is restricted to other end. Insertion is taken place at REAR end and deletion is taken place at FRONT end. It is First in first out (FIFO) means element inserted first is the first deleted.
2. **Directed graphs.** A data structure in which the component may be linked together using linear sequence of components is termed a directed graph.
3. **Tree.** A list in which the components may be lists as well as elementary data objects is termed a tree.
4. **Property list.** A property list is defined as a record with a varying number of components and component of property list may vary without restriction. Both the component name and their values must be stored. These are called as property name and the property values. ML and LISP uses this concept. In *C*, Pascal and Ada, a pointer data type is provided and programmer build his own linked structures.

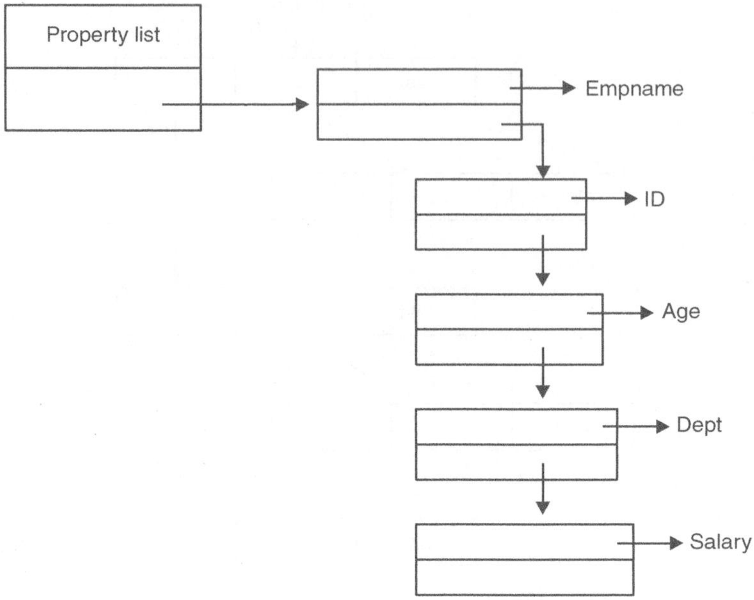

Fig. 4.19. Storage Representation of Property Lists.

4.13. FILES

A file is a collection of logically related records and a record is collection of heterogeneous data items. So a file is a collection of records in which different types of data items are stored. There are various situation where we use collection of records.

For example: In a university we can maintain the collection of records of various students. So there are different files that contains records of different students.

A file is represented on a secondary storage device such as disk or tape in which various records are stored.

4.13.1. Accessing a File

There are three possible modes of access to a file by a program.

1. **Input mode.** In input mode, the file is only read by the program.
2. **Output mode.** In output mode, the file is only written to by a program.
3. **Input/output mode.** In input/output mode, the file is both read from and written to during a program's execution.

4.13.2. Types of Files

There are different type of files.

1. Sequential files
2. Direct access files
3. Indexed sequential files

1. **Sequential files.** Sequential files are the most common type of files. It is a linear sequence of components of the same type. It is of varying length, with no fixed maximum length. The records are accessed consecutively from the file.

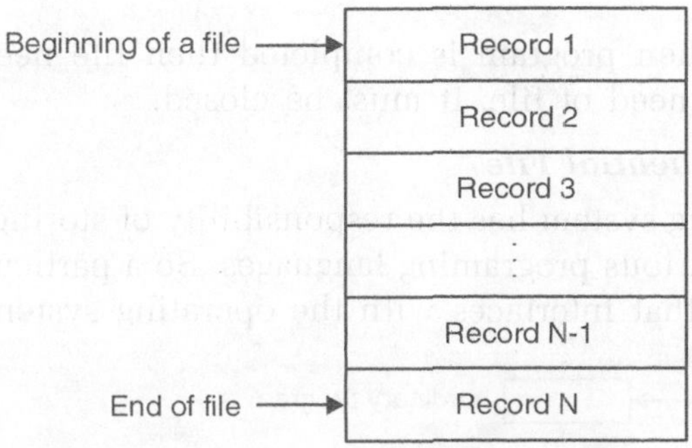

Fig. 4.20. Structure of Sequential File.

Consider the pascal example

xyz : file of Employee;

define a file named *xyz* whose components are of type Employee. It may be data structure type of fixed size or variable size that cannot be component of files. In sequential file, the records are inserted sequentially in file *i.e.,* one after another and they are also accessed sequentially from a file. If we have to access the Nth record in the sequential file then we have to first move to *N*-1 records one by one and then access the Nth record.

Specification. The main operations on sequential files are:

1. **Opening a file.** Before a file may be used, it must be opened. The open operation is given the name of file and the access mode *i.e.,* read or write. If the mode is read, it means file is already exist. If the mode is write, then a request is made to create a new file or if file already exist with the given name, it deletes all the components of the file and file pointer points to start of the file.
2. **Reading a file.** A read operation tranfers the contents of the current file component to a designated variable in the program. Variable may be an ordinary programmer defined variable or is a special variable. The read operation (called get in Pascal) assigns the next file component to file.
3. **Writing a file.** It creates a new component at the content position in the file and transfers the contents of a designated program variable to the new component. In Pascal we can write.

   Write (File name, Record name);

   The record will appear on the file in the same order as they are written.
4. **Updating a file.** Updating a file means changing the records of the file. These changes may include the insertion, deletion and modification of records.
5. **End of file.** A read operation fails if the file position pointer designates the end of file. In Pascal a function.

   eof : file → Boolean

   returns true if the file is positioned at its end and false otherwise.

In COBOL

Read filename AT END statement

specifies a statement to be executed if the read operation fails owing to an end of file condition.

6. **Closing a file.** When program is completed then file needs to be closed. It means when there is no need of file. It must be closed.

1. Implementation of Sequential File

In all systems, the operating system has the responsibility of storing the files. Files are created and manipulated by the various programing languages. So a particular programming language provides a data structure that interfaces with the operating system.

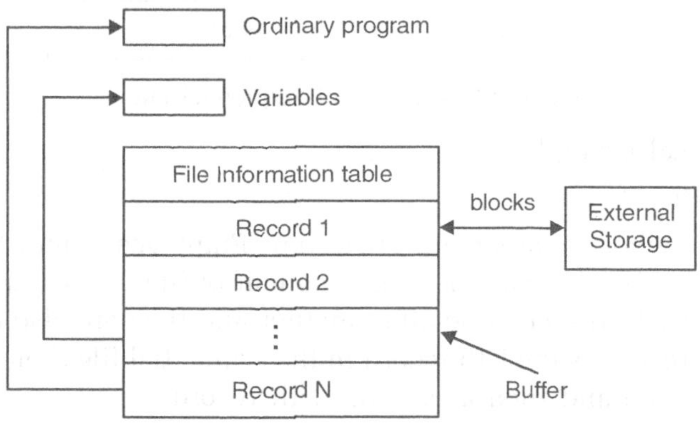

Fig. 4.21. File Representation Using Buffer.

When a file is opened during its execution, storage for file information table and a buffer must be needed-operating system stores location and characterstics of the file in the file information table. Buffer is a sequential representation of a queue.

When a read operation is performed the data is transferred. From the file into the buffer in blocks of components. When a write operation is performed the values of the variable is stored into the buffers.

2. Direct Access Files

The direct access file is organized so that a single component may be accessed at random. In sequential files the component must be accessed in sequence but in Direct access or random access the component must be selected randomly. Here a subscript is used to select a component is called key. Direct access file is organized as an unordered set of components with a key value which is associated with each component. A mapping function is applied to the key value to find the physical address of the records.

$$R \text{ (key value)} \rightarrow \text{Relative address}$$

When a write operation is given a component to copy to the file the key value to be associated with that component. Write operation creates a new component on the external storage device and copies the designated value into it.

When a read operation is given the key of the desired component in the file is used, the index is searched to find the desired location in secondary storage.

3. Indexed Sequential Files

It is combination of direct access files and sequential files. It is similar to direct access files with the additional facility to access component in sequence.

An indexed sequential file requires an index of key values, just as for a direct access file, but the entries in the index must be ordered by key values. When a component with a particular key value, then that pair in the index becomes the current component of the file. For example, the file-position pointer is positioned at that component.

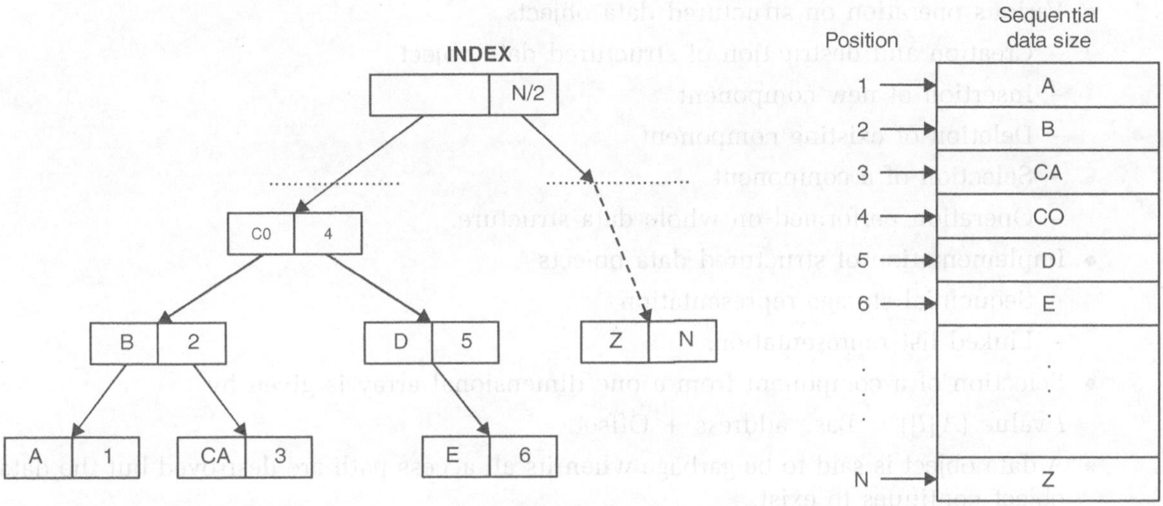

Fig. 4.22. Index Sequential Access by use of a Binary Search Tree and Sequential File.

Application of indexed sequential file. Because of its capability to support both sequential and direct access, indexed sequential organization is used frequently to support files that are used for both batch and interactive processing.

For example: Consider a credit card billing system with an indexed sequential master file of customer account information. An appropriate key for the file would be the account number of each record. The file could be accessed in batch mode, monthly to generate customer invoices and to build summary reports of account would appear in account number sequence.

The credit card management agency wants to use the master file of account information also to support interactive inquiry of the current credit status of any account. When a customer makes a purchase, the master file will be consulted. This mind of processing could not be supported well by sequential access. We need to access an individual account, given its account number, dictates use of the index of the indexed sequential file organization.

Some Important Terms

- Structured data objects or a data structure contains other data objects as its elements or components.
- A data object that are made up of other data objects as components, is termed as a structured data object.

- Various attributes of Data structure are
  - Type of component
  - Total number of components
  - Structure of the components
  - Names to be used to select a component
  - Maximum number of components.
- Various operation on structured data objects
  - Creation and destruction of structured data object
  - Insertion of new component
  - Deletion of existing component
  - Selection of a component
  - Operation performed on whole data structure.
- Implementation of structured data objects
  - Sequential storage representation
  - Linked list representation.
- Selection of a component from a one dimensional array is given by

  l value $(A\,[I]) = \text{Base address} + \text{Offset}$.
- A data object is said to be garbage when its all access path are destroyed but the data object continues to exist.
- A Dangling reference is problem with a data object is that when a data object is destroyed but its access path remain there.
- Type checking is more complex for structured data objects.
- A vector is a data structure composed of a fixed number of components of the same type organized as a simple linear sequence.
- A subscript is to be used to select each component.
- An Array can be one, two or multidimensional.
- The concept of virtual origin (V_0) gives an accessing formula.

  l value $(A\,[I]) = V_0 + I \times E$

  where V_0 is called virtual origin.
- A matrix can be implemented as
  - Row major order.
  - Column major order.
- For Row major order the accessing formula is

  l value $(A\,[I, J]) = \alpha + (I - lB_1) \times S + (J - LB_2) \times E$

  where α-base address

  S – length of row $= (UB_2 - LB_2 + 1) \times E$

  LB_1 = Lower bond of row

  LB_2 = Lower bond of columns

  UB_2 = Upper bond of columns

- The address of element $A[S_1, S_2, \ldots S_n]$ in multidimensional array is given by

$$l \text{ value } (A[S_1, S_2 \ldots S_n]) = V_0 + \sum_{i=1}^{n} (S_i \times m_i)$$

where V_0 = virtual origin $= \alpha - \sum_{i=1}^{n} (l_i \times m_i)$

- A Record is a collection of data items of hetrogeneous type means of different types.
- Component selection in records is given by the accessing formula.

$$l \text{ value } (R \,.\, I) = \alpha + \sum_{i=1}^{I-1} (\text{size of } R\,.\,i)$$

- Variant records are used for representing objects that have some but not all properties in common.
- A slice is a sub-structure of an array that is itself an array.
- A character string type is one in which the value consists of sequences of characters.
- Character string data types have three different forms:
  - Fixed length string
  - Limited dynamic length strings
  - Unlimited dynamic length strings.
- Operation performed on strings are:
  - String length
  - Concatenation
  - Comparison
  - Substring selection using subscripts
  - Pattern-matching
  - Formatting of I/o Data
  - Static and Dynamic string.
- Variable size data structures are those in which number of components of data structure changes dynamically.
- A union is a type that may store different type value at different times during the execution.
- Union use the memory same as the largest member of the structure.
- A pointer type is one in which the variables have a range of values that consists of memory addresses and a special value, null.
- Operation of pointer are:
  - Dynamic allocation
  - Dereferencing operation.
- A set is one whose variables can store unordered collection of distinct values.

- Basic operation on sets are:
  - Membership test
  - Insertion and deletion of single value
  - Union, Intersection and difference of sets.
- A list is a data structure that composed of ordered sequence of data structures.
- A file is a collection of logically related records.
- There are three modes of accessing a file:
  - Input mode
  - Output mode
  - Input/output mode.
- There are different types of files.
  - Sequential files
  - Direct access files
  - Indexed sequential files.

Review Questions

1. Explain the specification and implementation of structured data objects.
2. Explain the declaration of structured data objects.
3. Explain type checking of structured data objects.
4. Explain structured data objects and data types.
5. Define Vectors or Array. How multidimensional array is declared? Explain the row major and column major implementation of 2-D array.
6. Explain variant records. How they are implemented in memory?
7. Define character strings. Explain operations and implementation of character string.
8. Define Union. How it is different from structure?
9. Explain pointer and programmer-constructured data objects.
10. What are file? Explain different file organization techniques.
11. What are lists? What are different types of lists?
12. Write short-notes on:
    (*i*) Variable size data structures
    (*ii*) Sets
    (*iii*) Slices
    (*iv*) Array of Records
    (*v*) Structures and unions.
13. Explain programmer defined data objects.
14. Define the three string length options.
15. Explain the specification, implementation of multidimensional arrays.
16. Differentiate array and record data structure.
17. Explain the implementation of sets.

❑❑❑

Chapter 5

SUBPROGRAMS AND PROGRAMMER DEFINED DATA TYPES

In this chapter, we explore programming language support for data abstraction. Early languages, such as FORTRAN and COBOL, limit the creation of new data types to subprogram definition. But new language designs have provided better facilities for specify and implementing entire abstract data types. C^{++} and Java defines class which is abstract data types. By abstract data type we can create new data type. We begin by discussing the evolution of abstract data type concept and then discuss the concept of abstraction and abstract data type. Data encapsulation and Information hiding are also associated with abstraction. In this chapter, we also create programmer–defined data by use of subprograms. Procedures, subroutines and functions are defined and implemented.

5.1. DATA TYPE CONCEPT

Hardware cannot tell the difference between a bit string representing a real number, integer or character. In actual computer there is no provision for defining data types. A higher level language provides a basic data types such as real, integer and character string. Type checking concept discuss in chapter 2 ensures that operations cannot be applied on wrong data type.

In 1970, Pascal extends the concept of general type definitions applicable to a set of variable. Type definition defines the structure of a data object with its possible value binding. The possible value binding means the values associated with data objects.

In 1970, the set of data objects also includes the set of operations that are performed on data objects. To define a data object we require only the variable name and the data type of the data object. For primitive types such as real and integer, a language provides a facility to declare that type of variable and a set of operations that are performed on real and integer. The storage representation is hidden from the programmer. The programmer does not know, how they are represented in memory.

5.2. THE CONCEPT OF ABSTRACTION

Abstraction provides facility to programmers to focus on essential attributes or features and ignore the subordinate attributes or background detail. An abstraction is a representation of an entity that contain only the significant attribute of that entity. Attributes are also called features of an entity. In the abstraction, only that attributes are considered that are different from another attributes. Common attributes need not to be considered. Abstraction resolves the complexity of programming languages and simplify the process of programming. Programming language provides support for abstraction by using subprograms, subprogram libraries, classes, type definitions etc.

There are two fundamental kinds of abstraction that are used by programming languages.

(*a*) Process abstraction (*b*) Data abstraction

(*a*) Process Abstraction

Process abstraction means providing a way for a program to specify that some process is to be done, without providing the details of how it is to be done. Process abstraction is among the oldest in programming language design. All subprograms supports process abstraction. For example, when a program need to find the factorial of number, it usually uses a subprogram for finding factorial of number. When we need to find the factorial of a number. We call the factorial subprogram for a particular number passed as arguments.

Consider the following statements:

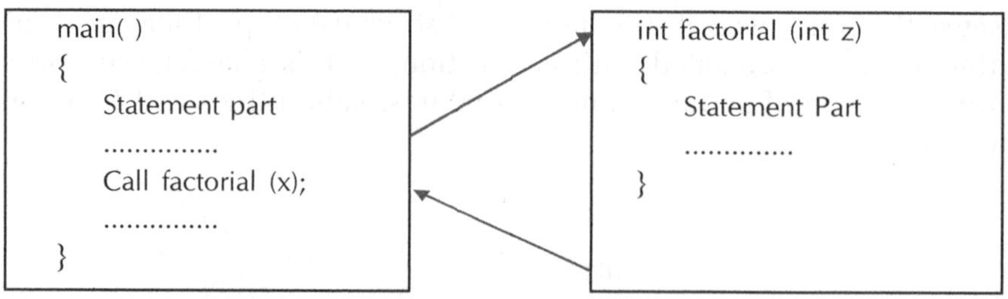

When we write the statement call factorial (x) then the pointer goes to factorial subprogram which calculates the factorial and results back to main program.

So in this example main program does not know the details of factorial subprogram. It only know about the input number that is scanned by the input statement and only the calling of subprogram. But it does not know how the factorial of a number is calculated.

(*b*) Data Abstraction

The motivations for data abstraction is similar to that of process abstraction. Data abstraction consists of a set of objects and a set of operations that are applied to that data objects. In the case of data abstraction, we also do not need to know how the operations are performed of the data objects and how they are implemented in the memory. Data abstraction provides facility of making large and complicated program more manageable. Object-oriented programming uses the concept of data abstraction and this concept is used in software development companies. By data abstraction, we can hide the detail of operations and the memory representation of operations from the programmer.

These process and data abstraction concepts are crucial to the programming languages because by these we can avoid the programmers from the details of data.

5.3. ABSTRACT DATA TYPES

An abstract data type is defined as:

(*a*) A set of data objects of a given type.

(*b*) A set of operations that are performed on these data objects.

(*c*) Encapsulation (binding of Data object and Operation) of the whole in such a way that the user of the type needs to know only the name and semantic of operation rather than how they are stored in memory.

Unnecessary details of the type can be hidden from units outside the encapsulation that uses the type. Program unit that use an abstract data type can declare variables of that type, even the representation is hidden from them. An instance of an abstract data type is called an object.

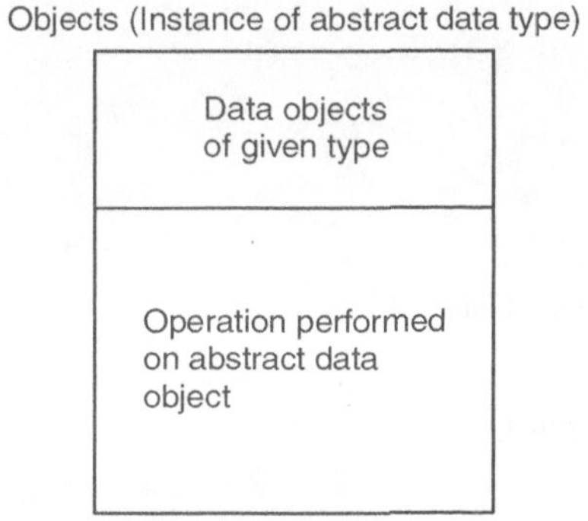

Fig. 5.1. Abstract Data Type.

Data objects are the variables of certain type and operations are the subprograms that performs operations on Data objects and object are used as instance of abstract data type.

Abstract data type is the primary component of object-oriented programming. In object oriented programming we use classes that are the abstract data type. By using classes in C^{++}, we can achieve abstraction. Basically, object-oriented programming is programming with abstract data type.

5.3.1. Floating-point as an Abstract Data Type

For primitive type such as real, integers, floating-point etc. provides a facility to declare a type of variables and a set of operation that are performed on these types. Basically, hardware defines which operations are performed on built in type and this is decided during language implementation.

The storage representation of floating-point is effectively hidden from the programmer. Programmer may use these type of data objects without knowing exactly how they are stored in memory. The floating-point type in high level languages employs the concept of information hiding. The actual format of the data value in a floating point memory cell is hidden from the user. We can't create new operations on data of the type because all operations are defined by hardware.

The user cannot directly manipulate the parts of the actual representation of floating-point objects because that representation is hidden.

5.3.2. User Defined Abstract Data Type

User defined data type means programmer can create their own data objects. Rather than built in type, now user can create their own data objects and decides what operations are performed on these data objects. So there are two characteristics of user-defined abstract data type.

1. A definition part that declare the variables of particular type and hides the detail of representation.
2. A subprogram part that contains operations that are performed on variables.

C^{++} and Ada uses classes to create user-defined abstract data type. Let's consider the declaration of class in C^{++}.

```
Class  Class_name
{

    Private:
        Data object_1;
            ⋮
        Data object_n;
    Public:
        Function_1 (Argument List)
            ⋮
        Function_n (Argument List)
};
```

In this we create a class having a name. By default all data in the classes are private. We can declare data object in private section and functions that contains operations performed on private data in public section. Only these function declared in public part can access the data. The detail of implementation of Data objects and functions are hidden from the programmer.

So by use of classes we can create the user defined abstract data type. We can create objects for accessing the data of the class.

5.3.3. Advantages of Abstract Data Type

1. Abstract data type binds the data to the functions so only these functions can use the data objects.
2. Functions outside the class cannot access the data.
3. It provide, facility to hide the information regarding the storage. So less burden on programmer.
4. We can add new data and functions at any time to the abstract data type.
5. Data is not free to move function to function, only function defined in the class uses the data only.

5.4. ENCAPSULATION AND INFORMATION HIDING

Encapsulation

To introduce abstract data type, we must need encapsulation as a support mechanism for abstract data type.

Encapsulation is binding of data and functions into a single unit (called class). Encapsulation is a grouping of data and subprograms that manipulate the data. An encapsulation, which is either separately or independently compilable provides an abstracted system and a logical organization for a collection of related computations.

Encapsulation are often placed in Libraries and made available for reuse in programs other than those for which they were written. In 'C', a collection of related function and data definitions can be placed in a file, which can be independently complied.

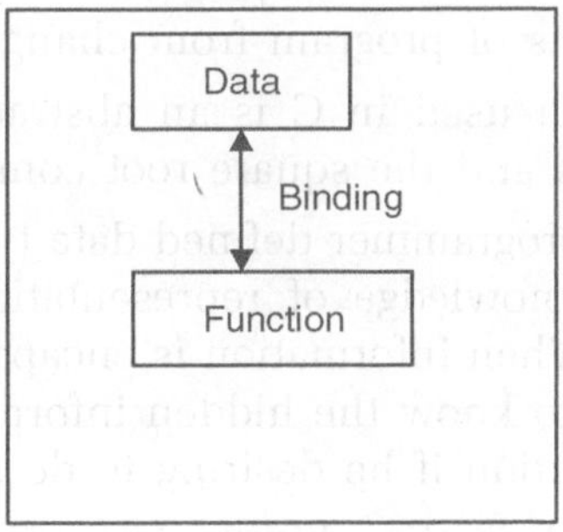

Fig. 5.2. Encapsulation.

In C++ classes, we can bind data and functions into single unit. So C++ uses the concept of encapsulation.

The data defined in a class are called data members and functions defined in a class are called member functions. All of the instances of a class share a single set of member functions, but each instances gets its own set of the class is data members.

For example:

```
Class  Class_name
{
    Private:
        Data member_1;
            ⋮
        Data member_n;
    Public:
        Member Function_1;
            ⋮
        Member Function_n;
};
```

This is the syntax of a class in C^{++}. We can create objects as

Class_name Objectname;

There are any number of objects are created for a class. Return type of objects is class name.

Information Hiding

To construct a large program, a form of divide and conquer strategy must be used. A program appears as a single collection of subprogram that does not impose an adequate level of organization. To organize the program into syntactic containers that include groups of logically related subprogram and data. These syntactic containers are called modules and process of designing them is called modularization.

Information hiding is term used for the central principle in the design of programmer defined abstractions. Each such program component should hide as much information as possible for the component user. It hides the design decisions and if the design decisions changes then it protect other parts of program from change.

For example: SQRT function used in C is an abstract operation because it hides the details of number representations and the square root computation algorithm from the user.

Similarly a user defined or programmer defined data type is also a successful abstraction if it may be used without the knowledge of representation of objects of that type or the algorithm used by its operation. When information is encapsulated in an abstraction then user of the abstraction does not need to know the hidden information and is not permitted to use or manipulate the hidden information if he desiring to do so.

The most common use of information hiding are:

1. To hide the physical storage layout for data so that if the physical storage layout is changed, the change is restricted to a small subset of the total program.
2. To make a program easier for the user to understand.
3. To make program portable between different languages and machines.

5.5. ENCAPSULATION BY SUBPROGRAMS

Subprograms are the fundamental building blocks of programs and are therefore among the most important concepts in programming language design. Two different views of subprograms are:

(*a*) At the program design level, we may ask about the sense in which a subprogram represents an abstract operation that the programmes defines that is different from built in type.

(*b*) At the language design level, the concern is with the design and implementation of the general facilities for subprogram definition and invocation.

Specification of a Subprogram

Specification of a subprogram includes three things:

1. The name of the subprogram.
2. The prototype or declaration (signature) of the subprogram by providing its number and type of arguments and number of results and data type of the results.
3. The statement part that tells us what action will be performed by a subprogram.

Consider the specification part by using 'C' code:

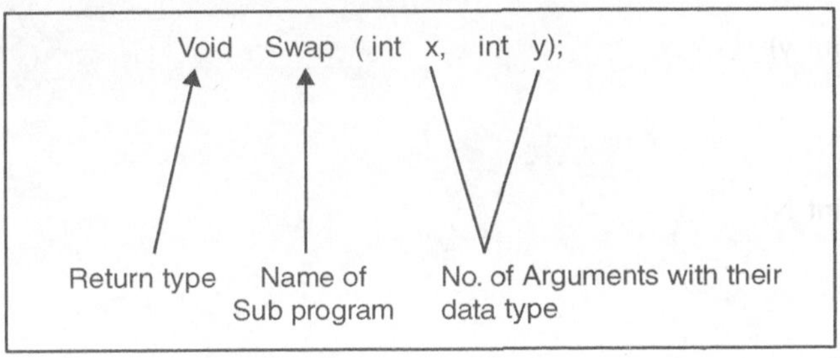

Fig. 5.3 Declaration or Prototype of Subprogram.

Definition part:

```
Void Swap (int x, int y)
{
    //Statement part containing logic of Swap two numbers.
}
```

Different languages having different syntax for representing declaration and definition of subprogram. Void indicating a null function means it does not return a value. In subprograms, there is implicit arguments and they produce implicit results. A subprogram may be history sensitive so that its result depend on the arguments given over the entire past history of its calls and not just on the arguments given in a single call.

Implementation part of a subprogram: A subprogram is a user defined operation. So it is implemented using the data structures and operation provide by programmer. The subprogram body is defined by programme and that body tell what is performed by the subprogram. In some languages (*e.g.*, Ada, Pascal) the body may also include definition of other subprograms that represent programmer-defined operation used only within the larger sub-programs.

When a subprogram is called it requires arguments of proper type that is provided in specification part. Return type of the results must also be known. Type checking is done at compile time, if the arguments and result type are provided at compile time. Otherwise dynamic or runtime type checking is used. The data declared within the subprogram are local to the subprogram. Other subprogram cannot use this local data.

5.5.1. Subprogram Definitions and Subprogram Activations

Specification: A subprogram definition tells what action has been performed by the subprogram. When a subprogram is called an Activation record is created by the subprogram. A subprogram definition is a static part *i.e.*, is fixed during execution. But the activation record is dynamic part *i.e.* during execution, each time a new activation is created. Subprogram activation is exist only during program execution. After that subprogram activation is destroyed. Its like a malloc function used in C that create new data objects during execution and after that it destroyed the objects that is created during runtime.

An activation has a life time, the time during execution between the call that creates it and the return that destroys it. A number of activations may be created during program execution, each time the subprogram is called. Different number of activations may be created for the same subprogram.

Implementation part: For implementation part consider the following example in 'C'.

```
Void Swap (int x, int y)
{
    Const a = 2;
    Float M (10), int N;
        ............
        ............
    N = a;
}
```

In this example, an activation is created during runtime. It includes:

1. Signature or name of subprogram is Swap, having two arguments x and y of integer type.
2. Declaration part contains two variable, Arrange M and variable N.
3. Constant 2 is defined.
4. Statement part containing code for subprogram body.
5. This subprogram have return type void means it does not return any value.

The subprogram definition allows the above storage area to be organized and executable code determined during translation. The code consists of two parts:

(*a*) **Static Code Segment:** It is static part that contains constants and executable code. This part is invariant during execution of subprogram. It has only one copy that is shared by all activations.

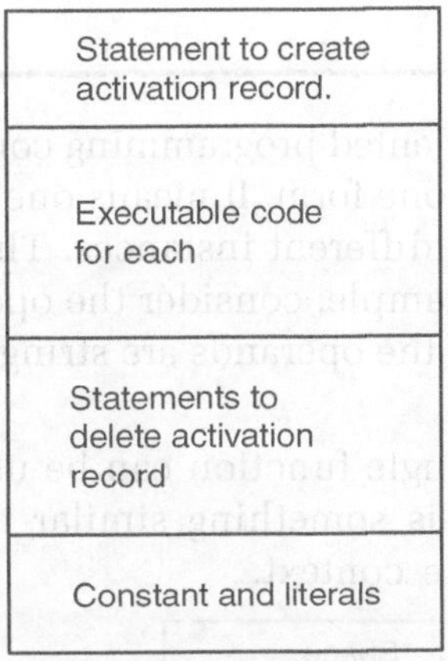

Fig. 5.4. Code Segment (Static Part).

It contains statements to create activation record, Executable code *i.e.* fixed during executions, statements to delete activation record and constants and literals declared in the declaration section of the subprogram.

(*b*) **Dynamic Activation Record:** It contains that part of the subprogram that is changes each time the subprogram is called. Like parameter passed to the subprogram, return points, temporary storage areas and linkages for referencing non-local variables. This part has the same structure for each activation but it contain different data values each time the subprogram in called.

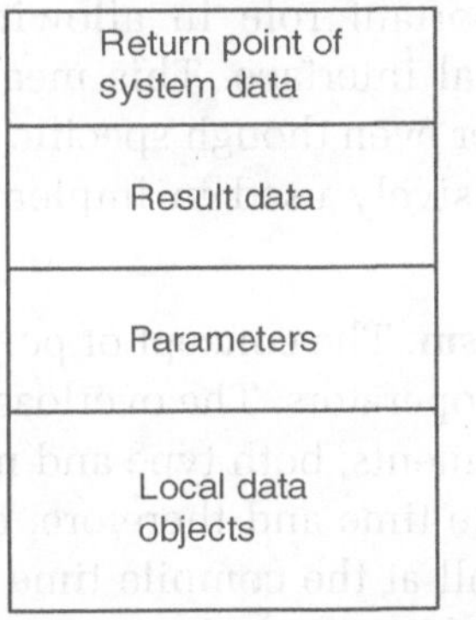

Fig. 5.5. Activation Record.

These activation records has different size and structures. They are dynamically created and destroyed during execution each time the subprogram is called and each time it terminates. The size and structure of activation record is determined during the translation. When a subprogram is called, a number of hidded actions take place that are concerned with the setting up of the activation record, the transmission of parameters, the creation of linkages for non-local referencing activities.

5.6. POLYMORPHISM

Polymorphism is important object-oriented programming concept. Polymorphism is a Greek term, means the ability to take more than one form. It means one name, multiple forms. An operation may exhibit different behaviours in different instances. The behaviour depends upon the type of data used in the operation. For example, consider the operation of addition for two numbers, the operation will generate a sum. If the operands are strings, then the operation would produce a third string by concatenation.

Figure 5.6, illustrates that a single function can be used to handle different number and different types of arguments. This is something similar to a particular word having several different meaning depending on the context.

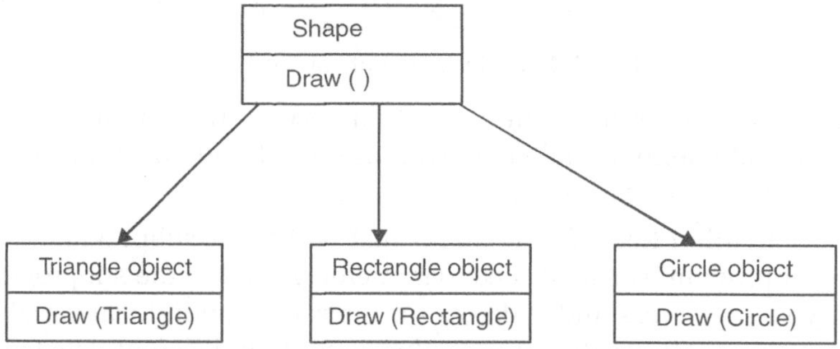

Fig. 5.6. Polymorphism.

Polymorphism plays an important role in allowing objects having different internal structure to share the same external interface. This means that a general class of operations may be accessed in the same manner even though specific action associated with each operation may differ. Polymorphism is extensively used in implementing inheritance.

It is of two types:

1. **Compile Time Polymorphism.** The concept of polymorphism is implemented using the overloading functions and operators. The overloaded member functions are selected for invoking by matching arguments, both type and number. This information is known to the complier at the compile time and therefore, compiler is able to select appropriate function for a particular call at the compile time itself. This is called early binding or static binding or static linking. Also known as compile time polymorphism, early binding simply means that an object is bound to its function call at compile time. Compile time polymorphism can be done by:

   (*a*) function overloading (*b*) operator overloading

2. **Runtime Polymorphism.** If member function is selected while program is running then this is called runtime polymorphism. In C^{++}, runtime polymorphism is also possible with the help of virtual function concept. In runtime polymorphism the function link with a class very late (*i.e.* after compilation), therefore this is also called late binding or dynamic binding. In this function is selected dynamically at runtime. Runtime polymorphism is done by virtual function.

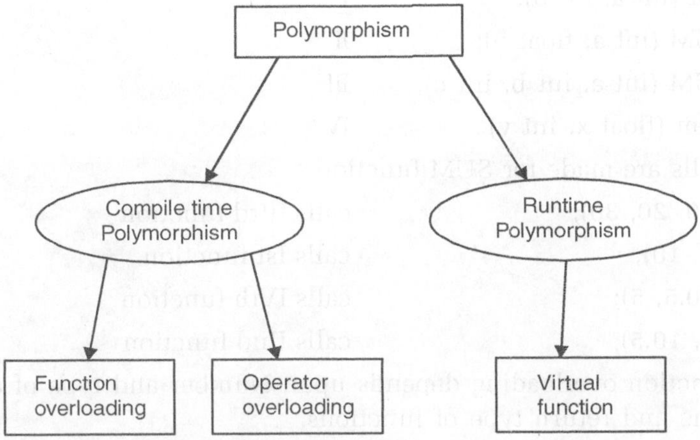

Fig. 5.7. Achieving Polymorphism.

5.6.1. Parametric Polymorphism

A generic or polymorphic subprogram takes parameter of different types on different activation. Overloaded subprogram provide a particular kind of polymorphism called ad-hoc polymorphism. A more general kind of polymorphism is provided by the function of APL. Because of the dynamic type binding of APL, the types of parameters can be left unspecified; they are simply bound to the type of the corresponding actual parameters.

Parametric polymorphism is provided by a subprogram that takes a generic parameter that is used in a type expression that describes the type of the parameters of the subprogram. Both ADA and C^{++} provide a kind of compile time parametric polymorphism. ADA provide parametric polymorphism through a construct that supports the construction of multiple version of program units to accept parameters of different data types. The different version of the subprogram are instantiated or constructed by the compiler upon request from the user program.

5.7. OVERLOADED SUBPROGRAM

An overloaded subprogram is subprogram that has the same name as another subprogram in the same referencing environment. Every version of an overloaded subprogram must have a unique protocol; that is, it must be different from the others in the order, type, number of parameters, or its return type if it is a function. The meaning of a call to an overload subprogram is determined by the actual parameter list.

C^{++}, Java and Ada include predefined overloaded subprogram. For example, Ada has several versions of the output function PUT. In Ada, the return type of an overloaded function is used to disambiguate calls. Therefore, two overloaded functions can have the same parameter profile and differ only in their return type.

In C^{++}, function overloading is used. In this, the function is overloaded depending upon the number and type of arguments and not on the return type. **For example:** Following four functions can be overloaded depended on arguments:

```
int SUM (int a, int b);              I
void SUM (int a, float b);           II
void SUM (int a, int b, int c);      III
void Sum (float x, int y)            IV
```

When four calls are made for SUM function

```
SUM (10, 20, 30);          calls IIIrd function
SUM (5, 10);               calls Ist function
SUM (10.5, 5);             calls IVth function
SUM (5, 10.5);             calls IInd function
```

So in C^{++} function overloading depends upon Number and type of arguments and not depends upon name and return type of functions.

5.8. GENERIC SUBPROGRAMS

A generic subprogram or polymorphic subprogram is one with a single name but several different definitions, distinguished by a different signature. A generic subprogram name is said to be overloaded. Subprograms may also be generic in the same manner. For example, in writing a set of subprograms for a university class registration program, two routines might be needed, one to enter a "section" in a table of class sections and another to enter a "student" in a class roll for a "section". Both subprogram might be defined using the name Register.

```
Procedure    Register (student: in integer
                       sect: inout section) is
begin
             Statement to enter student in a section roll list.
end;
Procedure    Register (S: in section;
                       Tab: inout class list) is
begin
             Student to enter section in a class list.
end;
```

The name Register is overloaded and has become the name of a Generic Register Subprogram. When a call to Register is made. Register (X, Y); the translator must resolve the type of the arguments X and Y with the appropriate types for the two Register procedures.

In the case if X is of type integer, then the call is a call on the first definition of the Register Subprogram and if X is of type section then it is a call on the second. Since this resolution is made during translation, in a language such as Ada there is no effect on the runtime organization of the language. Ada provide parametric polymorphism through a construct that supports the construction of multiple versions of program units to accept parameters of different data types. Generic subprograms introduce no major change in the language or its possible implementations, but can have great impact upon how the language gets used.

5.8.1. Generic Functions in C++

Generic functions in C++ have the descriptive name of template functions. By template we are enable to define generic classes and function. A template can be used to create a family of classes or functions.

For example, a class template for an array class would enable us to create arrays of various data types such as int array and float array. Similarly, we can define a template for a function, say Mul(), that would help us create various versions of Mul() for multiplying int, float and double type values.

A template can be considered as a kind of macro. When an object of a specific type is defined for actual use, the template definition for that class is substituted with the required data type. Template allow us to define generic classes. The general format of a class template is:

```
template<class T>
    Class  Class name
{
    // .................
    // class member specification;
    // with anonymous type T;
    // wherever appropriate;
    // .................
};
```

The class template definition is very similar to an ordinary class definition except the prefix template <class T> and the use of type T. This prefix tells the complier that we are going to declare a template and use T as a type name in the declaration.

A class created from a class template is called a template class. The syntax for defining an object of a template class is:

Class name <type> object name (arglist);

This process of creating a specific class from a class template is called instantiation. Like class templates, we can also define function templates that could be used to create a family of functions with different arguments types. The general format of a function template is:

```
template<class T>
return type function name (arguments of type T)
{
    // .................
    // Body of function;
    // With type T;
    // Wherever appropriate;
    // .................
}
```

The function template syntax is similar to that of the class template except that we are defining functions instead of classes.

The following template function shows the swapping of integer and float data.

```
#include<iostream, h>
using namespace Std;
template<class T>
void swap (T & x, T & y)
{
    T temp = x;
    x = y;
    y = temp;
}
Void fun (int m, int n, float a, float b)
{
    Count<"m and n before swap:"<<m"<<"<<n;
    Swap(m, n);
    Count<<"m and n after swap:"<<m<<" "<<n;
    Count<<"a and b before swap:" <<a<<" "<<b;
    Swap(a, b);
    Cout<<"a and b after swap:" <<a<<" "<<b;
}
int main( )
{
    fun (100, 200, 10.05, 20.10);
    return 0;
}
```

Output of Program will be

```
    m and n before swap:     100      200
    m and n after swap:      200      100
    a and b before swap:     10.05    20.10
    a and b after swap:      20.10    10.05
```

5.9. TYPE DEFINITIONS

In defining a complete new abstract data type, some mechanism is required for definition of a class of data object. In language such as C, Pascal and Ada, this mechanism is termed a type definition. Type definition does not define a complete abstract data type because it does not include definition of the operation on data of that type.

In a type definition, a type name is given, together with a declaration that describes the structure of a class of data objects. The type name then becomes the name for that class of data objects, and when a particular data object of that type is needed, we need to give only the type name, rather than repeating the complete description of the data structure.

In Pascal, for example, if several records A, B, and C are needed, each of which has the same structure, then the program may contain the type definition:

```
type   Employee = record
                Id : integer;
           Salary : integer;
end
```

Following by the declaration:

Var A, B, C : Employee.

So that the definition of structure of a data object of type rational is given only once rather than being repeated three times for each of A, B and C.

The same thing is done in C by following syntax.

```
Struct Employee Type
{
     int Id;
     int salary;
}
```

The objects are created as struct Rational Type A, B, C;

We would like the new data type to appear as an extension of the language and be syntactically and semantically similar to the primitive data types.

A type definition is used as a template to construct data objects during program execution. Type definitions allow the separation of the definition of the structure of a data object from the definition of the points during execution at which data objects of that structures are to created. It is a new form of encapsulation and information hiding. The type definition effectively hides the internal structure of data objects of that type.

Implementation: Implementation of type definition includes storage representation for data objects declared in type definition. The language translator enters the information from a type definition into a table during translation and when a type name is referenced in the declaration part, this table produce the appropriate executable code for setting up and manipulating the desired data objects during execution. The type definition is used to define data objects and create user defined data type. The same type definition information is called many times when the objects is created.

5.9.1. Type Definition with Parameters

Type definition with parameters means we can pass parameters to the data object definitions in the type definition. Array sizes have been the classical example of type parameters. We consider, the following Ada type definition

```
type student is
    record
        Class Roll: array (1....100) of student_ID;
```

```
        Age : integer;
    end record;
```

This definition of student define a student of at most 100 students to get larger type definition.

Another type definition with parameter is a parameterized type definition for student that allows the type definition to have a Maxsize parameter that determines the maximum class size:

```
type student(Maxsize : integer) is
    record
        Class Roll : array (1....Maxsize) of Student ID;
        Age : Integer;
    end record;
```

With this type definition, we can declare variable of maximum class size as:

A : Student (10) — gives maximum size 10.

B : Student (20) — gives maximum size 20.

Implementation: Type definition with parameters are used as a template to construct data objects during program compilation. Parameters in type definitions have an effect on the runtime organization of the language implementation in only a few cases. During compile time, the parameters of type definition is not determined. We can pass parameters to type definition during runtime.

5.9.2. Type Equivalence

Type Equivalence is different from type checking. Type Equivalence means whether a type A is same as type B *i.e.,* whether two type A and B are same. Second whether two data objects of the same type are equal. Type equivalence *i.e.* whether a type is same as another type. Type equivalence can be true in terms of

(*a*) **Name Equivalence:** Two data types are said to be equivalent only if they have the same name. It is method used in C++, Ada and for subprogram parameters in Pascal. Consider the following declaration of two arrays

```
type  X : array [1....10] of integer;
      Y : array [1....10] of integer;
```

Both have same structure but is of different type.

Name equivalence have some limitations like a single type definition must serve all or large parts of a program and every object used in an assignment must have a type name but no duplicate type.

(*b*) **Structural Equivalence:** Two data types are considered equivalent if they define data objects that have same internal structure. Consider the example, of declaration of two arrays

```
type  X : array [1....10] of integer;
      Y : array [1....10] of integer;
```

Now both have same internal structure. So, it is structural equivalence. Both have same number of components of equivalent type and in the same order. It also has some limitations. First one is two variables declared differently but they have same structure. Second it is very costly to determine that two data type is structurally equal. There are different questions that arise when two types are structurally equivalent.

5.9.3. Data Object Equality

Data object equality tells if two data objects are of same type then these two data objects are equal or not. Suppose two data object x and y have same integer type then whether x=y? or $x \neq y$?

For these we consider the following example.

We consider two type definition

Struct Stack	Struct Set
{	{
int top;	int number;
int Data [10];	int Data [10];
} X, Y	} A, B

X, Y, A and B have same structure means they are structurally equivalent. There are different conditions for x=y and A=B.

In case of stack if top refers to the top of the stock then X.top = Y.top and

for all I between 0 and top—I;

x. Data[I] = y. Data[I].

In case of set the conditions are

A. number = B. number

and A. Data[0] .. A[Data[Number—1]] is a permutation of B. Data[0] .. B[Data[Number—1]].

So for Data object equality there will be different conditions for these two type definitions. Although these data object are structurally equivalent but they have different conditions for this.

Some Important Terms

- An abstraction is a representation of an entity that contain only the significant attribute as that entity.
- Attributes are also called features of an entity.
- Abstraction is of two kinds
  - Process abstraction
  - Data abstraction.
- Process abstraction means providing a way for a program to specify that some process is to be done, with and providing the details of how it is to be done.
- Data abstraction consists of a set of objects and a set of operations that are applied to that data objects.

- Abstract data type is a primary component of object oriented programming.
- User defined data type means programmer can create their own data object.
- Two characteristics of user defined abstract data type are
  - A definition part that declare the variables of particular type
  - A subprogram part that contains operations that are performed on variables.
- Encapsulation is binding of data and functioning into a single unit known as class.
- Information hiding hides the design decisions and if the design decision changes then it protect other part of program from change.
- Subprogram are the fundamental blocks of programs.
- Subprogram is a user defined operation.
- A subprogram definitions tells what action has been performed by the subprogram.
- When a subprogram is called a activation record is created by the subprogram.
- A subprogram definition is static part but the activation record is dynamic part.
- Polymorphism means one name, multiple forms.
- Polymorphism is of two types
  - Compile time polymorphism
  - Runtime polymorphism.
- A generic or polymorphic subprogram takes parameter of different types on different activation.
- An overload subprogram is a subprogram that has the same name as another subprogram in the same referencing environment.
- A generic subprogram is one with a single name but several different definitions, distinguished by a different signature.
- A template can be used to create a family of classes or functions.
- Type definition does not define a complete abstract data type because it does not include definitions of the operations on data of that type.
- In a type definition, a type name is given together with a declaration that describes the structure of a class of data objects.
- Type definition with parameter means we can pass parameter to the data object definition in the type definition.
- Type Equivalence means whether a type A is same as type B.
- Type Equivalence can be true in terms of
  - Name equivalence
  - Structural equivalence.
- Data object equality tells if two data objects are of same type then these two data objects are equal or not.

Review Questions

1. Explain the evolution of data type concept.
2. Explain the concept of abstraction.
3. Explain abstraction, encapsulation and Information hiding.
4. What is an overloaded subprogram?
5. What is Parametric Polymorphism?
6. What do you understand by polymorphism? Distinguish between runtime and compile time polymorphism using suitable examples.
7. Explain generic subprograms.
8. Explain abstract data type in details.
9. Write short notes on:
   (a) Subprogram definition and subprogram activation.
   (b) Type definition
   (c) Encapsulation by subprograms.
10. Explain Generic function in C++.
11. Explain type definitions with parameters.
12. Write short notes on:
   (a) Type Equivalence
   (b) Data object equality.
13. Difference between overloaded subprogram and Generic subprograms.

❑❑❑

Chapter 6 SEQUENCE CONTROL

By use of user defined datatype we can combine operations and data into programs. There are control structures that provide the basis for convert this organization into complete executable programs. In this chapter, we discuss sequence control, in which control of the order of execution of the operations takes place. In this we discuss how sequence control takes place in expression, statements and subprograms. In subprogram sequence control we can also Studied Recursive subprograms. Some related terms to sequence control like coroutine and exception handling will also be discussed. In this chapter, basically we will discuss all the concepts related to sequence control.

6.1. SEQUENCE CONTROL

There are two types of operations, first one is built-in-type or primitive type and another one is user-defined operations. Built-in-operations are defined by the language implementor and user-defined operations are defined by the programmer.

Sequence control is defined as the order of execution of primitive and user-defined operations or sequence control tells us what is the order of execution of operations, which operation is performed first and which operation is performed in last.

Sequence control structures are categorized in three groups:

1. **Sequence control in expression:** Sequence control in expression tells us what structure is used in expression means which statements is used and what is the order of statements in expressions. It tells us various precedence rules of operators and parentheses. So sequence control in expression tells us how sequence of statement flows in expressions.
2. **Sequence control with in statements:** It tells us the structure used between statements or a group of statements. There are various types of statements like iterative statement, conditional statements, compound statements. So sequence control with in statements tells us the sequence among the statements.
3. **Sequence control in subprograms:** A simple subprogram have call and return statement structure. Sequence control in subprograms tells the structure used between subprogram and coroutines. So sequence control in subprograms tells the sequence of statements in subprogram. How the call and return statement is implemented and how the pointer changes in coroutines.

6.2. IMPLICIT AND EXPLICIT SEQUENCE CONTROL

Implicit or default sequence control: It is the sequence control structures that are defined by the language. Almost every language defines the sequence of statements in a program and controlling the sequence in which these statements are executed. In sequence control with in expression, programming languages defines the operations that controls the order of execution of operation in the expression. There is some precedence rules that tells the order of execution of operations.

For example: Consider the expression 5 + 10 * 2 in 'C'. Since there is no parenthesis that tells which operation is performed first. But 'C' language defines that has precedence higher then + operator. So it is solved first. The resultant will be 25.

So implicit sequence control tells the sequence of operations that are defined by one programming language. Since it is built in the programming language so it also called default sequence control.

Explicit sequence control: Explicit sequence control that are defined by programmer to modify the implicit sequence of operation defined by the language. Programmer can modify the implicit structure by the some explicit structure.

For example: Programmer provide parentheses with in expression to change the order of execution of operation.

In expression ((5 + 10) * 2) we can first solve the addition (+) operation and then multiplication (*) operator. So the resultant will be 30 instead of 25.

So programmer can change the implicit structure defined by programming language and provide explicit structure with in operations. Programmer provide go to statement that shift controls from a statement to another statement. **For example:**

```
1. Statement 1;
2. If (condition)
3. {
       Statement 2;
   }
4. else
5. {
       goto 1;
   }
```

In this statement if condition false then control goto statement 1.

6.3. SEQUENCE CONTROL WITH IN EXPRESSIONS

Expressions are the fundamental means of specifying computations in a programming language. The semantic rule determines the order of evaluation of operators in expressions. Programmer may understand the syntax and semantics of expression. To understand the expression evaluation, it is necessary to know the order of operator and operand evaluation. The operator evaluation order of expression is governed by the associativity and precedence rules of the language. Other issues related to expressions are type mismatches, coercions etc. Simple assignment statements specify an expression to be evaluated and a target location in which to place the result of the expression evaluation.

6.3.1. Sequence Control with in Arithmetic Expression

Arithmetic expression are found in mathematics. Evaluation of arithmetic expression is the goal of programming language. In programming language, arithmetic expression consists of operator, operands, Parentheses and function call.

The operators can be Unary, meaning they have a single operand, or binary, meaning they have two operands. C, C^{++} and Java include two concept of ternary operator which has three operands.

The various design issues for arithmetic expression are:

- What are the operator precedence rules?
- What are the operator associativity rules?
- What is the order of operand evaluation?
- Are there restrictions on operand evaluation side effects?
- Does the language allow user-defined operator overloading?

6.3.1.1. Tree-structure representation

For tree-structure representation functional composition of expression takes place. In functional composition an operation and its operands are specified. Functional composition gives the expression a characteristic structure of a tree, where the root node of the tree represents the main operation, nodes between the root and leaves represents the intermediate-level operation.

By tree-structure representation the various problems are solved. Like which operator is solved first, what is the order of operand evaluation. The tree representation clarifies the control structure of the expression.

Consider the tree representation of quadratic formula

Root = (–B + SQRT (B**2–4*A*C))/(2*A)

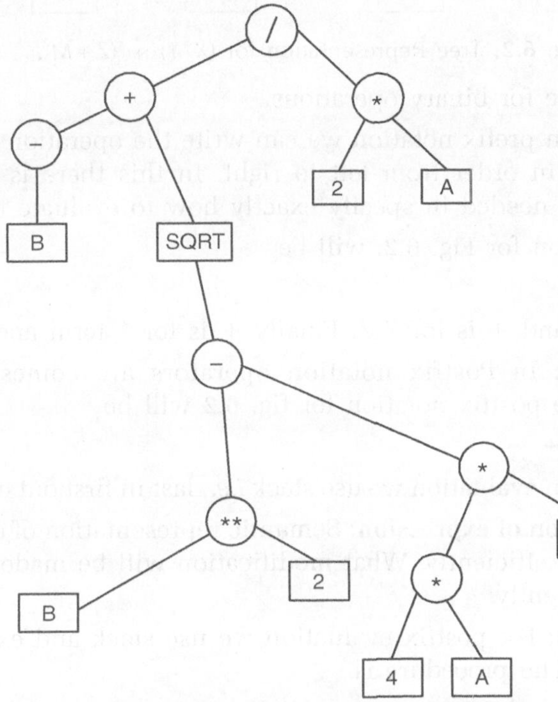

Fig. 6.1. Tree Representation of Quadratic Formula.

In this tree representation the order of evaluation undefined. This representation not tells whether—B should be evaluated before or after B**2. So this is the problem associated with tree representation.

Syntactic representation of expressions: For tree representation the order of evaluation of expression must be required. There are three notations that are used.

(*a*) **Infix notation:** Infix notations are well suited notations for expression. In this notation operators comes in between the operands. Infix notations are used in arithmetic, relational and logical operations.

Consider the example

(X*Y) + (Z + M)

The tree representation corresponding to this infix notation will be

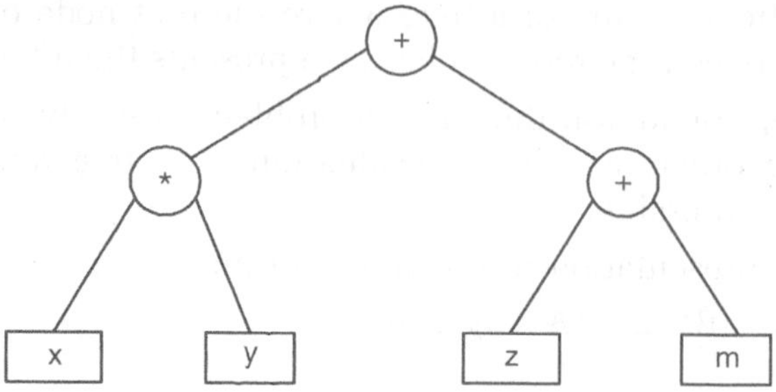

Fig. 6.2. Tree Representation for $(X*Y) + (Z+M)$.

It is more suitable for binary operations.

(*b*) **Prefix notation:** In prefix notation we can write the operation symbol first, followed by the operands in order from left to right. In this there is no ambiguity and no parentheses were needed in specify exactly how to evaluate the expression.

The prefix notation for Fig. 6.2. will be

+*XY+ZM.

*is for X and Y and + is for ZM. Finally + is for * term and + term.

(*c*) **Postfix notation:** In Postfix notation operators are comes after the operands. **For example:** The postfix notation for fig. 6.2 will be

XY* ZM ++.

for postfix notation evaluation we use stack *i.e.*, last in first out evaluation of operands.

Semantic representation of expression: Semantic representation of expression means how we evaluate the expression efficiently. What modification will be made in the order to make expression evaluation efficiently.

(*a*) **Postfix evaluation:** For postfix evaluation we use stack and expression E written in postfix notation. The procedure is

1. If the next item of E is an operand, place it on the stack.
2. If the next item of E is an operator, then pop top two operands in stack and apply the operator on that and result is stored on stack.

For example: Consider the postfix expression

E = 23*4+2/

Input	*Stack*	*Computation performed*
2	2	–
3	2, 3	–
*	6	2*3=6
4	6, 4	–
+	10	6+4=10
2	10, 2	–
/	5	10/2=5

The resultant after evaluation of E = 5.

(b) **Prefix evaluation:** For prefix evaluation we also use stack and expression E written in prefix notation. The procedure is:

1. If the next item in E is an operator, Push it on top of the stack. Set the argument count to be the number of operands needed by the operator.
2. If the next item in E is an operand, Push it on top of the stack.
3. If the top n entries in the stack are operand entries needed by the operator, then apply the top operator to these operands.

For example: Consider the prefix expression.

E = *3 + 4 6

Input	*Stack*	*Computation performed*
*	*	–
3	*3	–
+	*3+	–
4	*3+4	–
6	*3+4 6	4+6=10
–	*310	3*10=30
–	30	–

The resultant after evaluation of E = 30.

Infix evaluation: Evaluation of infix notation can lead to a number of problems. Consider the expression

3 + 4*5.

There is ambiguity what to do whether multiplication is solved before addition or addition is solved before multiplication. So, here the problem is operator evaluation order. There are various rules that language specify for order of evaluation of operators.

(a) **Precedence:** The operator precedence rules for expression evaluation define the order in which the operator of different levels are evaluated. The operator precedence rules for expressions are based on the hierarchy of operator priorities, as seen by the language designer. These rules of the common imperative languages are neraly all the same, because they are all based on mathematics. In these language exponentiation has the highest precedence, followed by multiplication and division on the same level, followed by binary addition and subtraction on the same level. Some language use Unary operator often called identity operator. Then these operator has higher precedence. C, C^{++} use Unary operator. We can specify Unary operator as

X + (–y) * Z is legal, but

X + (–Y) * Z

usually is not.

The precedence of the arithmetic operators of a few common programming languages are as follows:

Table 6.1. Precedence of Arithmetic Operators in Different Programming Language

	FORTRAN	C	Pascal	Ada
Highest	* *	Postfix + +, – –	*, /, div, mod	* *, abs
⋮	*, /	Prefix + +, – –	all +, –	*, /, mod
⋮	all +, –	Unary +, –		Unary +, –
⋮		*, /, %		binary +, –
⋮				
Lowest		binay +, –		

Here ** operator is exponentiation. The /and div operator are used in Pascal. The % operator of C is like mod operator of Pascal. abs operator of Ada is Unary operator that gives the absolute value of its operands.

(*b*) **Associativity:** For associativity we consider following example

M – N + O – P

We know addition and subtraction operator have the same level of precedence, the precedence rule say nothing about the order of evaluation of the operators in the expression. So here we use the rule of associativity of the language. The operator can either be left associative or right associativity, means that left most occurrence is evaluated first or right most occurrence is evaluated first, respectively.

Different imperative languages like FORTRAN, C, C^{++}, Pascal use different associativity rules.

Table 6.2. Shows the Associativity Rule of different Imperative languages.

Table 6.2. Associativity Rule of Different Languages

Language	*Associativity Rule*
FORTRAN	Left: *, /, +, – Right: **
Pascal	Left: All
C++	Left: *, /, %, binary +, binary – Right: ++, --, Unary –, Unary +
C	Left: Postfix ++, Postfix --, *, /, % of bianry +, binary – Right: Prefix ++, Prefix --, Unary +, Unary –

Consider the few example of Associativity

1. In the FORTRAN expression

   X - Y + Z

   The operators have left associative so left operator is evaluated first

2. In the FORTRAN expression

   X**Y**Z

   because ** (exponent) have right associative so right operator is evaluated first.

3. Consider the following FORTRAN expression

   –X–Y

   Because FORTRAN uses left associativity for both Unary and binary minus. So following expression is equivalent to

   (–A)–B.

(c) **Parentheses:** Programmer can change the precedence and associativity rules by placing parentheses in expression. The parenthesized part of an expression has higher precedence than other parts.

   For example:

   (5+4) * 5.

   In this expression * has higher precedence than +. But + operator is in parentheses so it is evaluated first.

(d) **Conditional expression:** In some languages if then else statements are used to perform a conditional expression assignment. In C, C^{++}, Java we use such type of conditional expression.

   For example:

   If (flag = 0)

   then Avg: = 0

   else Avg: = Sum/Flag;

This statement converts in a conditional expression of the form.

expression 1? expression 2: expression 3.

Where expression 1 is a Boolean expression. If it is true then value of whole expression is the value of expression 2.

Otherwise it is the value of expression 3.

Above example is considered as

Avg= (flag == 0)?)0 Sum/flag.

6.3.1.2. Execution time of tree structure used in expression

There are three forms of expressions *i.e.*, infix, prefix and postfix. There are two stages, in the first stage a tree representation of expression is formed and in second stage, the decision regarding evaluation process are taken. The decoding of infix expression are difficult and we translate it into an executable form during execution. We use following alternatives:

1. **Prefix and Postfix form:** In the semantic of prefix and postfix evaluation, we give two algorithms for evaluation of prefix and postfix expression. Both techniques uses stack for evaluation. Some languages allow prefix and postfix representation as a executable form of program.
2. **Tree format:** There are various tree traversal methods. By these algorithms, expressions may be executed directly in tree structure representation. Some languages like LISP uses tree format during execution.
3. **Object code sequence:** In this method, the expression are directly converted in object code (Machine code) and ordering of instructions is maintained by sequence control structure of expression. Machine code representation allows hardware interpreter to fast the execution time of expression.

Problems in order of evaluation of expression in tree representation

Tree representation of programs or expression is the main format of representing expressions. There are various operations performed during execution of tree format. So some problems occurs during evolution of order of expressions. These problems are discussed here.

1. **Side effects in operand evaluation:** Variables in expressions are evaluated by fetching their values from memory. A side effect of a function called a functional side effect, occurs when the function changes either one of its parameter or global variable.

   Consider the expression

   X + Function (X)

   If function does not change the value of X then the evaluation of two operands, X and Function (X) has no effect on the value of the expression. However, if function changes X, there is a side effect.

   In this, function returns the value of its arguments divided by 5 and changes its parameter to the value 20. We have

   X = 10;

   Y = X + Function (X)

   Then, if value of X is fetched first in the evaluation, its value is 10 and expression is

   Y = 10 + 2

   Y = 12

   {Function divides the value by 5 *i.e.*, 10/5=2 and set value of X=20}

   But if the second operand is evaluated first then

   Y = 20 + 2

   Y = 22

   Statements are allowed to have side effects. The assignment operation necessarily produces a side effect, a change in the value of a variable or data structure element.

   Disallowing functional side effects is difficult, and it eliminates some flexibility for the programmer. In C and C^{++}, we use functions. To eliminate side effects, we use a new subprogram type that is similar to the procedures of other imperative languages. To eliminate the problem the Java language definition guarantee that operands appear to be evaluated in left to right order.

2. **Errors in expressions:** Side effects are generated in programmer defined functions. But some error conditions may arise in the primitive operations. The most common error is created when the result of an operation cannot be represented in the memory cell where it must be stored. This is called overflow or underflow, depending on whether the result was too large or two small. Another error condition is division by zero is disallowed. These runtime errors are sometime called exceptions.

3. **Problem in evaluation of expressions:** When we evaluate a expression, there are two rules for evaluation of expression.

   First evaluation rule is eager evaluation rule or uniform evaluation rules. According to this rule all the operands are evaluated before applying an operation. In this all the operands are evaluated first. **For example:**

Consider the example

(X*Y) + (Z+X)

According to the eager evaluation rule we evaluate operands before any operators.

(*a*) Fetch the r-value of X.

(*b*) Fetch the r-value of Y.

(*c*) Fetch the r-value of Z.

(*d*) Multiply X and Y obtaining X_1.

(*e*) Add Z and X obtaining X_2.

(*f*) Add X_1 and X_2, obtaining t.

But this approach is not used in all cases. For conditional expression this eager rule fails.

Consider the example

```
If (A= =0)
{
        t = 1;
}
else
{
        t = (X*Y)/A;
}
```

In this example, dividing (x*y)/A even if A=0. Clearly in this case we do not wish all the operands evaluated before the operation is applied because if A is not equal to zero. In that case we need not fetch x and y. So we need to pass the operands to the conditional operation unevaluated and let the operation determine the order of evaluation. This rule is called Lazy-evaluation rule. In this never evaluate operands before applying the operation, we pass the operand unevaluated and the operation decide the evaluation.

4. **Short-circuit Evaluation:** A short-circuit evaluation of an expression is one in which the output of an expression is determine without evaluating all the operator and operands. **For example:**

   (x+5) * (y/10+1)

   In this, value of y is independent of x. So if x=0. Then multiplication with O and any value of (y/10+1) is also zero. So in this case we did not need to compute (y/10+1) If the value of x=0.

   Similarly (x<=10) and (y>5)

   In this case first part is independent of second. So if x>10. Then if one condition is false then another is also false so we no need to evaluate y.

6.3.2. Sequence Control with in Non-arithmetic Expression

In all languages Non-arithmetic expression are also used. In prolog and ML we use other form of expression evaluation that are used for character data.

6.3.2.1. Pattern matching

Pattern Matching is an operation that matches and assigns a set of variable to a predefined template. It is used in Prolog, ML and SNOBOL 4. It is like parse trees recognition by BNF grammar discussed in chapter 3.

For example. Lets consider the BNF grammar that recognizes odd length palindrome over the alphabet 0 and 1.

$X \rightarrow 0X0/|1X1|0|1$

Recognition of a valid string 11011 proceeds as

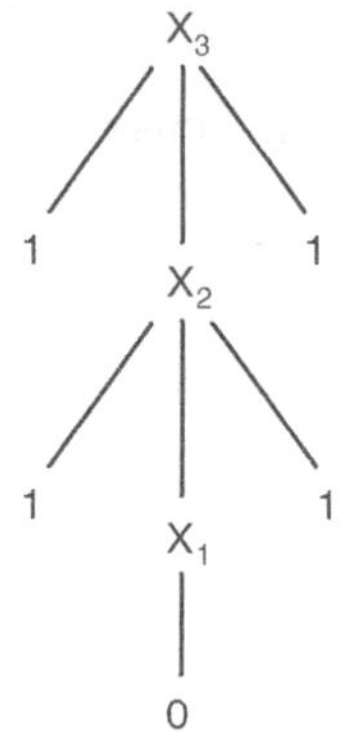

Fig. 6.3. SNOBOL 4 Pattern Matching.

X_1 matches the centre 0

X_2 matches $1X_1$ 1

X_3 matches $1X_2$ 1

From this three assignments of X_1 to 0, X_2 to $1X_11$, X_3 to $1X_21$ as shown in Fig. 6.3.

SNOBOL 4 is a language that have pattern matching based upon BNF grammars; totally dynamic including declaration, types, storage allocation. SNOBOL 4 was the first language that is available on almost every computer and have exactly the same semantics in every implementation. SNOBOL 4 uses string replacement for its pattern matching operation while prolog uses the concept of a relation as a set of n-tuples as its matching mechanism. There are some facts that specify known instances of these relations. From these we can derive other instances.

Consider the relation Parent with the fact

Parent (Amit, Ajay) → Amit is parent of Ajay

Parent (Seema, Ajay) → Seema is parent of Ajay.

If we want two parents of Ajay who are different we write:

Parent (X, Ajay), Parent (Y, Ajay), not (X=Y).

Where the comma separating predicates is an operator.

6.3.2.2. Term rewriting

In the programming language domain there are numerous application where Term Rewriting is used. For given a string $x_1, x_2...x_n$ and rewrite rule $Z \rightarrow y$ if $Z=x_i$, we say $x_1...x_{i-1}, Y...x_n$ is a term rewrite of $x_1, x_2...x_n$. Basically Term Rewriting is a restricted form of Pattern matching.

If we are deriving a string by using some BNF grammar, then it is also considered a case of rewriting process. For example, given the grammar.

$X \rightarrow 0Y/1$

$Y \rightarrow 0X$

We can generate the string 001 with the following derivation:

$X \Rightarrow 0Y$ using rule $X \rightarrow 0Y$

$0Y \Rightarrow 00X$ using rule $Y \rightarrow 0X$

$00X \Rightarrow 001$ using rule $X \rightarrow 1$

There are various languages where term rewriting is used. ML uses term rewriting as a form of function definition. ML will replace the function call by the appropriate definitions.

6.3.2.3. Unification

When we study the term Pattern matching there are two main points first one is facts and second is rules. A prolog data base consists of facts, as in

Parent (Amit, Ajay) → Amit is parent of Ajay

Parent (Seema, Ajay) → Seema is parent of Ajay

The rule is if we want two parents of Ajay who are different we write:

Parent (X, Ajay), Parent (Y, Ajay), not (x=y)

Where the comma separating predicates is an operator.

If an expression containing one or more variable *e.g.,* in shown above, like.

Parent (Amit, Ajay)

Then it is called a Query or Goal.

Prolog uses unification on the substitution of variables in relations, to pattern match in order to determine if the query has a valid substitution consistent with the rules and facts in the database.

6.3.2.4. Substitution

In many programming languages we use parameter passing and macro expansion. Behind these terms the basic principle is substitution. Substitution means the values of arguments and substituted in the arguments. Lets cosider the following C macro:

```
# define Quadratic (a,b,c) Printf ("quadratic %d%d%d%d",
    a, b, c, (b) * (b) – 4 * (a) * (c)
```

When we pass in Quadratic (1, 2 3) then results of this is

```
Printf ("quadratic %d%d%d%d", 1, 2, 3, (2) * (2) - 4 * (1) (3))
```

Substitution is the result of applying new values to macro template arguments. When we substitute the values in the macros the invocation of the macro expansion takes place.

6.3.2.5. Backtracking

Backtracking is a technique that is generally available in the programming languages. In generally, backtracking has generally tree like structure. In prolog, when a goal with multiple sub-goals is being processed, at any time we are trying to match a subgoal. If the match is to succeed, then one of the possible goal will succeed, only we do not necessarily know which one. If we first try an incorrect goal, that goal will fail. In backtracking, if we select a goal and that goal reaches to a fail, then we backtrack (*i.e.*, back to set of goals) and selects another subgoal to reach the goal.

Let we call the general backtracking algorithm.

Step 1: Set K=1 as a new goal

Step 2: Successively try to match $goal_k$ for k=1...N where N is no. of subgoals.

Step 3: This returns either success or failure.

Step 4: If $goal_k$ succeeds, then save k and this leads to success.

Step 5: If $goal_k$ fails for any k, then Backtrack to subgoals N–1 and try to next possible goal k+1 for that subgoal.

Step 6: If $subgoals_i$, N succeeds, than return success as the result of the parent $goal_k$.

Step 7: If $subgoal_i$, j goals for all k, then returns failure as the result of the parent $goal_k$.

6.4. SEQUENCE CONTROL WITH IN STATEMENTS

The statement part decides which computation is performed in the program and what is the output of the program. The basic statements are:

(a) Assignment statements

(b) Input-output statements

(c) Subprogram calls.

(a) Assignment Statements

Assignment statement provides the mechanism by which the user can dynamically change the bindings of values to variables.

The general form of Assignment statement is

<target_variable> <assignment_operator> <expression>

Different languages uses different assignment operators FORTRAN, BASIC, PL/I, C, C^{++} and Java use the equal sign for the assignment.

For example: X=10

Assigns the constant 10 to the variable X.

In C equality test operator is ==. and the inequality test operator is !=.

Some other languages line ALGOL 60 and Pascal use := as the assignment operator.

Different types of Assignment Statement are used by different languages.

(*i*) **Multiple Targets:** In this we can assign the value to more than one location. For example, in PL/I the statement.

S_1, S_2 = 0

assigns the value zero to both S_1 and S_2.

(*ii*) **Compound Assignment:** In this technique the destination variable also appearing as the first operand in the expression on the right side, as

Total = Total+A;

C, C^{++} and Java also uses this type of compound assignment.

Like

Sum = Sum + A;

In C, C^{++} Java we can also use Unary arithmetic operation like increment and decrement operation with assignment. The operators are ++ for increment and --for decrement.

Like

S = count++;

It assigns the value of count to S first; then count is incremented.

(*iii*) **Assignment with in expressions:** C allows assignment to appear with in expressions. An expression $E_1 = E_2$ is evaluated by placing the value of E_2 into the location of E_1.

For example: The expression

C=getchar ( )

assigns to C the input character read by the standard procedure getchar ( ). The value assigned to C also becomes the value of C=getchar ( ), so it can appear as a sub-expression with in a larger expression:

(C= getchar ( )) ! = EOF

Constant EOF, signifies the end of input file. This expression thus reads a value using getchar, save the value by assigning it to C, are then test is the Value equals the constant EOF.

(b) Input-Output Statements

All programming languages use some input statement that reads the data from user at a terminal or from files and some output statements that displays the data through the terminal to the user. Like in C we use Scanf and printf functions for Input-output. Also read (file, data) reads the data from file and write (file, data) writes the data to the file.

(c) Subprogram Calls

All programming language use some form of parameter transmission methods for passing parameter to the subprograms. Subprograms are called by passing parameter to the subprograms. These parameters are passed implicity to the subprogram. Subprogram calls we discuss later in this chapter.

6.4.1. Different Forms of Statement-level Sequence Controls

Basically there are three forms of statement level sequence control:

1. **Composition:** In composition a sequence of statements are placed with in a block and that statements are executed in sequence given in the block.

   Like, ALGOL 60 use the concept of composition whose general form is

```
begin
    Statement—1
    -------------
```

```
    Student—n
end
```

2. **Alternation:** In alternation, there are two sequence of statement and one conditional statement. If condition is true then one sequence is executed and if false, another sequence is executed but not both.
3. **Iteration:** By iteration, a sequence of statements may be executed several times depending upon the loop. If the loop is true for n time, then sequence of statement is executed n-times.

6.4.2. Handling Special Cases in Loops

In some language, all statements are not single entry/single exit. These statements are called loop invariants. There are different type of loops that are not single entry/single exit. These are:

1. **Break and continue statements in Loops:** Break and continue handles the special cases in loops:
   - A break statement sends control out of the enclosing loop to the statement following the loop. It can be used to jump out of a loop after establishing the conditions upon exit from the loop.
   - A continue statement repeats the enclosing loop by sending control to the beginning of the loop. It can be used to restart the loop after re-establishing the loop invariant, the condition that holds upon loop entry.

     One use of break statement is to break out of a loop after handling a special case, as

```
While condition do
    if special case then
        break;
    end if
        statements;
    end while
```

Use of break statement

In this if special case then break otherwise work normally.

```
While condition do
    if normal case then
        continue;
    end if
        statement
    end while
```

Use of continue statement

In this, the continue statement in the outline ensures that control flows back to the beginning of the loop immediately after taking care of normal as,

2. **Return Statement:** The return statement have the form

   return <expression>

Sends control back from a procedure to a caller, carrying the value of <expression>. If the return statement is not in a procedure, then the program halts.

For example:

```
for i = 1 to n do
if x = A[i] then return i;
else return 0;
```

3. **Goto statements:** Goto statement transfer the control explicitly to the another statement. Goto statement is of two types

   (*a*) **Unconditional Goto:** The syntax of unconditional Goto is

   Goto L.

   It interrupts the normal flow of control from one statement to the next in sequence; control flows instead to the statement labelled L somewhere in the program.

   (*b*) **Conditional Goto:** The syntax of conditional Goto is

   if X=0 then goto L.

   The control transfers to L if the condition (X=0) is true. Use of goto statements leads to an unstructured design of a program. The axiomatic correctness model of program design does not easily permit the inclusion of a goto statement.

6.4.3. Need of Structured Programming Design

The use of goto statement leads to an unstructured design of program. There are various disadvantages of goto statements.

1. **Difficulty in Understanding Code:** A program is easily understood if each group of statements serves a single purpose in the program. Using goto, we can combine two groups of statements so that identical statements are written only once and controlled is transferred to this common set during execution of each group. This makes of this code difficult.
2. **Lack of hierarchical structure:** Single entry/single exit design is more understandable design. If statements are organized in groups then they are easily understandable. But goto, break statement removes the concept the single entry/single exit concept. So it have lack of hierarchical structure design.
3. **Change the order of execution:** By use of goto statement, control jumps between different sequence of statements in irregular patterns. It is not the actual order of statement in which the program text is written. It is different from the actual design. So its order of execution is difficult to understand. This is irregular execution sequence of the program.

6.4.4. Structured Programming Design

The problem discussed in above, can cause problem to reader of a program to understand the actions that occur in the program. If the sequence is not in order then understanding the execution of program is also difficult.

The structured programming design is that which emphasizes.

1. Hierarchical design of program structure by use of composition, alternation and iteration.

2. The structure of the program text should help us understand what the program does.
3. A program is structured if the flow of control through the program is evident from the syntactic structure of the program text.
4. The program sequence in corresponds to the execution sequence of program.
5. Language must allow an underlying assignment oriented machine to be used directly and efficiently.

When the program is written in structure programming principle then it is easier to understand, debug and verify the correctness of program.

6.4.5. Structured Sequence Control or Control Flow

If the control flow is according to syntactic structure of the program text then it is easy to understand the execution of statements. Structured sequence control based on single entry/single exit concept.

There are different types of statements that follows structured sequence control.

1. **Compound statements:** Compound statements are examples of composition. Compound statement uses the collection of statements with in a block. It will be treated as a single statement that executed serially.

   Many language like ALGOL 60, C, C++, Java uses compound statements.

   A compound statement is written as

```
begin
    Statement 1;
    ..................
    Statement n;
end.
```

   It can be implemented in conventional computer by placing the blocks of executable code. Pascal followed ALGOL 60's design for compound statements but does not allow blocks.

2. **Selection statements:** A selection statement selects one of two alternative substatement for execution. There are various forms of selection statements.

   If statement: This statement has the form

   If (Boolean expression)

```
then
    begin
        statement
    end
```

   Most of the languages use single way selection that can select a compound statement or a sequence of statements.

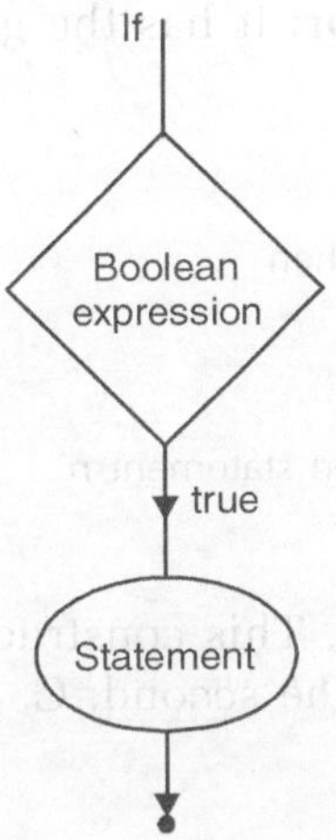

Fig. 6.4. If Statement Structure.

If then else or two-way selector: It has the general form

```
If (Boolean_expression) then
    Statement 1;
else
    Statement 2;
```

The statement following the then reserved word is called the then clause and the statement following the else reserved word is called else clause.

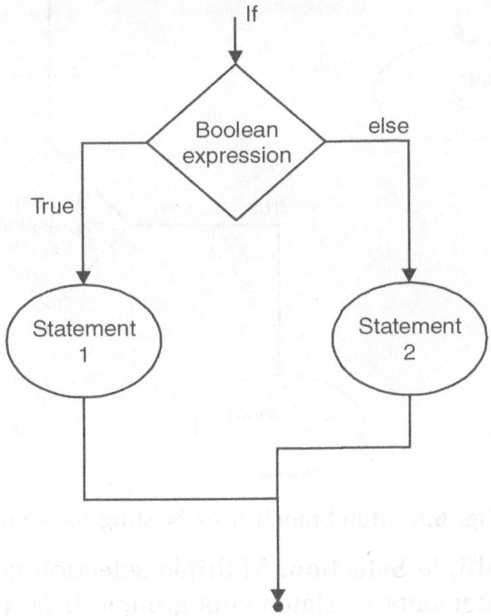

Fig. 6.5. If then else or two-way Selector.

Multibranch If or Nesting Selector: It has the general form

```
If (Boolean_expression 1) then
    Statement 1;
else if (Boolean_expression 2) then
    Statement 2
    ---------------
else if (Boolean_expression) then statement n
else statement n+1 end if.
```

It avoids nesting in the then parts. This construct depends or whether the else clause is matched with the first then clause or the second. C, C++, Java uses this concept.

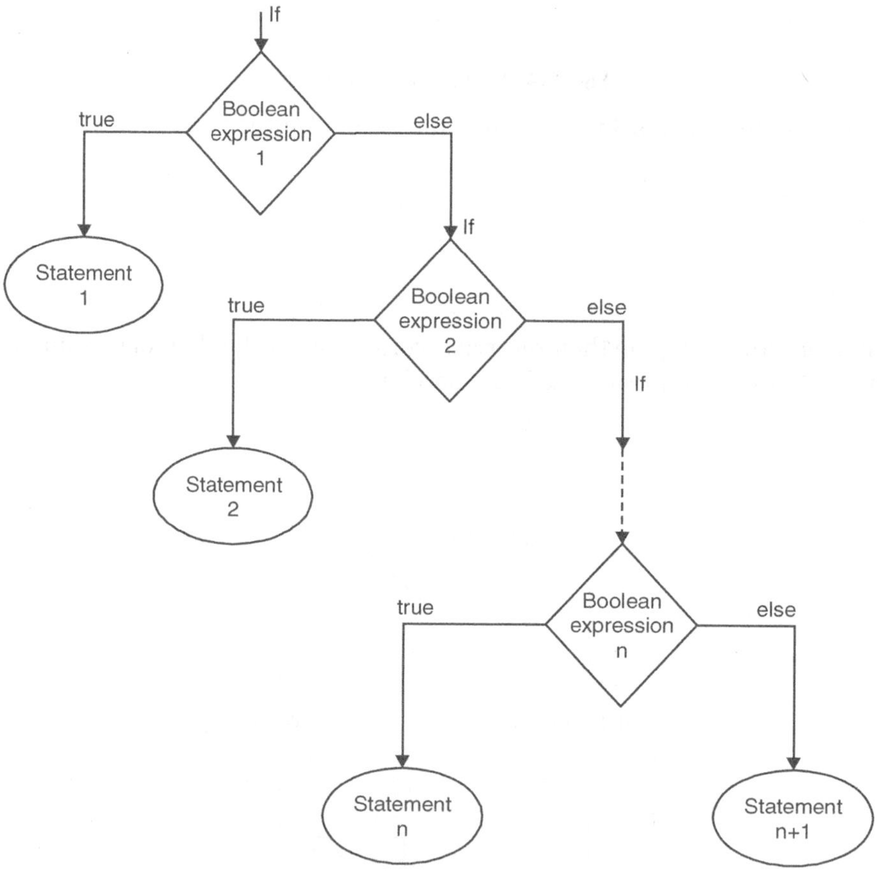

Fig. 6.6. Multibranch If or Nesting Selector.

Case statements or Multiple Selection: Multiple selection construct allows the selection of one of any number of statements or statements groups. It is, therefore, a generalization of a selector. Multiple selector can be single way and two way selector. A better form of multiple selector, named case, was suggested by C.A.R Hoare. This structure is encapsulated and has single entry. This restricts the control flow through the structure to a single selectable segment. The general form of Hoare's multiple selector is:

```
Case integer_expression of
  begin
      Statement 1;
      ..................
      Statement–n;
  end.
```

Where statements could be either single statements or compound statements.

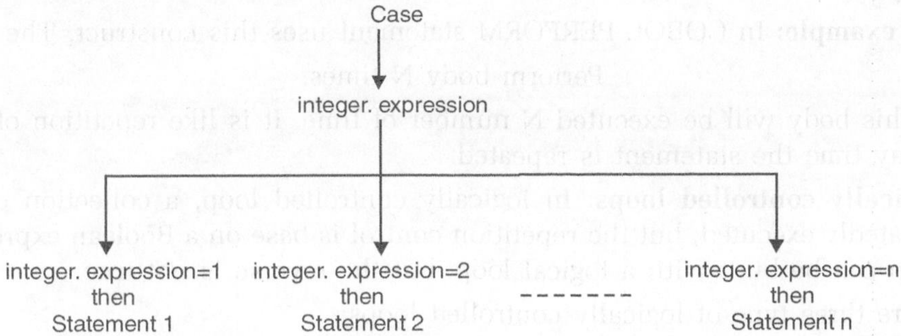

Fig. 6.7. Flow of Control in a Case Statement.

Semantics of the Pascal is as follows: The expression is evaluated, and the value is compared with the constants in the constant lists. If a match is found, control transfers to the statement attached to the matched constant. When statement execution is completed, control transfers to the first statement following the whole case construct.

In 'C' language switch construct using break is used. The syntax of switch is as follows

```
Switch (index) {
    Case 1: Statement 1;
            break;
    Case 2: Statement 2;
            break;
    Case 3: Statement 3;
            break;
    default: Printf ("Error message");
}
```

It is convenient to allow control to flow from one selector table code segment to another.

Case statements are commonly implemented using a jump table to avoid repeated testing of the value of the same variable. A jump table is a vector, stored sequentially in memory, each of whose components is an unconditional jump instruction. The expression forming the condition of the case statement is evaluated, and the result is transformed into a small integer representing the offset into the jump table from its base address.

3. **Iterative statements:** An iterative statement is one that causes a statement or collection of statements to be executed zero, one, or more than one times. It depends upon iterative statements, how many time the statements will be executed. The first iterative

constructs in programming languages were directly related to arrays. Several categories of iteration control statements have been developed. In iteration statements we have to keep two things in mind, first one is how is the iteration controlled and where should the control mechanism appear in the loop. The primary possibilities for iteration control are logical, counting, or a combination of the two. The main choices for the location of the control mechanism are the top of the loop or the bottom of the loop.

There are various form of iterative statement.

(*a*) **Simple iterative statement:** In simple iterative statement top specifies that how many time the body is executed. There is a fixed number of time the body is executed.

For example: In COBOL PERFORM statement uses this construct. The Syntax is

Perform body N times.

In this body will be executed N number of time. It is like repetition of a statement *i.e.,* how many time the statement is repeated.

(*b*) **Logically controlled loops:** In logically controlled loop, a collection of statements must be repeatedly executed, but the repetition control is base on a Boolean expression. Every counting loop can be built with a logical loop, but the reverse is not true.

There are three type of logically controlled loops:

(*i*) **While do statement:** The syntax of while do statement is

```
While (expression)
do
    statement.
```

This means evaluating the expression and if true, executes the statements. In the pretest version (while), the statement is executed as long as the expression evaluates to true (non-zero)

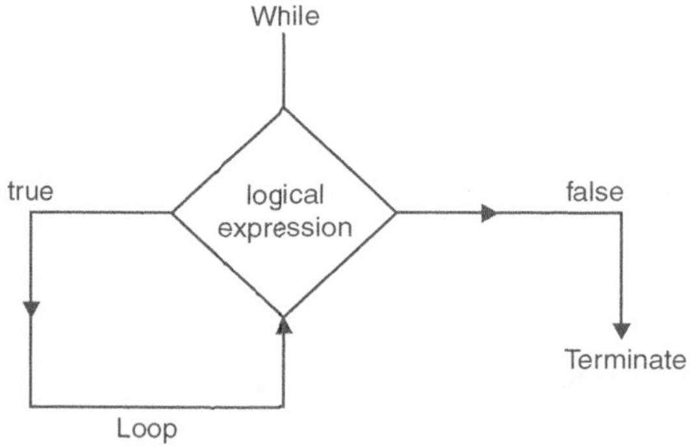

Fig. 6.8. Flow of Control in While-do Statement.

(*ii*) **do-while statement:** The syntax of do-while loop is

```
do
    loop body
while (expression)
```

In this do-while statement first statement part is executed and then condition is checked in the while loop. In do-while loop, one time statement is executed even if the condition is false.

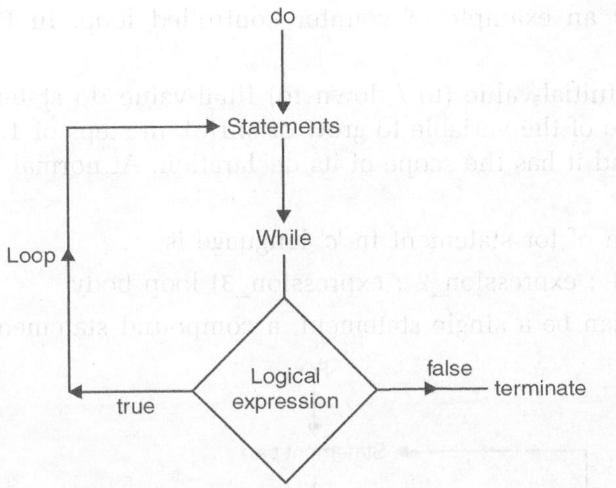

Fig. 6.9. Flow of Control in do-while Statement.

The basic difference between while and do while statement is that in while loop only if the logical expression is true then statement part is executed. But in do while loop, one time the statement part is executed.

(*iii*) **Repeat Until statement:** The syntax of repeat until is given as

Repeat

Statement

Until (expression)

It means execute the statement and then evaluate the expression, until the expression is true.

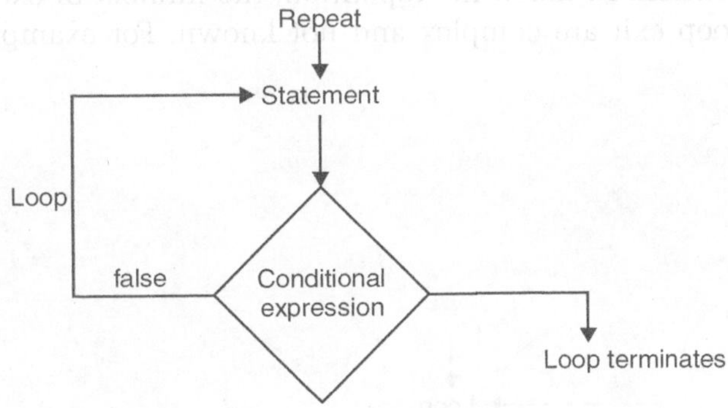

Fig. 6.10. Flow of Control in Repeat-until Statement.

In repeat until statement part is executed, until the expression is true. If the expression is false then the statement is executed in loop.

(*c*) **Counter-Controlled loops:** A counting iterative control statement has a variable, called the loop variable, in which the count value is maintained. It also includes some means of specifying the initial and terminal values of the loop variable and the difference between sequential loop variable values, often called the step size.

For statement is an example of counter controlled loop. In Pascal for statement has form.

For variable := Initial-value (to / down to) final-value do statement. The to / down to choice allow the value of the variable to grow or shrink in steps of 1. The loop variable must be an ordinal type, and it has the scope of its declaration. At normal loop-terminator/the loop variable is undefined.

The general form of for statement in 'c' language is

for (expression_1 ; expression_2 ; expression_3) loop body.

The loop body can be a single statement, a compound statement, or a null statement.

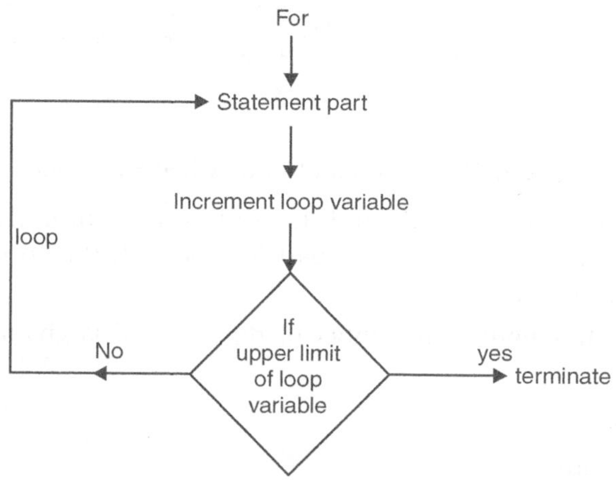

Fig. 6.11. Flow of Control in for Statement.

(*d*) **Indifinite repetition:** In indefinite repetition, the number of execution are not known. In this condition for loop exit are complex and not known. For example, in Ada

```
loop
- - - - - - - - - - - - - -
exit when condition;
- - - - - - - - - - - - - -
end loop;
and for (; ;) {body}
```

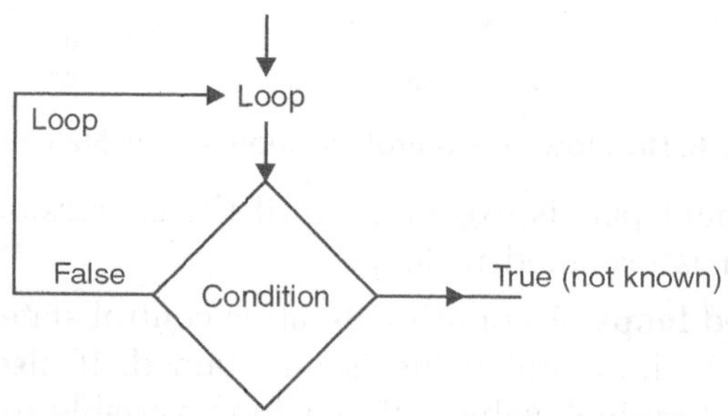

Fig. 6.12. Flow of Control in Indefinite Interation.

6.4.6. Problems in Structured Sequence Control

In the previous sections, we have studied that a goto statement is inadequate for the expression in structured sequence control. The goto statements are not suitable for structured sequence control because it not follows the sequence of structured sequence control. Some other problems are also arises in structured sequence control:

(1) **Multiple exit loops:** Every condition requires a termination of loop. Structured sequence control obeys the single entry-single exit principle. It avoids the multiple exits from loops. Every language, provides the features of multiple exit from loop. Like goto, break statements in '*c*', the exit statement in Ada etc.

(2) **do-while-do:** The most natural place to test whether to exit a loop comes not at the beginning or end of the loop but in the middle, after some processing has been done. The do-while-do construct is also called 'loop and a half'.

Unfortunately, no common language implements this structure, although in C, if (condition) break come close and Ada's exit when is similar.

(3) **Exceptional condition:** Exception may represent error conditions. In many programming languages special exception handling statement is used.

A goto statement is used. Exception are like unexpected end of file condition, subscript range errors etc. Where exception handling constructs are not used then a goto statement is used.

6.4.7. Prime Programs

The prime program was developed by Maddnx as a generalization of structured programming to define the unique hierarchical decomposition of a flowchart. There are generally three classes of nodes in the program graph.

(*a*) **Function node:** A function nodes represent a single arc entering and a single arc leaving a node. It represent computation by a program and represented by boxes. Generally it is for representing an assignment statement.

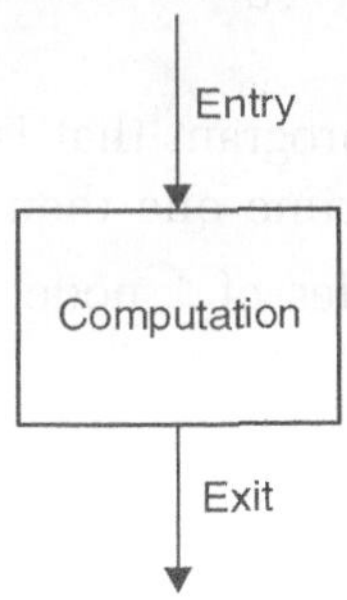

Fig. 6.13. Function Node.

(*b*) **Decision node:** It is represented as diamond shaped boxes with one input and two output arc representing, true and false. In this control flows out of a decision box on either the true or false branch.

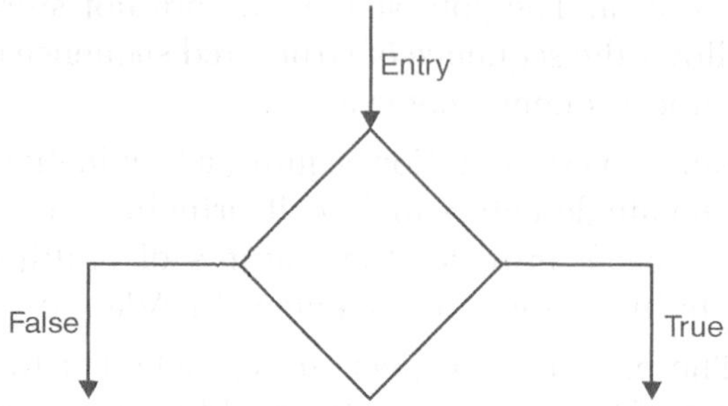

Fig. 6.14. Single-entry and Multiple Exit Decision Node.

(*c*) **Join node:** A join node, two arcs flow together and comes to a point and there is single exit point.

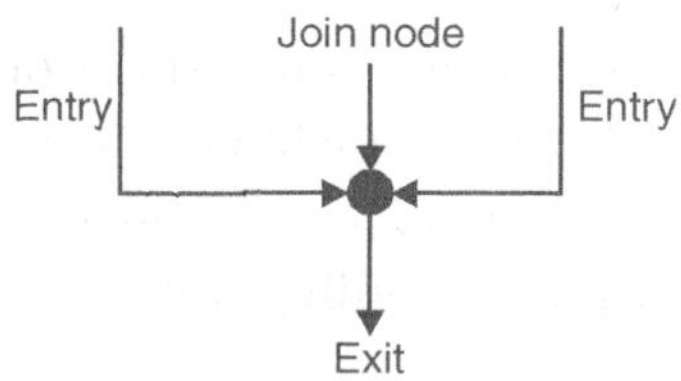

Fig. 6.15. Join Node Representing Multiple Entry and Single Exit.

The theory of prime programs can be used to describe a consistent theory of control structures. Every flowchart consists of function node, decision node and join node.

Proper program: Proper program represents the formal model of a control structure of flowchart. It has a single entry arc, a single exit arc and a path from entry to exit arc. Proper programe uses the structured concept. Proper programs are different from unstructured programs.

Prime Program: A prime program is a proper program that cannot be subdivided into smaller proper programs. If a proper program is divided into smaller proper subprogram then it is not a Prime program.

Composite Program: A proper program that is not a prime is called composite program *i.e.*, if a proper program is not the prime one then it is composite program.

In below we show some examples of 1 node, 2 node, 3 node prime program.

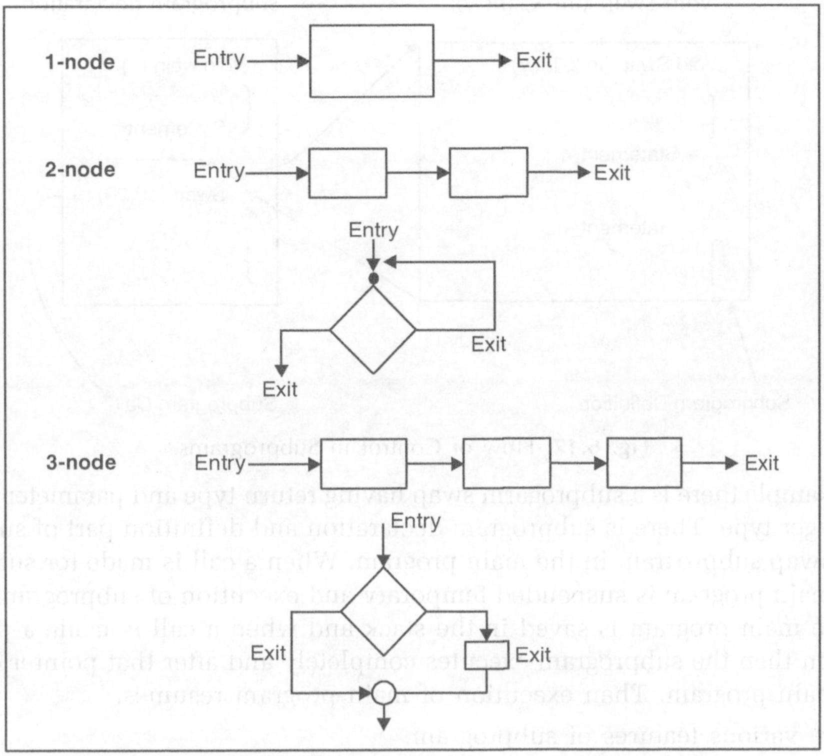

Fig. 6.16. Representation of Prime Programs.

6.5. SUBPROGRAM SEQUENCE CONTROL

Subprograms are the fundamental building blocks of programs and it is the most important concept in programming language. A subprogram structure consists of three parts.

(*a*) **Subprogram header:** It is the first line of the definition, it specifies that the following syntactic unit is a subprogram definition of some particular kind.

(*b*) **Subprogram definition:** It describes the interface to and the actions of the subprogram abstraction. It defines what action the subprogram perform.

(*c*) **Subprogram call:** It is the explicit request that the subprogram be executed. A subprogram becomes active when it is called and perform the desired action.

Generally specification of subprogram consists of its return type, name for the subprogram and a list of parameters.

The protocol of a subprogram is its parameter profile plus, if it is a function its return type. In languages in which subprograms have types, those types are defined by the subprogram is protocol. Subprogram can have declaration as well as definition. Subprograms declaration are common in C programs, where they are called prototypes. These are two ways that a subprogram can gain access to the data that it is to process: through direct access to nonlocal variable or through parameter passing.

Consider the following 'C' example that differentiate Declaration, Definition and calling of Subprograms.

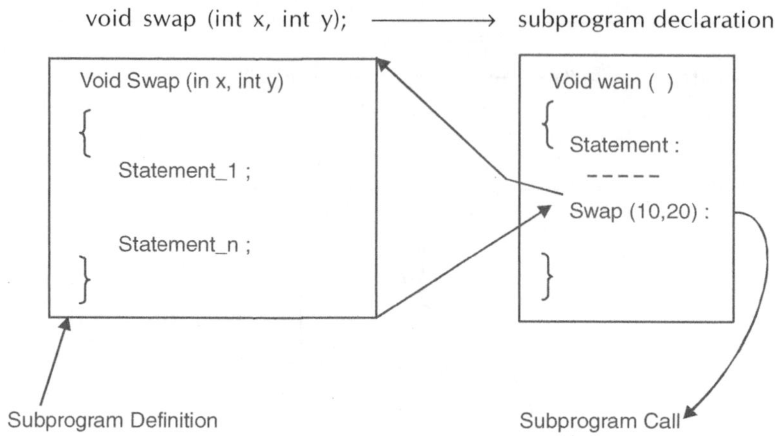

Fig. 6.17. Flow of Control in Subprograms.

In this example there is a subprogarm swap having return type and parameter list containing *x* and *y* of integer type. There is subprogram declaration and definition part of subprogram and a call to this swap subprogram in the main program. When a call is made for subprogram then execution of main program is suspended temporary and execution of subprogram starts and all the data of the main program is saved in the stack and when a call is made a pointer goes to the subprogram then the subprogram executes completely and after that pointer comes back to the original main program. Then execution of main program resumes.

There are various features of subprogram.

(*i*) Subprogram cannot be recursive.

(*ii*) Subprogram must execute completely at each call.

(*iii*) Explicit call statement is used to call the subprogram.

(*iv*) When subprogram is called then immediately control transfer to the point of call.

(*v*) Subprogram has single execution sequence.

6.5.1. General Subprogram Characteristics

All subprograms except coroutines have the following characteristics:

(1) Subprograms have a single entry point.

(2) When a subprogram is called then execution of main program stops and execution of subprogram starts. We can say that only one subprogram is in execution at any given time.

(3) When execution of subprogram terminates then control returns to the main program.

Some language like FORTRAN have multiple entries but is kind of entry is unimportant because it does not provide any different capabilities.

6.5.2. Procedures and Functions

There are two types of subprograms procedures and functions.

Procedures are collections of statements that define parameterized computations. These computations are performed by single call statements. It defines new statements. It produce results in the calling program unit by two methods. First, if the variable are not formal parameter but are still visible in procedure and calling program unit, the procedure can change them.

Second, if the subprogram has formal parameters that allow the transfer of data to the caller, those parameters can be changed. Pascal language uses the concept of procedures.

Functions resemble procedure by structurally but are semantically modelled on mathematical function. If function is a mode, It produce no side effects that is, it modifies neither its parameters nor any variables defined outside the function. One important property of function is, function should return a value *i.e.*, it always returns values. Functions are called by its actual parameters. Function define new user-defined operators.

Most common imperative languages provide both functions and procedures. C and C^{++} have only function. However, these functions can behave like procedures. They can be defined to return no value by defining its return type to be void. The methods of Java and C++ are similar to the functions of C.

6.5.3. Simple Subprogram Call-Return

Generally, subprogarm sequence—control means a mechanism for transfer of control between program and subprogram. Simple subprogram call-return means that all local variables are static and subprograms are not nested. When main program CALL the subprogram then execution of main program stops and execution status of main program is saved and transfer the contrtol to the subprogram. When the subprogram completes it execution then control returns to the main program. In this case the subprogram is not nested means if main calls the subprogram then the subprogram cannot call to the another subprogram.

Implementation: For implementation of simple call-return subprograms we need to consider the following points:

(1) Subprogram definition is different from the subprogram activation. An activation record is created each time a subprogram is called.

(2) An activation record consists of two parts:

(*a*) A code segment containing the executable code and constants.

(*b*) An activation record containing local data, other data items and parameter.

(3) Code segment is fixed during execution *i.e.*, it is invarient during execution. The activation record part is dynamic *i.e.*, changes each time the subprogram is called means each time a new activation record is created when a subprogram is called.

(4) When subprogram completes its execution then activation record is destroyed.

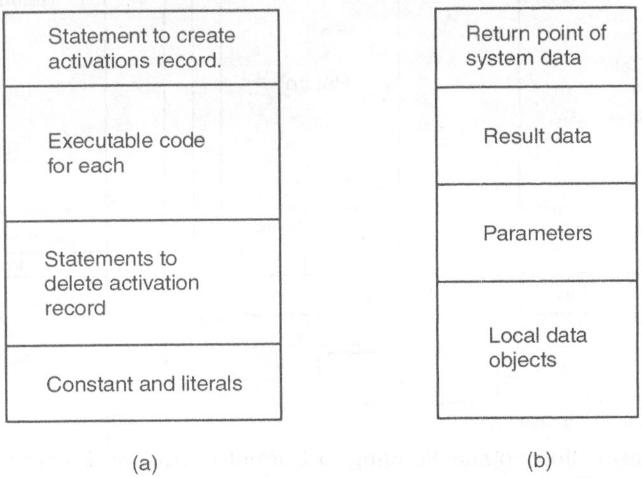

Fig. 6.18. Subprogram Activation (a) Code Segment (b) Activation Record.

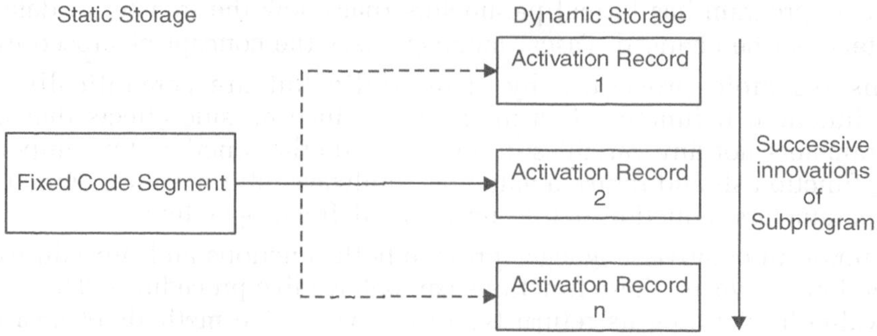

Fig. 6.19. Static Storage for Code Segment and Dynamic Storage for Activation Records.

Figure 6.19. shows that the code segment is fixed for different activation record. It means if a subprogram is called multiple times then the code segment is only one and there is different activation records for this.

The execution of simple call-return subprograms we need to keep track of the point at which a program is executed. For this we need two systems defined pointer variables.

(1) **Current Instruction Pointer (CIP):** Current instruction pointer points to the current instruction that is currently being executed by hardware or software interpreter. In case of subprograms call there are various statements and expressions. These statements are represented by instructions of some sort in the executable code produce by translator. We need to check which instruction is currently being executed. So for this, we use current instruction pointer which tells which instruction is currently executed.

(2) **Current Environment Pointer (CEP):** For all activations there is only one code segment. If multiple activations of same programs may exist during execution, then a pointer

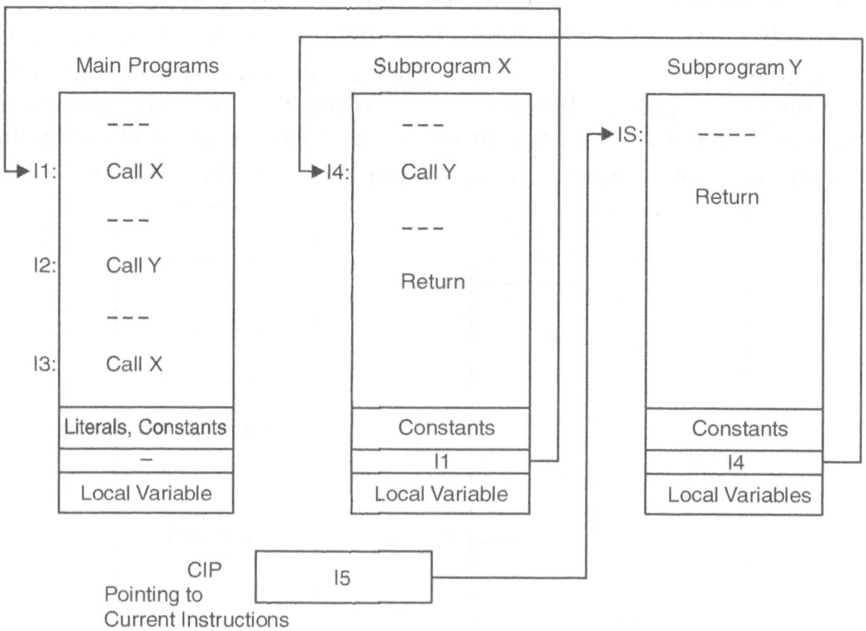

Fig. 6.20. Current Instruction Pointer Pointing to Current Instruction Executing in Subprogram *y*.

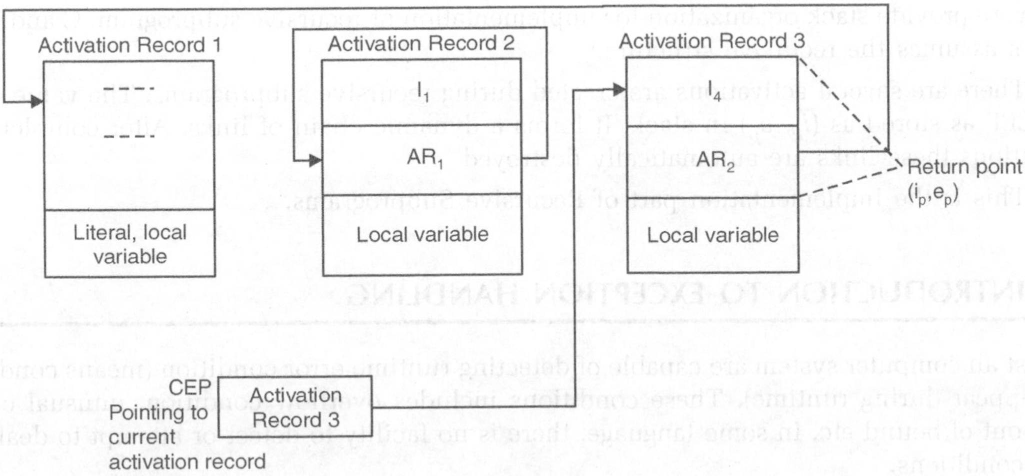

Fig. 6.21. Activation Records Corresponding to Fig 6.20 and CEP Points to Current Activation Record which is Executing.

to the current activation record is also needed that tells instruction being executed is belong to which activation. So a pointer to an activation record is needed and this pointer that points to current activation-record (current referencing environment) during execution is known as current environment pointer (CEP).

In Figs. 6.20 and 6.21 shows the CIP that is pointing to current instruction being executing and CEP that is pointing to current activation record. The return point contains space for two pointers (i_p, e_p) names instruction pointer and environment pointer. During call instruction it contains old values of (i_p, e_p) of the CIP and CEP in the return point. After the call instruction it contains the new values of the CIP and CEP.

6.5.4. Recursive Subprograms

Recursion, in the form of subprogram call, is the most important sequence control structure used in programming.

Specification part: There are basically two type of Recursive Subprograms.

(*a*) **Direct recursive:** If a subprogram calls itself then it is called direct recursive.

(*b*) **Indirect recursive:** If a subprogram calls another subprogram then it is called indirect recursive.

If a recursive call is made then it creates a second activation record during the life time of first activation record. If second activation leads to another recursive call, then three activations may exist simultaneously, and so on. These activations are destroyed after completing the execution. The recursive subprograms use stack to store the data while executing the recursive subprograms.

Implementation part: In recursive subprogram, there are multiple activation records is created. As studied is section 6.5.3., we need CIP and CEP pointers that points to the current instruction and current activation record. In recursive subprogram a nested chain is built in which the lifetime of one activation record, contains the lifetime of another activation record and after the completion of execution, the activaton records are destructed. Some computer hardware provide stack organization for implementation of recursive subprogram. C and Pascal always assumes the recursive structure.

There are several activations are created during recursive subprograms. The value of CIP and CEP as stored as (i_p, e_p) in stack. It forms a dynamic chain of links. After completion of activations these links are automatically destroyed.

This is the implementation part of Recursive Subprograms.

6.6. INTRODUCTION TO EXCEPTION HANDLING

Almost all computer system are capable of detecting runtime error condition (means conditions that appear during runtime). These conditions includes overflow condition, unusual events, array out of bound etc. In some language, there is no facility to detect or attempt to deal such error conditions.

In this case while appearing such a condition a control is transferred to the operating system and a runtime error is appearred on the screen. But some languages deals with these error conditions, they detect where these conditions appers and what to do while appearing these conditions. For example, A FORTRAN READ statement can intercept input errors and end of file conditions. In both cases error is detected by the input device hardware.

6.6.1. Exception and Exception Handlers

Exception is defined as any unusual condition, erroneous or not, some error conditions that are detected by hardware or software during execution and that require processing. Exceptions are the runtime conditions like overflow, End of file etc., that appeared during execution. Rather than continue with normal program execution, a subprogram needs to be called to perform some special processing called exception handling.

These includes:

(1) Error conditions to process an error such as an arithmetic operation overflow or reference to an array element with a subscript out of bounds.

(2) Unpredictable condition that arise during normal program execution such as the production of special output heading at the end of a printer page or an end of file indicator on an input file.

(3) Tracing and monitoring during program testing such as printing trace output during program testing when the value of a variable changes.

Exception handler: The subprogram that performs the special processing is termed as Exception handler.

An exception handler is defined as the unit or segment that performs the special processing to handle the execution.

An exception handler is involved with an explicit call. The definition of each exception handler typically contains a set of declaration of local variables, if any, and a sequence of executable statements.

The usual form of an exception clause is given below:

```
begin
    –statements
when exception
    - call exception handler
end ;
```

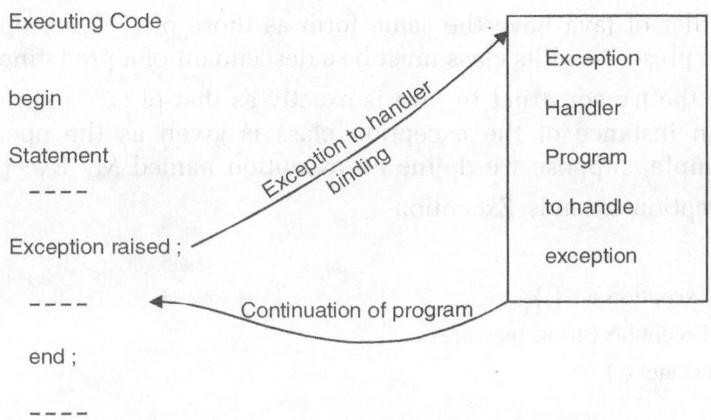

Fig. 6.22. *Control flow during exception handling*

6.6.2. Exception Handling in C + +

C^{++} uses a special construct that is introduced with the reserved word try for exception handling. A try construct includes a compound statement called the try clause and a list of exception handler. The general form of this construct is

```
try
{
    // code that is expected to raise an exception
}
Catch (formal parameter)
{
    // a handler body
}
...
Catch (formal Parameter)
{
    // a handler body
}
```

Each of the catch functions are exception handlers. A catch function can have only a single formal parameter which is similar to a formal parameter in a function definition in C^{++}, including the possibility of it being only an ellipsis (...). In C^{++} exceptions handler can include any C^{++} code. C^{++} exceptions are raised only by the explicit statement throw, whose general form is

throw [expression];

The brackets are meta symbols used to specify that the expression is optional. A throw without an operand can only appear in a handler. The type of the throw expression selects the particular handler which of course must have matching type formal parameter.

A handler with a formal parameter of type T, const T, T & (a reference to an object type T), or const T and matches a throw with an expression of type T.

6.6.3. Exception Handling in Java

The exception handler of Java have the same form as those of C^{++}, except the parameter of every catch must be present and its class must be a descendant of a predefined class, throwable.

The syntax of the try construct in Java is exactly as that of C^{++}. Throwing an exception is quite simple. An instance of the exception class is given as the operand of the throw statement. **For example,** suppose we define an exception named My Exception as

```
Class My Exception extends Exception
{
    Public MY Exception ( ) { }
    Public MY Exception (string message)
    { Super (message) ; }
}
```

This exception can be thrown with

```
throw new My Exception ( );
```

The creation of the instance of the exception for the throw could be done separately from the throw statement, as in

```
My Exception      My Exception object = new My Exception ( );
...
throw My Exception object;
```

If an exception is thrown in the compound statement of the try construct, it is bound to the first handler (catch function) immediately following the try clause whose parameter is the same class, as the thrown object, or an ancestor of it. If a matching handler is found, the throw is bound to it and it is executed. All exceptions that are derived from Exception simply by defining the handler with an Exception type parameter, as in

```
Catch (Exception generic object)
{
    ...
}
```

6.7. COROUTINES

A coroutine is a special kind of subprogram that has multiple entries. A subprogram that return to their calling program before completion of execution is termed as coroutines. When a coroutines receives control from another subprogram, it executes partially and then is suspended when it returns control. At a later point, the calling program may resume execution of the coroutines from the point at which execution was previously suspended.

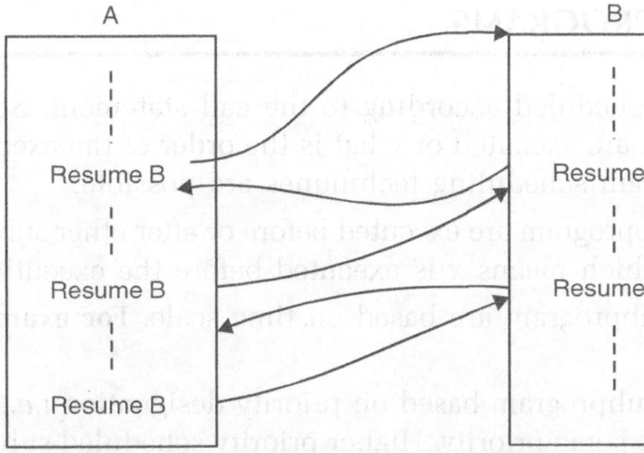

Fig. 6.23. Control Transfers between Coroutines A and B.

If A calls subprogram B as a coroutines, B executes a while and returns control to A, just as any ordinary subprogram would do. When A again passes control to B via a resume B, B again executes awhile and return control to A, just as an ordinary subprogram. Thus to A, B appears as an ordinary subprogram. However, the situation is very similar when viewed from subprogram B. B, in the middle of execution, resumes execution of A. A executes awhile and return control to B. B continues execution awhile and return control to A. From subprogram B, A appears very much like an ordinary subprogram. The name coroutine derives from this symmetry.

Implementation: In coroutines, the control transfers with the help of resume instruction. In specifies the restart of some activation of the coroutines. In coroutine, there is only one activation exist at a time. So implementation of coroutines is similar to call-return structure we discussed in previous section. A single location *i.e.*, resume point is reserved for old i_p, value of the CIP. When control transfers to another coroutines then the new value of i_p is stored. The execution of a resume B instructions in coroutine A involves following steps:

(*i*) The current value of CIP is saved in resume point location of the activation record of A.

(*ii*) The i_p value in the resume point locations of B is fetched from B's activation record and assigned to the CIP to effect the transfer of control to the proper instruction in B.

6.7.1. Coroutine and Subprograms

Table 6.3. Difference between Coroutine and Subprogram

Coroutine	*Subprograms*
1. A coroutine is a special kind of subprogram that has multiple entries.	1. A subprogram usually has a single entry.
2. A coroutine executes partially when is called by another coroutines.	2. A subprogram executes completely when is called by another subprogram.
3. When it is called it begins execution where it is previously suspended.	3. When subprogram is called it begins execution from the start of subprogram.
4. It is invoked by a resume instruction.	4. It is invoked by a CALL statement.

6.8. SCHEDULED SUBPROGRAMS

Basically subprogram are scheduled according to the call statement. Scheduled subprograms means how the subprogram are executed or what is the order of the execution of subprograms. There are various subprogram scheduling techniques are possible:

(1) Some schedule subprogram are executed before or after other subprogram. **For example:** Call x before y, which means x is executed before the execution of y.

(2) Some schedule subprogram are based on time scale. **For example:** CAll x at time = current time + 5.

(3) Some scheduled subprogram based on priority designation *i.e.*, some subprogram are called according to some priority. Higher priority scheduled subprograms are executed before Lower priority subprogram.

(4) Some scheduled subprogram are executed according to some Boolean conditions are true or false.

Call x when (A < 7 and B = 0).

In this subprogram x is called when the boolean condition is true *i.e.*, when value of parameter A is less than 7 and parameter B is equal to zero.

The most common approach to subprogram scheduling is based on a type of generalized coroutines. Generalized subprogram scheduling is a feature used is SIMULA, GPSS etc.

Some Important Terms

- In sequence control, control of the order of execution of the operation takes place.
- Sequence control is defined as the order of exceution of primitive and user-defined operations.
- There are three types of sequence control structures.
  - Sequence control in expression.
  - Sequence control with in statements.
  - Sequence control in subprograms.
- Implicit sequence control structures are defined by the language.
- Explicit sequence control are defined by programmer to modify the implicit sequence of operation defined by the language.
- Expressions are the fundamental means of specifying computations in a programming language.
- Arithmetic expression consists of operators, operands, parentheses and function calling.
- In infix notations operators comes in between the operands.
- In prefix notation, the operation symbols followed by the operands in order from left to right.
- In postfix notation operators are comes after the operands.
- The operator precedence rules for expression evaluation define the order in which the operator of different levels are evaluated.

- Pattern matching is an operator that matches and assigns a set of variable to a predefined template.
- Term Rewriting is a restricted form of pattern matching.
- Substitution means the values of arguments are substituted in the arguments.
- Backtracking has generally tree like structure.

  The basic statements are

  - Assignment statements
  - Input-output statements
  - Subprogram calls.
- Assignment statement provides the mechanism by which the user can dynamically change the bindings of values to variables.
- Input statements reads the data from user at a terminal or from files.
- Output statements displays the data through the terminal to the user.
- There are three forms of statement level sequence control:
  - Composition
  - Alternation
  - Iteration
- A break statement sends control out of enclosing loop to the statement following the loop.
- A continue statement repeats the enclosing loop by sending control to the beginning of the loop.
- Goto statement transfer the control explicitly to the another statement.
- There are different types of statements:
  - Compound statements.
  - Selection statements.
  - Iterative statements.
- Problems in structured sequence control
  - Multiple exit loops.
  - do-while-do.
  - Exceptional condition.
- Prime program used as generalization of structured programming to define the unique hierarchical decomposition of a flowchart.
- There are there classes of nodes in the program graph:
  - Function node.
  - Decision node.
  - Join node.
- A prime program is a proper program that cannot be subdivided into smaller proper progarms.
- If a proper program is not the prime one then it is composite program.

- Subprograms are the fundamental building blocks of programs.
  - A subprograme structure consists of three parts
  - Subprogram header.
  - Subprogram definition.
  - Subprogram call.
- Subprogram Executes completely in each call.
- Subprogram have a single entry point.
- There are two types of subprograms
  - Procedures
  - Functions
- Procedures are collections of statements that define parameterized computations.
- Functions resemble procedure by structurally but are semantically modelled on mathematical function.
- Simple subprogram Call-Return means that all local variables are static and subprograms are not nested.
- Each time a subprogram calls, a activation record is created.
- A code segment containing the executable code and constants.
- An activation record containing local data, other data items and parameter.
- A code segment is fixed during execution *i.e.*, it is invariant during execution.
- The activation record part is dynamic *i.e.*, changes each time the subprogram is called.
- Current instruction pointer (CIP) points to the current instruction that is currently being executed by hardware or software interpreter.
- Current-environment Point (CEP) points to the current activation record (current referencing environment).
- Return points contains space for two pointer (*ip*, *ep*) means instruction pointer and environment pointer.
- If a subprogram calls itself then it is called direct recursive.
- If a subprogram calls another subprogram then it is called indirect recursive.
- Exception is defined as any unusual condition, erroneous or not, some error condition that are detected during execution.
- A subprogram needs to be called to perform some special processing called exception handling.
- The subprogram that performs the special processing is termed as Exception handler.
- C^{++} uses try, catch and throw keywords for exception handling.
- A coroutine is a special kind of subprograms that has multiple entries.
- A coroutine uses Resume statement to transfer controls.
- A coroutine executes partially when is called by another coroutine.
- Scheduled subprograms tells what is the order of the execution of subprograms.
- A subprogram uses call statement to transfer control to another subprogram.

Review Questions

1. Explain Implicit and Explicit Sequence control.
2. What is sequence control? Explain sequence control for arithmetic expressions.
3. Explain sequence control within non-arithmetic expression.
4. What is sequence control? Explain sequence control within statements.
5. Explain the terms:
   (a) Pattern Matching.
   (b) Unification.
   (c) Backtracking.
6. What is the structured sequence control? Explain the advantages and disadvantages of structural sequence control.
7. Explain subprogram sequence control in detail.
8. Explain simple subprogram call-return.
9. What do you mean by Recursive subprograms? Explain the implementation of Recursive subprograms.
10. What is an Exception? Explain the concept of Exception handling in detail.
11. Explain Exception handling in C++?
12. Explain Exception handling in Java?
13. Explain the term coroutines. What is the difference between subprogram and coroutines?
14. Write short notes on:
    (a) Current Instruction pointer
    (b) Current Environment pointer
    (c) Scheduled subprograms.
15. Explain the terms:
    (a) PRIME PROGRAMS
    (b) Proper program
    (c) Composite program.
16. What are the different forms of statement level sequence control?

❑❑❑

Chapter 7 CONCURRENCY

This chapter discuss the various concepts regarding concurrency, categories of concurrency and synchronization methods. There are various kinds of concurrency at the subprogram, or Unit level, and at the statement level. We also discuss competition and cooperation synchronization. The concurrent processes may be executing truly simultaneously, in the case that they run on separate processors, or their execution steps may be interleaved to produce the appearance of concurrency. The intention of this chapter is to discuss the aspects of concurrency that are most relevant to language design issues, rather than to present a definitive study of all of the issues of concurrency.

7.1. INTRODUCTION TO CONCURRENCY

Concurrency means execution of multiple interacting computation task.

A task is a unit of program, similar to a subprogram, that can be in concurrent execution with other units of the same program. Each task in a program can provide one thread of control. Tasks are sometimes called processes.

Three characteristics of tasks distinguish them from subprograms. First, a task may be implicitly started, whereas a subprogram must be explicitly called. Second, when a program unit invokes a task, it need not wait for the task to complete its execution before continuing its own. Third, when the execution of a task is completed, control may or may not return to the unit that started that execution.

7.1.1. Level of Concurrency

Concurrency is divided into four levels:

(*i*) **Instruction level:** In instruction level, two or more machine instructions are executing simultaneously.

(*ii*) **Statement level:** In statement level, two or more source language statements are executing simultaneously.

(*iii*) **Subprogram level or unit level:** In this, two or more subprogram units are executing simultaneously.

(*iv*) **Program level:** In program level, two or more programs are executing simultaneously.

7.1.2. Categories of Concurrency

There are two distinct categories of concurrent unit control:

(*i*) Physical concurrency.

(*ii*) Logical concurrency.

(*i*) **Physical concurrency:** In Physical concurrency, several program units from the same program execute simultaneously on more than one processor. In indicates the multiple independent threads of controls. A thread of control in a program is the sequence of program points reached as control flows through the program.

(*ii*) **Logical concurrency:** The logical concurrency occurs when the execution of several programs takes place in an interleaved fashion in a single processor.

7.1.3. Motivation for Studying Concurrency

There are at least two reasons to study concurrency.

1. It provides a method of conceptualizing program solutions to problems.
2. The second reason to discuss concurrency is that multiple processor computers currently are being used, although that use is not widespread.

7.1.4. Advantages of Concurrency Control Mechanism

The concurrent computing provides the following advantages:

1. Concurrent control mechanism increase programming flexibility.
2. Concurrent execution increases the throughput of the system because the number of tasks completing their execution increases.
3. Some problems and problem domains are well suited to representation as concurrent tasks on processes.

7.2. INTRODUCTION TO SUBPROGRAM LEVEL CONCURRENCY AND SYNCHRONIZATION

Subprogram level concurrency is defined as the execution of two or more subprogram units simultaneously. First we discuss the fundamental concept of a task.

1. **Task:** A task is a program unit that can be concurrent execution with other program units.

   Tasks fall into two categories:

   (*a*) **Heavy weight tasks:** Heavy weight tasks execute in their own address space and have their own runtime stacks.

   (*b*) **Light weight tasks:** Light weight tasks all run in the same address space and use the same runtime stack.

2. **Different states of tasks:** Tasks can be in several different states, which are:

   (*a*) **New state:** A task is in the new state when it has been created but not started execution.

   (*b*) **Ready or runnable:** A task is ready to run in this state but is not currently running. It is stored in a queue often called the task ready queue.

   (*c*) **Running:** A running task is one that is currently executed *i.e.*, its code is being executing.

   (*d*) **Blocked:** A task that is blocked has been running, but that execution was interrupted by one of several different events. The most common is an Input or Output operation. In addition to these kinds of blocking, some languages provide operations for the program to specify that a task has been blocked.

   (*e*) **Dead:** A dead task is no longer active in any sense. A task dies when its exeution is completed or explicitly killed by program.

3. **Disjoint:** If a task does not communicate with or affect the execution of any other task in the program in any way, it is said to be disjoint.

4. **Synchronization:** Synchronization is a mechanism that defines the orders in which the tasks executes. Synchronization is basically controls are orders of execution of tasks.

   There are two types of synchronization:

   (*a*) Cooperation Synchronization.

   (*b*) Competition Synchronization.

   (*a*) Cooperation Synchronization: Cooperation synchronization between two task X and Y is required when task X must wait for task Y to complete some specific activity before task X can continue its execution. A simple form of cooperation Synchronization is producer-consumer problem. Produced data are usually placed in a storage buffer by the producing unit and removed from that buffer by the consuming unit. The sequence of stores to and removals from the buffer must be synchronized. The consumer unit must not be allowed to take data from buffer when it is empty and similarly producer cannot be placed new data when the buffer is full. This is called the problem of cooperation synchronization because the users of shared data structure must cooperate if the buffer is to be used correctly.

(*b*) **Competition Synchronization:** The competition synchronization between two tasks X and Y is required when both require the use of some resources that can be simultaneously used. Specifically, if task X needs to access shared data location Z while task Y is accessing Z, task X must wait for task Y to complete its processing of Z, regardless of what that processing is. So for competition synchronization, tasks may need to wait for the completion of any other processing by any task currently occurring as specific shared data.

5. **Liveness:** A program has the characteristic of liveness if it continues to execute, eventually leading to completion. In more general terms, liveness means that if some event say program completion is supposed to occur, it will occur, eventually that is, progress is continually made.

6. **Deadlock:** Suppose task A and task B both needs the shared resources X and Y to complete their work. Further, suppose that task A gains possession of X and task B gains possession of Y. After some execution, task A need resource Y to continue, so it request Y but must wait until B release it. Likewise, task B requests *X* but must wait until A releases it. Neither relinquishes that execution of the program will never complete normally. This particular kind of loss of liveness is called deadlock.

7.2.1. Design Issues of Concurrency

The main important design issue for concurrency are competition and cooperation synchronization. Another design issues of concurrency are how to control task scheduling *i.e.*, when task start and end execution, and how and when tasks are created. A number of languages have been designed to support concurrency, beginning with PL/I in the middle 1960s and including the contemporary languages Ada 95, Java, and C#.

7.3. METHODS FOR SYNCHRONIZATION

There are various methods for Synchronization. The methods for synchronization provides mutual exclusion to the shared resources. To gain possession of a shared resource, a task must request it. When a task is finished then another task possesses that resource. There are three methods for providing mutual exclusive access to a shared resources.

These methods are:

(*i*) Semaphores.

(*ii*) Monitors.

(*iii*) Message passing.

7.3.1. Semaphores

A semaphores is a very simple mechanism that can be used to provide synchronization of tasks. Each process has a segment of code, called a critical section, in which the process may be changing common variables, updating a table, writing a file, and so on. The important feature of the system is that, when one process be executing in its critical section, no other process is to be allowed to execute in its critical section. Thus the execution of critical section by the processes is mutually exclusive in time.

A semaphore is a data structure consisting of an integer and a queue that stores task descriptors. A task descriptor is a data structure that stores all of the relevant information about the execution state of a task. The concept of a semaphore is that, to provide limited access to a data structure, we can place some conditions around the code that accesses the structure. These conditions allows only one task to access a shared data structure at a time.

A semaphore is an implementation of this condition that allow only one task to access the critical section at a time. There are two operation provided by semaphores *i.e.*, wait and signal.

The general structure of a process is:

```
Repeat
        Entry Section
            Critical Section

        Exit Section
            remainder section
 Until false
```

Fig. 7.1. General Structure of a Typical Process P_i.

Each process must request permission to enter its critical section. The section of code implementing this request is the entry section. The critical section may be followed by an exit section. The remaining code is the remainder section.

A semaphore S is an integer variable that, apart from initialization, is accessed only through two standard atomic operations: wait and signal. These operations were originally termed P (for wait; from the Dutch proberen, to test) and V (for signal; from verhogen, to increment). The classical definitions of wait and signal are

```
Wait (S): while S ≤ 0 do no-op;
      S = S – 1;
Signal (S): S = S + 1;
```

Modifications to the integer value of the semaphore in the wait and signal operations must be executed indivisibly.

Use of Semaphore: We can use semaphores to deal with the *n*-process critical-section problem. The *n* processes share a semaphore, mutex (standing for mutual exclusion), initialized to 1. Each process P_i is organized as shown as in Fig. 7.2.

```
repeat
        Wait (Hutex);
                critical section
        Signal (mutex);
                remainder section
Until false;
```

Fig. 7.2. Mutual-exclusion Implementation with Semaphore.

We can also use semaphores to solve various synchronization problems. Let us consider two running processes: P_1 with a statement S_1, and P_2 with a statement S_2 and we require that S_2 be executed only after S_1 has completed. We can implement this scheme readily by letting P_1 and P_2 share a common semaphore synchronization, initialized to 0, and by inserting the statement.

```
S1;
signal (synch);
```

In process P_1

```
wait (synch);
S2;
```

In process P_2

Because synch is intialized to 0, P_2 will execute S_2 only after P_1 has invoked signal (Synch), which is after S_1.

Implementation of Semaphore: The main problem associated with mutual exclusion solutions is busy waiting. While a process is in its critical section, any other process that tries to enter its critical section must loop continuously in the entry code. Busy waiting wastes CPU cycles that some other process might be able to use productively. This type of semaphore is also called a spinlock (because the process "spins" while waiting for the lock).

To overcome the need for busy waiting, we can modify the definition of the wait and signal semaphore operations. When a process executes the wait operation and finds that the semaphore value is not positive, it must wait. However, rather than busy waiting, the process can block itself. The block operation places a process into a waiting queue associated with the semaphore, and the state of the process is switched to the waiting state.

A process that is blocked, waiting on a semaphore S, should be restarted when some other process executes a signal operation. The process is restarted by a wake up operation, which changes the process from the waiting state to the ready state.

To implement semaphores under this definition, we define a semaphore as record:

```
type semaphore = record
value: integer;
L : list of process;
end;
```

Each process has an integer value and a list of processes. When a process must wait on a semaphore, it is added to the list of processes. A signal operation removes one process from the list of waiting processes and awakens that process. A semaphore operations can now be defined as shown in Fig. 7.3.

```
Wait (S):
   S.value = S.value - 1;
if (S.value < 0)
   then begin
   add this process to S.L;
   block;
end
```

```
Signal (S):
S.value = S.value + 1;
if (S.value ≤ 0)
then begin
remove a process P from S.L;
wake up (P);
end;
```

Fig 7.3. Implementation of Semaphore.

The block operation suspends the process that invokes it. The waheup (*p*) operation resumes the execution of a blocked process P. The list of waiting process can be easily implemented by a link field in each process control block (PCB). Each semaphore contains an integer value and a pointer to a list of PCBs.

7.3.1.1. Deadlocks and starvation

The implementation of a semaphore with a waiting queue may result in a situation where two or more processes are waiting indefinitely for an event that can be caused only by one of the waiting processes. The event in question is the execution of a signal( ) operation. When such a state is reached, these processes are said to be deadlocked.

To illustrate this, we consider a system consisting of two processes, P_0 and P_1, each accessing two semaphores, S and Q, set to the value 1:

```
P0              P1
Wait (S);       Wait (Q);
Wait (Q);       Wait (S);
  ⋮               ⋮
Signal (S);     Signal (Q);
Signal (Q);     Signal (S);
```

Suppose that P_0 executes wait (S) and then P_1 executes wait (Q). When P_0 executes (Q), it must wait until P_1 executes signal (Q). Similarly, when P_1 executes wait (S), it must wait until P_0 executes signal (S). Since these signal () operation cannot be executed, P_0 and P_1 are deadlocked.

In a deadlock state, every process in the set is waiting for an event that can be hold by another process in the set. The events mainly here are resource acquisition and release.

Another problem related to deadlocks is indefinite blocking, or starvation, a situation in which processes wait indefinitely with in the semaphore. Indefinite blocking may occur if we remove processes from the list associated with a semaphore in LIFO (Last in first out) order.

7.3.1.2. Solution of bounded-buffer problem using semaphore

Bounded-Buffer problem is a common paradigm for cooperating processes. A producer process produces information that is consumed by a consumer process. For example, a compiler may produce assembly code, which is consumed by an assembler. The assembler, in turn, may produce object modules, which are consumed by the loader. The producer - consumer problem also provides a useful metaphor for the client-server paradigm. We generally think of a server as a producer and a client as a consumer. For example, a web server produces (that is, provides) HTML files and images, which are consumed (that is, read) by the client webbrowser requesting the resources.

To allow producer and consumer processes to run concurrently, we must have available a buffer of items that can be filled by the producer and emptied by the consumer. A producer can produce one item while the consumer is consuming another item. The producer and consumer must be synchronized, so that the consumer does not try to consume an item that has not yet been produced. The bounded buffer assumes a fixed buffer size.

In this case, the consumer must wait if the buffer is empty, and the producer must wait if the buffer is full. Our solution allowed at most Buffer size - 1 items in the buffer at the same time.

We assume that the pool consists of *n* buffers, each capable of holding one item. The mutex semaphore provides mutual exclusion for accesses to the buffer pool and is initialized to the value 1. The empty and full semaphore counts the number of empty and full buffers. The semaphore empty is initialized to the value *n*; the semaphore full is initialized to the value 0.

The code for the producer process is shown below:

```
do
{
    // Produce an item in next P
    ...
    Wait (empty);
    Wait (mutex);
    ...
    // add next P to buffer
    ...
    Signal (mutex);
    Signal (full);
} While (TRUE);
```

Fig. 7.4. The Structure of the Producer Process.

The code for consumer process is shown below:

```
do {
    Wait (full);
    Wait (mutex);
    ...
    // remove an item from buffer to next C
    ...
    Signal (mutex);
    Signal (empty);
    ...
    // consume the item in next C
    ...
} while (True);
```

Fig. 7.5. The Structure of the Consumer Process.

We can interpret this code as the producer producing full buffers for the consumer producing empty buffers for the producer.

7.3.2. Monitors

Semaphores represent an early approach to provide synchronization. However, some of the problems of semaphores in a concurrent environment is to encapsulate shared data structures with their operation and hide their representation. Semaphore provide a convenient and effective mechanism for process synchronization, using them incorrectly can result in timing errors that are difficult to detect.

Timing errors can still occur when semaphores are used. Lets consider following problems.

- Suppose that a process interchanges the order of wait ( ) and signal ( ) operations on the semaphore mutex are executed, resulting in the following execution:

```
Signal (mutex);
...
Critical Section
...
Wait (mutex);
```

In this situation, several processes may be executing in their critical sections simultaneously, violating the mutual-exclusion requirement.

- Suppose that a process replaces signal (mutex) with wait (mutex). That is, it executes

```
Wait (mutex);
...
Critical Section
...
Wait (mutex);
```

In this case, a deadlock will occur.

- Suppose that a process omits the wait (mutex), or the signal (mutex), or both. In this case, either mutual exclusion is violated or a deadlock will occur.

These examples shows various types of errors that can be generated when we use incorrect use of semaphore.

Use of Monitors: A monitor is an Abstract Data Type (ADT) which represents a set of programmer-defined operations that are provided mutual exclusion within the monitors. The monitor type contains the declaration of variables whose values define the state of an instance of that type, along with the functions and procedures that operate on the data. The syntax of monitors is.

```
Monitor    Monitor Name
{
    || Shared variable declarations
    Procedure P1 (...) {
        ...
    }
    Procedure P2 (...) {
        ...
    }
        :
    Procedure Pn (...)
    {
        ...
    }
    initialization code (...)
    {
        ...
    }
}
```

Fig. 7.6. Syntax of a Monitor.

One of the most important feature of monitors is that shared data is resident in the monitor rather than in any of the client units. A monitor is an interface between concurrent user processes and provides a set of procedures callable by users. The representation of a monitor type cannot be used directly by the various processes. Thus, a procedure defined within a monitor can access only those variables declared locally within the monitor and its formal parameters. Similarly, the local variables of a monitor can be accessed by only the local procedures.

The monitor ensures that only one process at a time is active within the monitor. All accesses are resident in the monitor, the monitor implementation can be made to guarantee synchronized access by allowing only one access at a time.

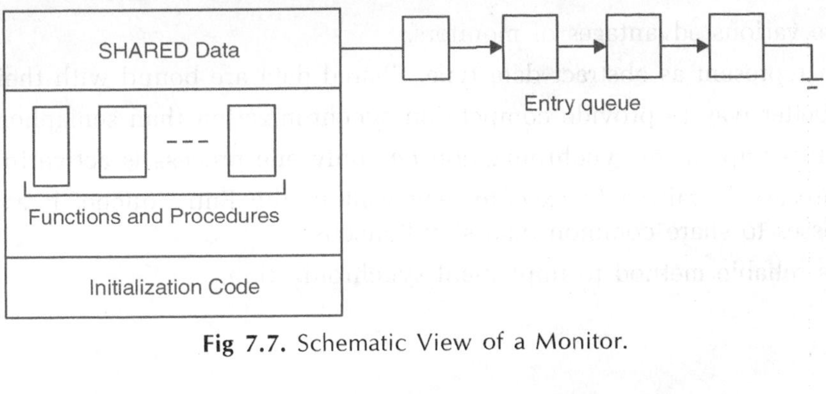

Fig 7.7. Schematic View of a Monitor.

Shared variables are accessible through the monitor's procedures. The language performs locking so only one process can access the monitors. All the critical sections are put inside monitor procedures. Only that process is active in monitor that enters from the queue. Monitors are a better way to provide competition synchronization than are semaphores. The cooperation synchronization is still a problem with monitors. Ada provides two ways to implement monitors.

Monitor Condition Variables: The monitor construct as defined so far, is not sufficiently powerful for modeling some synchronization schemes. For this purpose, we need to define additional sychronization mechanism. These mechanisms are provided by the condition construct. A programmer can define one or more variables of type condition:

Condition *x*, *y*;

The only operations that can be invoked on a condition variables are wait ( ) and signal ( ). The operation

x. wait ( );

means that the process invoking this operation is suspended until another process invokes

x. signal ( );

The *x*. signal ( ) operation resumes exactly one suspended process. If no process is suspended, then the signal ( ) operation has no effect; that is, the state of *x* is same as if the operation had never been executed. Contrast this operation with the signal ( ) operation associated with semaphores, which always affects the state of monitors.

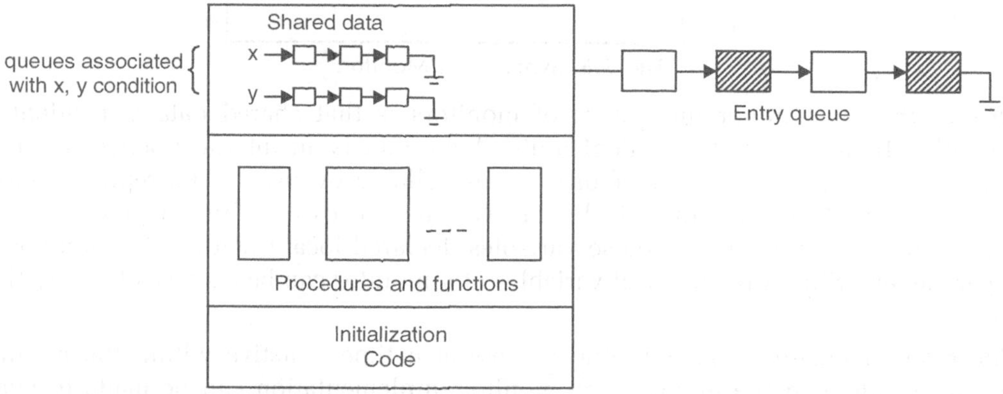

Fig 7.8. Monitor with Condition Variables.

There are various advantages of moniters.

1. It can represent as abstract data type. Shared data are bound with their operation.
2. It is better way to provide competition synchronization than semaphores.
3. Monitors implement synchronization *i.e.*, only one process is active in the monitor.
4. All processes waiting to execute may wait in the Entry queue. It avoids multiple processes to share common data simultaneously.
5. It is a reliable method to implement synchronization.

7.3.3. Message Passing

In the message passing model, the communicating processes exchange messages with one another to transfer information. Monitors and semaphores are basically designed for machines that uses a shared memory. Monitor is a safe method for providing competition synchronization for shared data access in concurrent units that share a single memory. Messages can be exchanged between the processes either directly or indirectly through a common mailbox. Message passing can be either synchronous or asynchrouous.

Message passing provides a mechanism to allow processes to communicate and to synchronize their actions without sharing the same address space and is particulary useful in a distributed environment, where the communicating processes may reside on different computers connected by a network.

A message passing facility provides at least two operations: send (message) and receive (message). Messages sent by a process can be of either fixed or variable size. If only fixed size messages can be sent, the system-level implementation is straight-forward. This restriction, however, makes the task of implementation more difficult. If processes P and Q want to communicate, they must send messages to and receive message from each other; a communication link must exist between them. There are several methods for implementing a link and send ( )/receive ( ) operations:

1. Direct and Indirect communications.
2. Synchronous and asynchronous communication.
3. Buffering.

1. Direct and indirect communication

Direct naming: In direct communication, each process that wants to communicate must explicitly name the recipient or sender of the communication. In this scheme, the send ( ) and receive ( ) primitive are defined as:

- Send (A, message) – Send a message to process A.
- Receive (B, message) – Receive a message to process B.

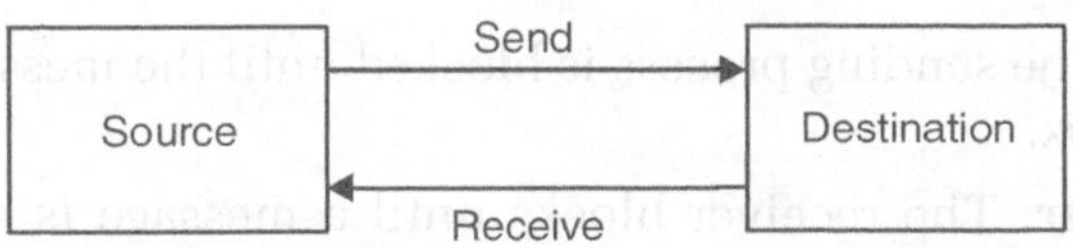

Fig 7.9. Message Send and Message Receive Primitive.

In this method a link is established automatically between every pair of processes that want to communicate. The processes need to know only each other's identity to communicate. Between each pair of processes, there exists exactly one link.

This scheme exhibits symmetry in addressing that is, both the sender process and the receiver process must name the other to communicate. A varient of this scheme employs assymmetry in addressing. Here, only the sender names the recipient; the recipient is not required to name the sender.

In this scheme, the send ( ) and receive ( ) Primitives are define as

- Send (A, message) – Send a message to process A.

- Receive (id, message) – Receive a message from any process; the variable id is set to the name of the process with which communication has taken place.

The disadvantage of these scheme is the limited modularity of the resulting process definitions.

Indirect communication: In this scheme, the messages are sent to and received from mailboxes, or ports. A mailbox can be viewed abstractly as an object into which messages can be place by processes and from which messages can be removed. In this method, a process can communicate with some other process *via* a number of different mailboxes. Two processes can communicate only if the processes have a shared mailbox. The send ( ) and receive ( ) primitives are defined as follows:

- Send (A, message) – Send a message to mailbox A.
- Receive (A, message) – Receive a message from mailbox A.

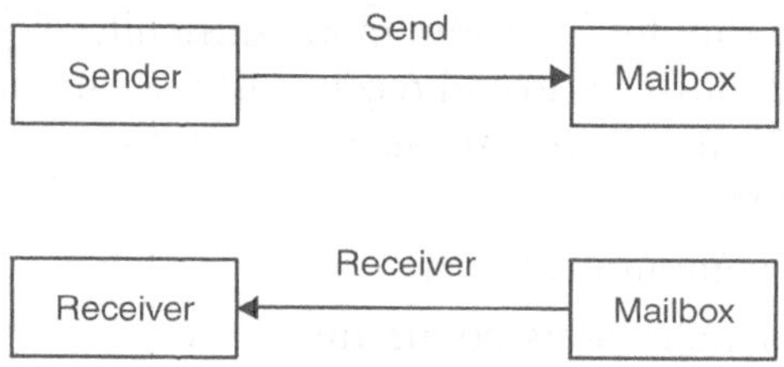

Fig 7.10. Message Send and Receive Primitives.

In this scheme, a link is established between a pair of processes only if both members of the pair have a shared mailbox. A link may be associated with more than two processes and between each pair of communicating processes, there may be a number of different links, with each link corresponding to one mailbox.

2. Synchronous and asynchronous communication

Message passing may be either blocking or nonblocking - also known as synchronous and asynchronous.

- **Blocking Send:** The sending process is blocked until the message is received by receiver or by the mailbox.
- **Blocking Receiver:** The receiver blocks until a message is available.
- **Nonblocking Send:** The sending process sends the message and resumes operation.
- **Nonblocking Receive:** The receiver retrieves either a valid message or a null.

3. Buffering

Buffering can be implemented in three ways:

- **Zero capacity:** In this, the queue has a maximum length of zero; thus , the link cannot have any message waiting in it. In this method, sender must block until the recipient receives the message.
- **Bounded buffer:** In bounded buffer, the queue has finite length *n*; thus, at most *n* messages can reside in it. If the queue is empty then a new message can be placed in the queue. If the queue is full then a new message must wait until the space is available in the queue.

- **Unbounded Buffer:** The queue's length is potentially infinite; thus, any number of messages can wait in it and the sender never blocks.

7.3.3.1. Message passing models

There are four types of message passing models.

1. **Point to point message passing:** It is the simplest message passing technique in which one process sends a message to another. It can passed message synchronously or asynchronously. In this method a single source sends a message to a single receiver.
2. **One to many or broadcasting:** In this method of message passing, one sender can sends a message to more than one receivers. Its also called broadcasting because it broadcasts the message to more than one receiver.

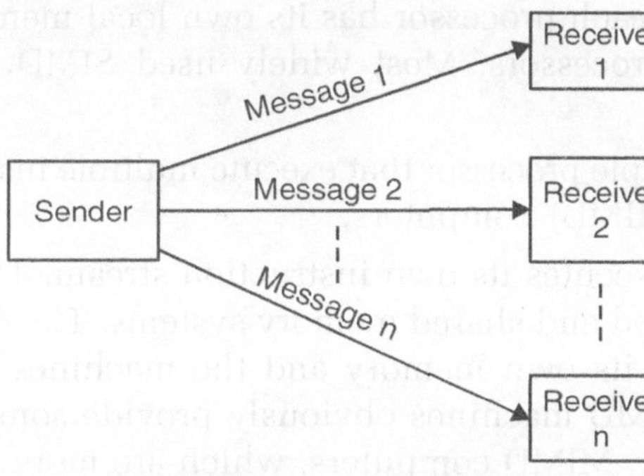

Fig 7.11. Broadcasting a Message.

3. **Rendezvous:** In some situations, if task A wants to send a message to B, and B was willing to receive a message, the message can be transmitted. This actual transmission is called rendezvous. Note that a rendezvous can occur only if both the sender and receiver want it to happen. The information of message can be transmitted in either or both directions.
4. **Remote procedure calls:** RPC is used to call a procedure in the remote location. In this method the parameters of procedure is passed as argument or by message passing and execution of procedure takes place in remote locations. RPCs are much like the processes used to accomplish rendezvous. RPCs have been considered for use with modula-2 and implemented in the V operating system and in concurrent CLU etc.

7.3.3.2. Advantages of message passing system

1. Message passing provide sharing of data values through passing the values as messages.
2. In distributed system this method is used because no shared memory is required.
3. The message passing model allows concurrent units to be distributed, which monitors do not allow.
4. It is used by many systems like Mach the basis of Apple's new Macintosh OS.
5. In this no critical sections are required to be maintained.

7.4. MULTIPROCESSOR ARCHITECTURES

Different computer architectures have more than one processor and can support form of concurrent execution. The first computer that had multiple processors actually had one general purpose processor and one or more other processors that were used only for input and output operations.

In the 1960s, machines have multiple complete processors. These processors were used by the job scheduler of the operating system, which distributed separate jobs from a batch-job queue to the separate processors.

Computers that have multiple processors that execute the same instruction simultaneously, each on different data, are called Single-Instruction Multiple-Data (SIMD) architecture computers. In these type of architecture, each processor has its own local memory. One processor controls the operation of the other processors. Most widely used SIMD machines are called vector processors.

Computer in which multiple processor that execute multiple instructions are called Multiple-Instructions Multiple-Data (MIMD) computers.

Each MIMD computer executes its own instruction stream. The different configuration of MIMD machines are distributed and shared memory systems. The distributed MIMD machines, in which each processor has its own memory and the machines are distributed over a large area. The shared memory MIMD machines obviously provide some means of synchronization to prevent the shared memory. MIMD computers, which are more expensive and more general than SIMD computers, clearly support unit-level concurrency.

7.5. SYNCHRONIZATION IN JAVA

In this section, we explore a modern implementation of concurrency control, using Java as the language of illustration.

Java Threads: A thread can be in one of five states. Created, runnable, running, blocked, or terminated. A thread makes transitions from one state to another, largely ignoring the transition from the runnable state to running, since this is handled by the underlying Java virtual machine.

In Java, every thread is an implementation of the Runnable interface, and so it must contain a run ( ) method. The simplest way to create a thread is to define a subclass that inherits from the Java Threads class:

```
Public class Mythread extends Thread {
    Public Mythread ( ) { ... }
    .........
}
```

An object of this subclass can then be created by declaring and constructing it using a new operation:

```
Thread  thread = new Mythread ( );
```

To make this thread runnable, its start method must be invoked:

```
Thread. Start ( );
```

Starting a thread means transferring control to its run method and then continuing execution. Each class that extends the Thread class must thus provide a run method. However, it does not need to provide a start method, since one is provided by the Thread class.

A thread's run method normally contains a loop, since exiting run method terminates the thread.

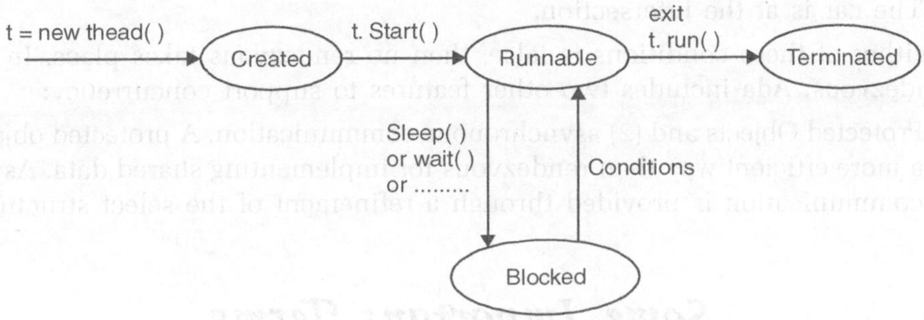

Fig 7.12. States of a Java Thread.

7.6. CONCURRENCY IN OTHER LANGUAGES

Concurrency is supported by many programming languages besides Java. In this we briefly summarizes the key language features for concurrency among the languages, C#, C^{++}, High performance Fortran, and Ada.

(*i*) **C#:** C# is similar to Java in its approach to concurrency; it reflect the monitor concept. C# has two operations, called Monitor. Enter (0) and Monitor. Exit (0), which provide explicit entry and exit from an object's monitor, and thus a direct looking ability on the object.

(*ii*) **C++:** The C++ Standard Library provides no support for concurrency. However, Independent C++ Library projects have extended the standared Library in various ways. One such project is called Adatpive communication Environment (ACE), and it provides C++ supports for networks, communication, and concurrency.

(*iii*) **High performance Fortran:** High performance FORTRAN (HPF) has features that allow the programmer to supply the compiler with information that helps it optimize code in a multiprocessing environment.

Here is a summary of those feature.

Feature	*HPF specification*
1. Number of processors	1. ! HPF $ Processors Procs (*n*)
2. Distribution of data	2. ! HPF $ DISTRIBUTE (type) ONTO Procs :: identifiers
3. Align two arrays	3. ALIGN array 1 with array 2.
4. Concurrent looping	4. FORALL (identifier = begin: end) statement.

In this table, type can be Block, meaning "distribute to processors in blocks" or CYCLIC meaning "distribute to processor serially". The FORALL statement is used to specify a loop whose iterations can be executed concurrently.

(*iv*) **Ada:** A rendezvous is a concept developed during the design of Ada. It is simple concept that we have already discussed, that suggests that two tasks can communicate only when both are ready. For instance, consider a car approaching an intersection with a stop light. The car can pass through the intersection only if both:

1. The light is green, and
2. The car is at the intersection.

If either of these conditions is false, then no rendezvous takes place. In addition to rendezvous, Ada includes two other features to support concurrency:

1. Protected Objects and (2) asynchronous communication. A protected object provides a more efficient way than rendezvous for implementing shared data. Asynchronous communication is provided through a refinement of the select structure.

Some Important Terms

- Concurrency means execution of multiple interacting computation tasks.
- A task is a unit of program, similar to a subprogram, that can be in concurrent execution with other units of the same program.
- Level of concurrency:
  - Instruction level.
  - Statement level.
  - Subprogram level.
  - Program level.
- Categories of concurrency:
  - Physical concurrency.
  - Logical concurrency.
- Tasks falls into two categories:
  - Heavy weight tasks.
  - Light weight tasks.
- Different states of Tasks:
  - New state
  - Ready or Runnable
  - Running
  - Blocked
  - Dead
- If a task does not communicate with or affect the execution of any other task in the program in any way, it is said to be disjoint.
- Synchronization is a mechanism that defines the order in which the task executes.

- Synchronization is of two type:
  - Cooperation Synchronization
  - Competition Synchronization
- Cooperation Synchronization between two task X and Y is required when task X must wait for task Y to complete some specific activity before task X can continue its execution.
- Competition Synchronization between two tasks X and Y is required when both require the use of some resources that can be simultaneously used.
- A simple form of cooperation Synchronization is producer-consumer problem.
- A program has the characteristics of liveness if it continues to execute, eventually leading to completion.
- When two or more processes are waiting indefinitely for an event that can be caused only by one of the waiting processes. These processes are said to be deadlocked.
- Methods for synchronization are:
  - Semaphores
  - Monitors
  - Message passing
- A semaphore is a data structure consisting of an integer and a queue that stores task descriptors.
- Two operation provided by semaphores are wait and signal.
- Each process has a segment of code, called a critical section, in which the process may be changing common variables, updating a table, writing a file and so on.
- While a process is in its critical section, any other process that tries to enter its critical section must loop continuously in the entry code is called Busy waiting.
- A situation in which processes wait indefinitely within the semaphore is called starvation.
- Bounded-Buffer problem is a common paradigm for cooperating process.
- A monitor is an Abstract Type (ADT) which represents a set of programmer defined operations that are provided mutual exclusion within the monitors.
- The monitor ensures that only one process at a time is active within the monitor.
- Monitors are a better way to provide competition synchronization than are semaphores.
- In message passing model, the communicating processes exchange message with one another to transfer information.
- There are several methods to implement message passing.
  - Direct and indirect communication
  - Synchronous and asynchronous communication
  - Buffering
- A mailbox can be viewed abstractly as an object into which message can be placed by processes and from which messages can be removed.
- Four types of message passing models are:
  - Point to point message passing.

- One to many message passing.
- Rendezvous
- Remote Procedure Calls.

- Computers that have multiple processors that execute the same instruction simultaneously, each on different data, are called Single-Instruction Multiple Data (SIMD) architecture computers.
- Computer in which multiple processor that execute multiple instruction are called Multiple-Instruction Multiple Data (MIMD) computers.
- A Java thread can be in one of five states—
  - Created
  - Runnable
  - Running
  - Blocked
  - Terminated
- Different Language supporting concurrency are
  - C#
  - C++
  - High performance FORTRAN
  - Ada

Review Questions

1. Define concurrency, level of concurrency and categories of concurrency.
2. Define the term synchronization. Differentiate between cooperation and competition synchronization.
3. Explain the synchronization in Java and other Language supporting concurrency.
4. Explain synchronization through semaphores.
5. Define task, disjoint task, synchronization, competition and cooperative synchronization, liveness and deadlock.
6. Explain concurrency in detail.
7. Differentiate between semaphore and monitors.
8. What is semaphore? How can the concurrent process coordinate using semaphore? Explain.
9. Write short on
   (*i*) Message Passing
   (*ii*) Monitors
   (*iii*) Multiprocessor systems.
10. Explain advantages of message passing systems.
11. Explain differnt type of message passing models.

❑❑❑

Chapter **8**

DATA CONTROL

By using control structures, we can combine operations and data into set of programs. There are two aspects: first is sequence control, *i.e.*, control of the order of execution of the operations, both primitive and user defined that we will discussed in chapter 7. Another is control of the transmission of data among the subprograms of a program that is called Data Control. In data control we can control the passing of data among the subprograms. There are several methods of parameters transmission like call by value, call by reference, call by name, call by value result and call by result. These methods comes under the data control and will be discussed in this chapter. This chapter also includes the other terms related to data control like what are the attributes of data control, Referencing environment, static and dynamic scope, block structure etc. There are many terms that are related to data control. So this chapter covers all the details of data control.

8.1. DATA CONTROL AND ATTRIBUTES OF DATA CONTROL

Data control controls the passing of data among the subprograms of a program. The data control feature of a programming language controls the data at different points during the execution of program. At each point during execution of an operation, we need data on which the operation can be performed.

The data control feature of a language determine how data may be provided to the operations and how the results may be saved after execution of the operations. Data control is concerned with the binding of identifiers to particular data objects and subprograms. Data control structures may be categorised according to the referencing environment of data. There are various parameter transmission methods to provide the data to the functions that we will study in this chapter. These methods tells how the data is provided to the subprograms.

8.2. NAMES AND REFERENCING ENVIRONMENT

There are two basic ways that tells how a data object is available as an operand for an operation.

1. **Direct transmission:** In direct transmission, the result of an operation may be directly passed to another operation as an operand. In this, the data object is allocated storage temporarily during its life-time and may never be given a name.

   Consider the example.

   $X = a + b * c;$

   $Y = a + b;$

   In these two statements first y will be computed and result of this second statement will be passed to the first statement.

   Direct transmission is used for data control within expressions. The problem is the names given to the data object during transmission.

2. **Transmission through reference:** In this way, the parameter is passed through reference. A data object is given a name and in the second expression that name is treated as an operand. So when the data object is specified a name. That name will be used as an operand in the other expression. This is done as reference. A reference variable may be treated as two aliases of same name is created.

8.2.1. Naming of Program Elements

Naming of program element means what kinds of names are given to data object during program. It depends upon the language that categories the names. There are different type of name that are given to data object. There are two categories:

(*a*) **Simple name:** A simple name designates an entire data structure as an element.

(*b*) **Composite name:** A composite name may be a component of a data structure.

For example: When we create a Array in C as int A [3][3];

In this when we treated simply A, it is a simple name and when we takes it as A[2][3] *i.e.*, a component of it then it is called composite name.

The different name given to a language data object are:

1. Variable name.
2. Formal parameter.
3. Actual parameter.
4. Subprogram name.
5. Names for data object of a particular type.
6. Constants.
7. Exception name.
8. Literal constant.
9. Primitive operations.
10. Statement name.
11. Indentifies.

8.2.2. Associations of Identifiers

An association is a binding between identifiers and particular data object and subprogram. Association means how names are attached to a particular data object and subprogram. There are different stages during execution where we provide association.

1. When the main program is executed, then identifier associates with variable declared in the main program and bind each subprogram name is the main program to a particular subprogram definition.
2. When a main program executes, it invokes all the referencing operations associated with it.

   For example, X = function (Y) + 2

   In this form association takes place X, Y, Z and function name F.
3. In subprogram execution, a new set of association is created in the subprogram that involves variable names, formal parameter associated with a particular data object. Some association is created on entry of the subprogram and some is created after the subprogram execution (in the main program).
4. When the subprogram returns control to the main program, all its association may be inactive and the execution of the main program resumes.

8.2.3. Referencing Environments

A referencing environment of a subprogram contains a set of identifier association of subprograms that are available for use in referencing during its execution. The referencing environment of a subprogram is invariant *i.e.*, It may not be change as the activations of subprogram are created or destroyed. The values of data object changes for different association but the association of names with data object and subprogram do not change. There are several components of the referencing environment of a subprogram.

1. **Simply local environment:** The local referencing environment contains the association that are created on beginning of subprogram. These association includes Local variables, formal parameters and subprograms that are defined within that subprogram.
2. **Global referencing environment:** In the global referencing environment association are created at the beginning of the main program and are available to be used in the different subprogram.

   The global environment is part of the non-local environment. In global referencing environment global variables are created at the beginning of program and is used by different subprograms.
3. **Non-local referencing environment:** In non-local environment the associations are not created in the subprogram beginning. In non-local referencing environment associations are created at the start of execution and termed as non-local referencing environment of the subprogram.
4. **Predefined referencing environment:** In predefined referencing environment, some associations are defined directly by the language definition and these associations are directly used by different subprograms and main program. Predefined association may be hidden in the program. Like SORT function used in 'C' language.

Consider the following example that illustrate the use of local, nonlocal and global referencing environment.

```
int main( )
{
    int X, Y, Z;
    ...
    Void subprogram_1 (int x)
    {
        int m;
        ...
        Void subprogram_2 (int Z)
        {
            int m;
            ...
            Z = Z * y;
        }...
        subprogram_2 (y);
    }...
    subprogram_1 (x);
}...
```

Fig. 8.1. A 'C' Language Program to Illustrate the use of Referencing Environment.

In this program we can find following referencing environment.

(*i*) **For main:** Local referencing environment consist of *x*, *y*, *z* and subprogram_1.

(*ii*) **For subprogram_1:** (*a*) Local referencing environment consists of *x*, *m* and subprogram_2.

(*b*) Non-local referencing environment consists of *y*, *z* and subprogram_1 in main program.

(*iii*) **For subprogram 2:** (*a*) Local referencing environment consists of *m* and *z*.

(*b*) Non-local referencing environment consist of *x*, subprogram_2 in subprogram_1, *y*, subprogram_1 in main program.

8.2.4. Visibility of Associations

If an association for an identifier is part of the referencing environment for that subprogram then association is said to be visible. In other words if association belongs to a referencing environment of subprogram then it is called visible. If a association is not belongs to a referencing environment of the subprogram that is currently executing then the association is said to be hidden.

The dynamic scope of an association consists of the set of subprogram activations within which it is visible.

8.2.5. Different Type of References

A reference to an identifier is to find the association of identifier in a particular referencing environment.

Different type of references are:

(*a*) **Local references:** A reference to an identifier is said to be local if it belongs to a local environment.

(*b*) **Non-local reference:** A reference to an identifier is said to be non-local reference if its association is in a non-local environment.

(*c*) **Global references:** A reference to an identifier is said to be global reference if its association is in a global reference.

8.2.6. Referencing Operations

By referencing operation, we can find the data object or subprogram belonging to referencing environment. A referencing operation is an operation with the signature.

Referencing operation: id × referencing.environment → data object or subprogram.

By giving an identifier and a referencing environment (like global, local, non-local etc), we can find the appropriate association for that identifier in the environment and returns the associated data object.

8.3. CONCEPT OF ALIASING

If a data object have several associations in different referencing environment by a different name then it is called **aliasing.** Each name is termed an alias for the data object.

If a data object has different names, but a unique one in each referencing environment then there is no problem. But if it refer to the same data object using different names within the same referencing environment then serious problem occurs. Aliasing creates problem for the programmer because it makes difficult to understand a program.

Consider the following Pascal program.

```
Program main( );
Procedure S1(var X: Real);
    begin
        ...... (X is visible, Y is not)
    end;
Procedure S2;
    var Y: Real;
    begin
        .......
        S1(Y); {y is visible, x is not}
        .......
    end;
```

(a) No aliasing

```
Program main( );
    var y: Real;
Procedure S1(var x: Real)
    begin
        ....... (x and y refer to same data object)
    end;
Procedure S2;
    begin
        .......
        S1(y); {y is visible, x is not}
        .....
    end;
```

(b) x and y are aliased in S1

Fig 8.2. Concept of Aliasing.

In this example, in Fig. 8.2 (*a*) there is no aliasing because the data object having same name cannot appear in the same referencing environment. Aliases having same name are not appeared in a subprogram. But in Fig. 8.2. (*b*), aliasing creates problem in subprogram s1. Where *x* and *y* refers to same data object and appears in the same subprogram. So there is a problem for programmer.

8.4. SCOPE OF VARIABLE

The scope of a variable is the range of statements during which the variable is visible. In other words, scope of a variable defines the range of variable to a referencing environment. The scope rule of a language determining how a particular name is associated with a variable. The scope of a name is the collection of statements which can access that name binding. A name is visible to a reference if its referencing includes that reference and the name is not redeclared in an inner scope.

The scope and lifetime of a variable appear to be related. The scope of each variable is from its declaration to the end of the method. The lifetime of that variable is the period of time beginning when the method is entered and ending when execution of the method terminates, scopes and lifetime are also unrelated when subprogram calls are involved.

In most of the cases, the binding of a name to a scope can be of two types:

1. Static scope or static scoping.
2. Dynamic scope.

8.4.1. Static Scoping

In static scoping, a name is bound to a collection of statements in accordance with its position in the source program. Static scoping is so named because the scope of a variable can be statically determined; that is, prior to execution. Thus static scoping can be performed at compile time and is independent of the execution history of the program.

Static scoping improves program readability and supports a better level of compile time checking. Most languages including C/C++, Java, Python, and Ada, use static scoping. Because it is based on grammatical structure of a program. There are two categories of static scoped languages: those in which subprogram cannot be nested are called disjoint and another in which subprograms can be nested called nested scope.

The simplest case of what constitute a scope consists of the early versions of Fortran, in which a compilation unit constituted a single scope, which could not be nested. Departing from Fortran, an Algel 60 compilation unit constituted a scope within which functions and procedures introduced new scopes and could be nested. But C/C++ do not allow nested function. The C language neither supports packages nor classes.

The scope in which a name is defined is called its defining scope. A reference to a name is non local if it occurs in a nested scope of the defining scope; otherwise the reference is local.

Consider the following sorting program in 'C' language.

```
1.  void sort(int a[ ], int size)
2.  {  int i, j;
3.     for(i = 0; i<size; i++)
4.     for(j = i+1; j<size; j++)
5.     if(a[j] < a[i])
6.     {   int z;
7.         z = a[i];
8.         a[i] = a[j];
9.         a[j] = z;
10.    }
11. }
```

Fig. 8.3. Example scopes in 'C' Language.

The scope of the temporary variable Z includes lines 6-9, which is also its defining scope. Since there are no nested blocks within lines 6-9, all references to Z are local . Thus, Z can only be referenced by the statements enclosed by the braces on lines 5 and 10. This use of a compound statements to declare a variable improves the readability of the program, since the scope of the variable is limited. The scope for *a* and size is lines 2-10, that is, everything between the braces on lines 1 and 11.

Similarly, the scope for *i* and *j* is the same block, but references to *i* on lines 3-5 and to *j* on lines 4-5 are also local. But the reference to these names on lines 7-9 are nonlocal, since lines 6-10 is a nested scope within the defining scope for *i* and *j*.

Consider the following Ada Procedure:

```
Procedure sort is
        A : Integer;
Procedure sub1 is
        begin ... of sub1
        ... A ...
        end; ... of sub1
Procedure sub2 is
        A : Integer;
        begin ... of sub2
        ...
        end; ... of sub2
        begin ... of sort
        ...
        end; ... of sort
```

Fig. 8.4. Ada Procedure.

The correct declaration is found for the variable where he is declared in the subprogram sub1. If no declaration is found for variable there, the search continues in the declaration of the subprogram that declared subprogram sub1, which is called its static parent. If it is not found there then the search continues to the next larger enclosing unit and so on unit a declaration for x is found. The static parent of subprogram sub1, and its static parent, and so forth up are called the static ancestors of sub1.

In Fig. 8.4, under static scoping the reference to the variable A in sub1 is to the A declared in the procedure sort. This is true because the search for A begins in the procedure in which the references occurs, sub1, but no declaration for A is found there. The search thus continues in the static parent of sub1, sort, where the declaration of A is found.

The Importance of static scoping: The static scoping is very important. The main importance of static scoping are:

1. Static scope determine the scope of variable during translation of the program. Without it the scope of variable is not determined during translation of program.
2. Static scope rules allow many different type of connection to be established between references to names and their declaration during translation.
3. Static scoping makes program execution much faster and more reliable because type errors are detected at compile time.
4. The static scoping makes program easier to understand and read because the binding is done before translation.
5. In static scoping, some variables declaration can be hidden from some subprograms because there scope is outside that subprogram.
6. Most programming language like C, FORTRAN, Ada, Pascal and COBOL uses static scoping.

8.4.2. Dynamic Scope

In dynamic scoping, a name is bound to its most recent declaration based on the program's execution history. Dynamic scoping is based on the calling sequence of subprograms, not on their spatial relationship to each other. Dynamic scoping is used in early versions of LISP, APL, Snobal and Perl, it has proved to be particularly error prone and has largely been abandoned. Dynamic scoping is no longer a common feature of modern languages, except common LISP and Perl which also support static scoping.

A dynamic scope rule defines the dynamic scope of each association in terms of the dynamic course of program execution. A typical dynamic scope rule states that the scope of an association created during an activation of subprogram P included not only that activation but also any activation of a subprogram called by P, or called by a subprogram called by P and so on. Unless that later subprogram activation defines a new local association for the identifier that wides the original association.

Consider again the procedure SORT from section 8.4.1. which is shown again here:

```
Procedure sort is
        A : Integer
Procedure sub1 is
        begin ... of sub1
        ... A ...
        end; ... of sub1
Procedure sub2 is
        A : Integer;
        begin ... of sub2
        ...
        end; ... of sub2
        begin ... of sort
        ...
        end; ... of sort
```

Assume that dynamic scoping rules apply to non-local references. The meaning of the identifier A referenced of sub1 is dynamic if it cannot be determined at compile time. It may reference the variable from either declaration of A, depending on the calling sequence.

One way the correct meaning of A can be determined at runtime is to begin the search with the local declarations. This is also the way the process begins with static scoping, but that is where the similarity between the two techniques ends. When the search of local declarations fails, the declarations of the dynamic parent, or calling procedures, are searched. If a declaration for A is not found there, the search continues in that procedure's dynamic parent and so on, until a declaration for A is found. If none is found in any dynamic ancester it is a runtime error.

If, sort calls sub2, which calls sub1. In this case, the search proceeds from the local procedure, sub1, to its caller, sub2, where a declaration for A is found.

Perl's dynamic scoping is unusual, in fact it is not like that we have discussed, but the semantics are often that of dynamic scoping.

The importance of dynamic scoping: The importance of dynamic scoping is as follows:

1. By dynamic scoping, there is no need to determine scope at compile time.
2. The effect of dynamic scoping on programming is profound.
3. A statement in a subprogram that contains a reference to a non-local variable can refer to different non-local variables during different execution of the subprogram.

8.5. EVALUATION OF STATIC SCOPE

By static scoping, we can access non-local data that works well in different situations. For this consider a program structure and all its scopes created in main program and procedures.

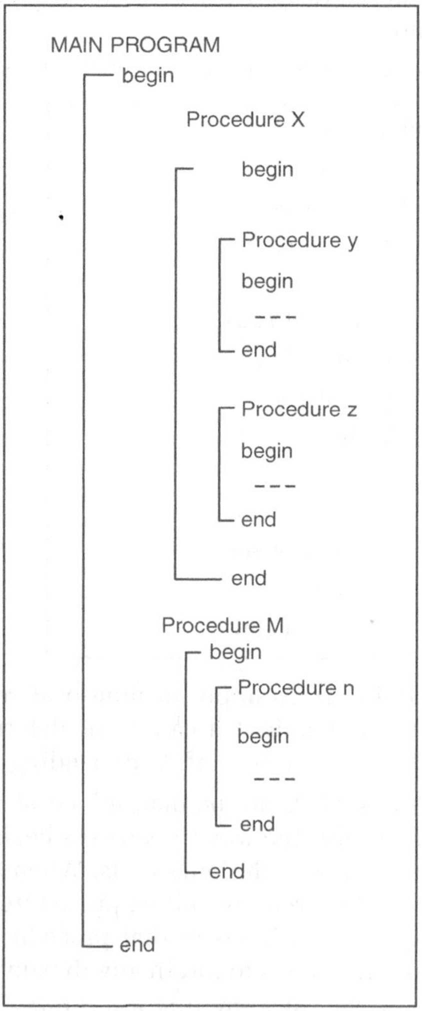

Fig 8.5. The Structure of a Simple Program.

This program contains an overall scope for main, with two procedure that define scope inside main, X and M. Inside X are scopes of procedures Y and Z. Inside M is the scope of procedure *n*. The required procedure access is as: main can call X and M. X can call y and z and M can call *n*.

The tree representation is shown as,

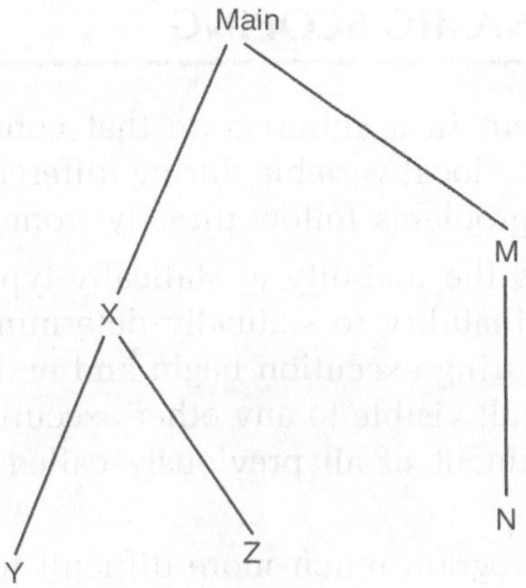

Fig 8.6. Tree Representation of Program in Fig 8.5.

The structure of this program might appear to be a very natural program organization that clearly reflects the design needs. The desirable calls in the program shown below.

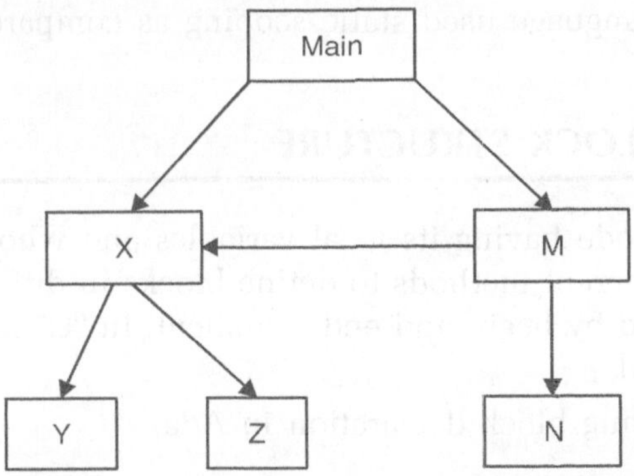

Fig 8.7. Desirable Calls for Program in Figure 8.5.

A program could call a subprogram that should not have been callable, which would not be detected as an error by the compiler. Access to procedures should be restricted to those that are necessary.

The problem with static scoping is that, if after the program has been developed and tested, a modification of its specification is required. Suppose that procedure N must now gain access to some variables of the scope of *z*. One way to provide that access is to move *n* inside the scope of *z*. But then N can no longer access the scope of M, which is essential. Another solution is to move the variable defined in *z* that are needed by N into main. This would allow access by all procedures, which would be more than is needed and thus creates the possibility of incorrect accesses. One final problem with moved the declaration of A to main is that it is harmful to readability to have the declaration of variables so far from their uses. The problem associated with variable visibility with static scoping are also present for subprogram access. In the tree of figure 8.6, suppose that due to some specification change, procedure N calls Z. This can be possible by moving Z to nest directly in main.

This static scoping restricated the program designs that bear little resemblance to the original, even in areas of the program in which changes have not been made.

8.6. EVALUATION OF DYNAMIC SCOPING

By Dynamic scoping, a statement in a subprogram that contains a reference to a non-local variable can refer to different non-local variable during different executions of the subprogram. Several kinds of programming problems follow directly from dynamic scoping.

First is dynamic scoping is the inability to statically type check references to non-local. This problem results from the inability to statically determine the declaration for a variable references as a local. Second, during execution begin and ending of subprogram, all the local variables of the subprogram are all visible to any other executing subprogram. Subprogram are always executed in the environment of all previously called subprograms that have not yet completed their executions.

Dynamic scoping makes program much more difficult to read and accesses to nonlocal variable in dynamic scoped languages take longer time to access the variable than the static scope.

Therefore, it is clear why dynamic scoping is not as widely used as static scoping. Program in static scoping are earier to read, more reliable and execute faster as compared to dynamic scope. Therefore, most language used static scoping as compared to dynamic scoping.

8.7. CONCEPT OF BLOCK STRUCTURE

A block is a section of code having its local variables and whose scope is limited to a set of statements. There are different methods to define blocks in different language like in Ada and Pascal block are delimited by begin and end statement. In "C" language blocks are declared in between the braces { and }

Consider the following block declaration in Ada.

```
...
declare Exchange : Integer
begin
Exchange: = First;
First: = second;
Second: = Exchange;
end;
...
```

In C-based language allow any compound statements (a statement sequence surrounded by matched braces) to have declarations and this define a new scope.

In 'C' we can write same sequence as

```
if (A [i] < A [i + 1])
{ int Exchange;
```

```
Exchange = A [i];
A [i] = A [i + 1];
A [i + 1] = Exchange;
}
```

The concept of block structure is found in block-structured languages such as pascal, PL/I and Ada.Block structured languages have a characteristic program structure and associated set of static scope rules. In block-structured language, each program or subprogram is organized as a set of nested blocks. The nesting of block is accomplished by allowing the definition of one block to entirely contain the definition of other blocks.

The class and method definitions in object-oriented language used nested static scopes. The Classes of C++, Java and C# treat their instance variables differently from the variables defined in their methods. The scope of a variable defined in a method starts at the definition.

8.7.1. Static Scope Rules Associated with Block Structured Languages

The static scope rules associated with a block structured program are as follows:

1. At the beginning of a block, the declaration of variable is given that defines the local referencing environment for that block. Any identifier declared in this section is considered as local variable to that block.
2. If an identifier is referenced in a block and no local declaration is given. Then their declaration is referenced to the block that immediatly encloses the first block (Parent of that block), if it is not found then next parent block is referred and so on. If no declaration is found there then its reference is taken as an error.
3. If inner block also exist to a block. Then the block is hidden from the outer block and cannot be referenced from it.
4. Every block should have a name. By this name it will be the part of local referencing environment of the containing block. In 'C' language subprogram is declared as:

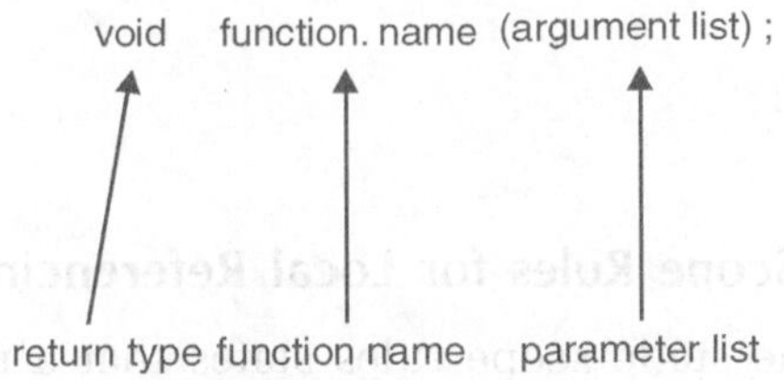

By using this static scope rule, a variable may occur in many different block but information in the inner block is hidden from outer blocks. This static scope rules for block structure programs allow every reference to a name within any block to be associated with a unique declaration. The compiler for the language may provide static type checking and other simplification of runtime structure based on static scope rule. Therefore many languages like Pascal, Ada, 'C' used block structure as a program structure. By using block structure the program design is highly structured.

8.8. LOCAL DATA AND LOCAL REFERENCING ENVIRONMENT

Data that are defined inside the subprograms are called local data. Variable are basically defined in the subprogram and they are called Local variables.

Subprograms are generally allowed to define their own variables, therefore local referencing environment. Access to local variables is restricted to the subprogram in which they are defined. The local environment of a subprogram consists of the various identifiers declared in the need of subprogram. Variable names, formal parameter names and subprograms names are the concern here. Subprogram name means the names of subprograms that are defined locally within the subprogram (*i.e.*, nesting of subprograms). Local variables can be either static or stack dynamic that are we discussed before. If local variables are stack dynamic, they are bound to storage when the subprogram begins execution and unbound from storage when the execution terminates.

There are several advantages of stack dynamic local variables, the first one be the flexibility they provide the subprogram. Recursive subprograms have stack dynamic local variable. The storage for local variables of all subprograms can be shared.

There are several disadvantages of stack dynamic variables are, the first one is the cost of the time required to allocate, initialize and deallocate variables for each activation. Second accesses to stack-dynamic local variables must be indirect whereas accesses to static variables can be direct.

There are various advantages of static local variable. These variable are very efficient because they can accessed the data faster. Consider the following example of 'C' (or C++) function, where variable X is static and count is stack dynamic.

```
int ABC (int a[ ], int b)
{ Static int X = 0;
    int count;
    for (count = 0; count < b; count P+)
    X = X + a [b];
    return X;
}
```

8.8.1. Static and Dynamic Scope Rules for Local Referencing Environment

1. **Static scope rule:** The static scope rules states that a reference to an identifier A in body of subprogram S is related to the local declaration for A in the need of Subprogram S. For implementation of static scope rule, a table of local declaration for identifiers are made by compiler. It appears in the head of S. While compiling the body of S, it refers to this table when declaration of an identifier is required.
2. **Dynamic scope rule:** The dynamic scope rule states that a reference to A during execution of S refers to the association for A in the current activation of S *i.e.*, there are several activations of S but only current activation is considered.

There are two ways to implement the dynamic scope rule and each gives a different semantics to local references. Consider subprograms S1, S2, S3 with a local variable A declared in S2 as in Fig. 8.8.

```
Subprogram S1;
...
end;
Subprogram S2;
Var A : integer: = 10;          – Initial value of A
begin
        write (A);              – Write the value of A
        Call S1;                – Call subprogram S1
        A = A + 1;              – Increment A
        write (A);              – write the value of A again
end;
Subprogram S3;
        ...
        call S2;
end;
```

Fig 8.8. Local Referencing Environment.

Subprogram S3 calls S2 which in turns call S1, which later returns control to S2, which completes its execution and returns control to S3. Lets consider the execution of A during this execution sequence:

1. When S3 executes, A is not visible in S3 since it is local to S2.
2. When S3 call S2. A becomes visible and it is bound with a value 10. As S3 executes, the first statement references A and writes its value 10.
3. When S2 call S1, the association for A hidden from S2. When S1 returns control to S2 the association becomes visible again.
4. When S2 resume its execution, A is referenced and increment and then its value is printed.
5. When S2 returns control to S3, the association again hidden.

There are two different meaning for this association.

1. **Retention:** The association for variable A might be retained until S2 is called again just as while S2 call S1. If the association is retained then when S2 called a second time, S2 is still associated with the same data object which has its old value. This means value of A is retained.
2. **Deletion:** In second, means that association for A might be deleted. It means if value is not retained then the value is deleted. Then binding of variable is broken and its data object is destroyed and storage is deallocated. When A is called again then association of A is created.

These two are different approaches to the semantics of local environment and lifetime of the environment C, Pascal, Ada uses deletion approach while COBAL and FORTRAN uses the retention approach.

8.8.2. Implementation of Local Referencing Environment

For implementing local referencing environment, a local environment table consists of pairs, each containing an identifier and the associated data object. Consider the local environment table for S2 in Fig. 8.8.

Name	Type	L value contents
A	Integer	Local value
S2	Procedure	Pointer to code Segment

Fig 8.9. Local Environment Table for Subprogram S2.

This table does not imply that the actual identifiers are stored during program execution. Usually they are not using local environment tables, implementation of the retention and deletion approaches to local environments is straight forward.

Retention: The implementation of the retention approach to local environment is straight forward using this tables. The table is kept as the part of the code segment. Since the code segment is allocated storage statically and remains in existence throughout execution, any variables in the local environment part of the code segment are also retained. If a variable has an initial value, then the initial value may be stored in the data object when the storage is allocated. Assuming each retained local variable is declared at the start of the definition of subprogram, the compiler can determine the size of each variable in the local environment table and compute the offset of the data object. With this implementation of retention for the local environment, no special action is needed to retain the values of the data object. Also no special action is needed to change from one local environment to another as one subprogram calls another.

Deletion: For implementation of the deletion approach to local approach to local environment is straight forward by using local environment table. When the local environment of a subprogram is deleted between calls and it is recreated a new entry on each call, then the local environment table containing the deleted variables is allocated storage as part of the activation record for subprogram. Assuming the activation record is created on a central stack on entry to subprogram and deleted from the stack on exit, the deletion of the local environment follows automatically. Current environment pointer (CEP pointer) is maintained during execution so that it points to the base address of the activation record in the stack for the subprogram that is currently executing at any point.

Both retention and deletion approaches are easy to implement in our general model of subprogram implementation as above several additional points are to be noted.

1. For simple call-return structure, retention and deletion in the absence of recursion lead to essentially the same implementation, as there are more than one activation record, which may be allocated statically.
2. Subprogram name in local environment may always be treated as retained.
3. A formal parameter name represents a data object that is reinitialized with a new value on each call of the subprogram.
4. Variables are either retained allocation or deleted allocated storage in the activation record.

8.8.3. Advantages and Disadvantages of Retention and Deletion

Retention and deletion are used by many languages. The retention approach provide the capability of history sensitive in the results on each call that determine the inputs. Retention approach consumed the space . Deletion approach is used by recursive subprograms. Deletion provides a saving in storage space in that local environment table exist only for those subprograms that are in execution or suspended execution. The Deletion approach cannot carry the data from one call to the another call. In case of subprogram execution local environment table maintains the retention.

8.9. PARAMETERS

Subprograms derive their great usefulness in both mathematics and programming language by their ability to accept parameters. For example, a square root function would not be very useful if it lacked the ability to accept an argument specifying the value whose square root is to be computed.

Argument: An expression which appears in a function or procedure call is termed an argument.

Parameter: An identifier which appears in a function or procedure is termed a parameter.

Explicitly transmitted parameters and results are the method for sharing data objects among subprograms. In non-local referencing environment sharing is achieved by non-local names visible to a subprogram, data objects transmitted as parameters and results are transmitted without a name attached. The sharing of data through parameter is most useful when a subprogram is to be given different data to process each time it is called. Sharing through a non-local environment is more appropriate where the same data object are used on each call.

8.9.1. Actual and Formal Parameters

The argument of a subprogram may be obtained both through parameters and through non-local references. Similarly the results of a subprogram may be returned through parameters, through assignments to non-local variables or through explicit function values. Thus the terms argument and result apply to data sent to and returned from the subprogram through a variety of language mechanisms.

The Algol/Pascal tradition is to use the term actual parameter for an expression in the call and formal parameter for a parameter in a function declaration. The C/Java tradition is to use the terms argument for the former and parameter for the latter. Some texts use parameter as a synonym for argument. This text follows the C/java tradition.

Formal Parameter: A formal parameter is a particular kind of local data object within a subprogram. The subprogram definition ordinarily lists the names and declarations for formal parameters as part of the specification part (*i.e.*, in the heading). A formal parameter name is a simple identifier and the declaration ordinarily gives the type and other attributes, as for an ordinary local variable declaration. Consider the 'C' procedure heading:

```
Void sub (int A, int B);
```

Here A and B are formal parameters and these two parameters are of integer type.

Actual Parameter: An actual parameter is a data object that is shared with the caller subprogram. An actual parameter may be a local data object belonging to the caller, it may be a formal parameter of the caller, it may be a nonlocal data object visible to the caller or it may be a result returned to a function involved by the caller and transmitted to the subprogram. An actual parameter is represented at the point of call of the subprogram by an expression, termed as an actual parameter expression that ordinarily has the same form as any other expression in the language.

```
Consider the following C/C++ program.
    int a, b;
    void B (int w)]
    {  int j, k;
       i = 3 * w;
       w = w - 1;
    }
    void A (int x, int y)
       {  int i, j;
          B (h);
       }
    void main ( )
    {  int a, b;
       h = 5, a = 3; b = 2;
       A (a, b);
    }
```

Fig 8.10. Example C/C++ Program.

In this the call in main to function A;

A (*a*, *b*) matches the argument a with the parameter *x*, and the argument *b* with the parameter of perl does not permit the declaration of parameters in a function header. Instead, Pearl makes the parameters available in an array named @-. The parameter can be accessed positionally using the above array.

8.9.2. Correspondence between Parameters

In all programming language, when a subprogram is called with a list of actual parameter, a correspondence must be established between the actual parameter and the formal parameters listed in the subprogram definition. There are two methods to establish correspondence between parameters.

1. **Positional correspondence:** In positional correspondence pairing of actual and formal parameters are based on their respective positions in the actual and formal parameter list. The first actual and first formal parameter are paired, then second and so on.

   For example

```
Void swap (int x, int y)
{
     ...
     statements
}
```

```
void main ()
{ ...
    swap (a, b);
}
```

In this example pairing of integer variable *x* is done with actual parameter a because they are in first position in formal and actual parameter and similarly pairing of *y* and *b* is done.

2. **Correspondence by explicit name:** In some languages, like in Ada the formal parameter to be paired with each actual parameter may be named explicity in the calling statement. For example, in Ada, one could call Swap with the statement:

    Swap ($a \Rightarrow$ X, $b \Rightarrow$ Y);

    which pairs actual parameter X with formal parameter *a* and actual parameter of with formal parameter *b* during the call of swap subprogram.

    Most languages uses positional correspondence exclusively. The number of actual and formal parameter must correspond so that pairing is unique.

8.10. PARAMETER PASSING MECHANISMS

Parameter passing mechanisms or methods are the ways by which parameters are transmitted to and/or from called subprogram. The value associated with the parameters during the life of a called function are determined on the basic of how these arguments are passed to the function by the call.

8.10.1. Semantic Models of Parameter Passing

There are three distinct semantics models by which formal parameter are characterized.

(*i*) **In Mode:** By In mode, formal parameter can receive data from the corresponding actual parameter. In mode is used by formal parameter to receive data from actual parameter.

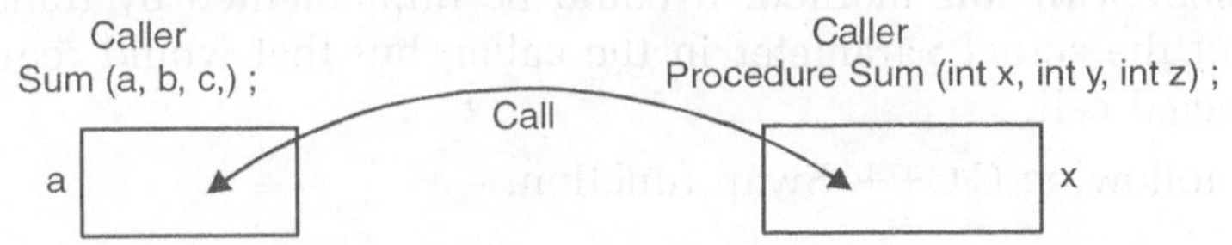

Fig 8.11. An In Mode of Parameter Passing.

(*ii*) **OUT Mode:** By An Out mode, the formal parameter can transmit data to the actual parameter. It is used to return the results from the subprogram by formal parameters.

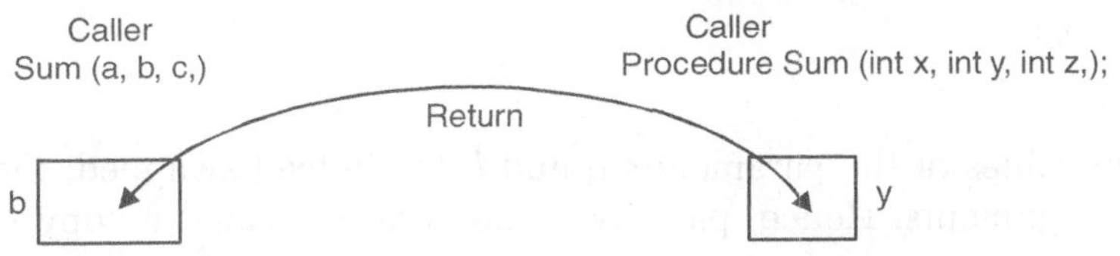

Fig 8.12. An Out Mode of Parameter Passing.

(*iii*) **IN OUT Mode:** By an In-Out mode we can do both *i.e.*, formal parameter can receive data from the corresponding actual parameter and formal parameter can transmit data to the actual parameter.

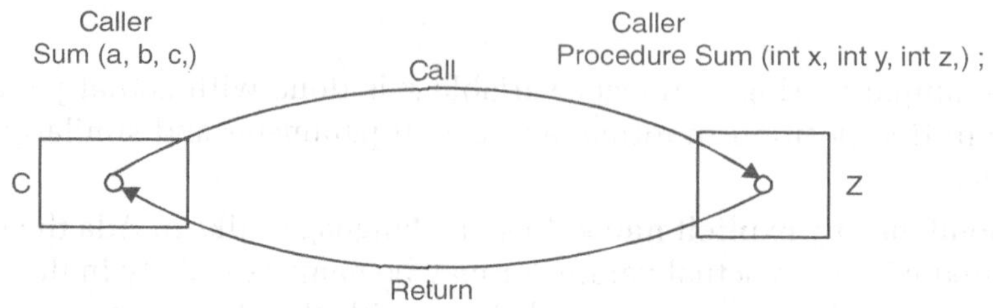

Fig 8.13. An IN OUT Mode of Parameter Passing.

8.10.2. Implementation Models of Parameter Passing

There are five principle way to pass an argument to a function:

1. Pass by value.
2. Pass by reference.
3. Pass by value-result.
4. Pass by result.
5. Pass by name.

Among these, the first two are the most prominent.

1. Pass by value

Passing an argument by value means that the value of the argument is computed at the time of the call and copied to the corresponding parameter. When a parameter is passed by value, the value of the actual parameter is used to initialize the corresponding formal parameter, when then act as a local variable in the subprogram, thus implementing in-mode semantics.

Pass by value is normally implemented by actual data transfer, because accesses are usually more efficient with this method. It could be implemented by transmitting an access path to the value of the actual parameter in the caller, but that would require that the value be in a write-protected cell.

Consider the following C/C++ Swap function.

```
Void Swap (int a, int b)
{
    int temp = a;
    a = b;
    b = temp;
}
```

Although the values of the parameters *a* and *b* are indeed swapped, these values are not copied out of the arguments. Hence, pass by value is after termed a copy in mechanism.

The main disadvantage of the pass-by value method if physical moves are done is that additional storage is required for the formal parameter, either in the called subprogram or in some area outside both the caller and the called subprogram.

2. Pass by reference

Pass by reference is a implementation model for input-mode parameters. Pass by reference method transmits an access path, usually just an address, to the called subprogram. This provides the access path to the cell storing the actual parameter. Thus the called subprogram is allowed to access the actual parameter in the calling program unit. To transmit a data object as a call-by-reference parameter means that a pointer to the location of the data object is made available to the subprogram. The data object itself does not change position in the memory.

Passing an argument by reference means that the memory address of the argument is copied to the corresponding parameter, so that the parameter becomes an indirect reference to the actual argument. The advantage of pass by reference is that the passing process itself is efficient, in terms of both time and space.

In language that support multiple parameter passing mechanism the distinction between a value and a reference parameter must be made explicit within the function declaration. For instance, in C++ a preceding ampersand (&) is written to indicate a reference parameter, and its absence indicates a value parameter. Arguments are passed by reference in cases when the actual value of the argument must be changed during the life of the call. Passing by reference is also preferred when the actual value of the argument must be changed during the life of the call.

The Swap function in C/C++ is written as

```
Void Swap (int & a, int & b)
{ int temp = a;
  a = b;
  b = temp;
}
```

Here when swap is called the statement is written as swap (*x*, *y*);

Where *x* and *y* are actual parameter. When a call is made then *a* and *b* variables points to the address of *x* and of variable. So when *a* and *b* are changes their memory locations then *x* and *y* are also changed.

3. Pass by result

Pass by result is an implementation model for out-mode parameters. A parameter transmitted by result is used only to transmit a result back from a subprogram.

An argument passed by result is implemented by copying the final value computed for the parameter out to the argument at the end of the life of the call. When a parameter is passed by result, formal parameter acts as a local variable, but just before control is transferred back to the caller, its value is passed back to the caller's actual parameter.

One problem with the pass by result model is that there can be an actual parameter collision. Another problem that can occur with pass by result is that the implementor may be able to choose between two different times to evaluate the addresses of the actual parameters at the time of call or at the time of the return.

4. Pass by value result

It is the combination of pass by value and pass by result. It is an implementation model for input-mode parameters in which actual values are moved.

An argument passed by value result is implemanted by coping the argument's value into the parameter at the beginning of the call and then copying the computed result back to the corresponding argument at the end of the call. In pass by value result, the value (*i.e.*, *r*-value) of the actual parameter is copied into the formal parameter data object at the time of call so that the effect is the same as if an explicit assignment of actual parameter were executed.

Pass by value result method developed from Algol-w, a language developed by Nicklans Wirth as a successor to ALGOL during the 1960s prior to his development of Pascal.

As a comparison of pass by reference versus pass by value result, consider the following similar C++ and Ada functions:

```
Void f (int & x, int & y)
{
    x = x + 1;
    y = y + 1;
}
```

```
Procedure f(x, y : in out integer) is
begin
        x : = x + 1;
        y : = y + 1;
end f;
```

The call *f*(*a*, *b*) has the effect in both cases of incrementing both *a* and *b* by one. However, the call *f*(*a*, *a*) will leave the a prior value of *q* incremented by 2 in the C++ (Pass by reference) case and by 1 (Pass by value result) in the Ada case.

5. Pass by name

Pass by name is an inout-mode parameter transmission method that does not correspond to a single implementation model. It is an example of late binding in that the expression in the call is not evaluated until it is used by the function. It views a subprogram call as a substitution for the entire body of the subprogram.

An argument passed by name behave as though it is textually substituted for each occurrence of the parameter. Its implementation view as a macro expansion. It was originally used by Algol 60. The basic call by name rule may be stated in terms of substitution. The actual parameter is to be substituted everywhere for the formal parameter in the body of the called program before execution of the subprogram begins.

The basic technique for implementing call by name is to treat actual parameters as simple parameterless subprogram. Whenever a formal parameter corresponding to a by-name actual parameter is referenced in a subprogram. This results evaluation of the actual parameter in the proper referencing environment and the return of the resulting value as the value of the subprogram.

8.10.3. Parameter Passing Methods in Different Languages

There are different programming languages and these languages uses different parameter passing methods.

FORTRAN used Input-Output mode of parameter passing, but it does not specify whether pass by reference or pass by value result should be used.

ALGOL 60 introduced the pass by name method. It also allow pass-by value as an option. Because of the difficulty in implementing them, Pass-by name parameters were not carried from ALGOL 60 to any subsequent languages that become popular.

C uses pass-by value and pass-by reference semantics by using pointers as parameter. In C and C++ formal parameter can be typed as pointers to constants. C++ uses a special pointer type, called a reference type. C++ also allow reference parameters to be defined to be constants.

As with C and C++, all Java parameters are passed by value. However, because objects can only be accessed through reference variables, object parameters are in effect passed by reference.

Ada is unique in that it does not specify how parameters are passed, but rather how they are used: in, out, or in-out. In Ada an in parameter is one that is referenced, but is not modified. As such, either pass-by value or by reference can be used depending on the size of the argument.

In contrast, an out parameter is one whose value must be set by the called routine before it can be referenced. Another way of viewing an out parameter is that its input value is never referenced. An out parameter could be implemented using either call by result or by reference, depending on its size. Finally an in-out parameter is one whose value may be referenced before it is assigned and one whose value may be reassigned before returning. In-out parameter may be implemented using either pass by value-result for primitive data types or pass-by reference for arrays and records.

8.10.4. Implementation of Parameter Transmission Methods

When a subprogram is called a new activation of subprogram receives a different set of parameters. Therefore, the storage for formal parameters is allocated as part of activation record.

ALGOL 60 use runtime stack for communication of parameter. A runtime stack is a stack of activation records used to model the semantics of function call and return. A runtime stack is initialized and maintained by runtime system, which is a system program that manages the execution of programs.

The various actions associated with parameter transmission are spilt into two groups, those associated with the point of call of the subprogram in each calling subprogram and those associated with the entry and exit in the subprogram itself. At the point of call, in each calling subprogram, each actual parameter expression is evaluated, and the list of pointers to actual-parameter data objects is setup.

Pass-by value parameters have their values copied into stack locations. The stack locations then serve as storage for the corresponding formal parameters. Pass-by result parameters are implemented as the opposite of pass-by value. Pass-by value results parameters can implemented directly from their semantics as a combination of pass-by value and pass-by result. The stack location for the parameters is initialized by the call and is then used like a local variable in the called subprogram.

Pass-by reference parameters are perhaps the simplest to implement. Regardless of the type of the actual parameter, only its address must be placed in the stack. In the case of literals, the address of the literal is transmitted. Pass-by name parameters are usually. Implemented with parameterless procedures or code segment called thunks. A thunk must be called for every reference to a pass by name parameter in the called subprogram. The thunk evaluates the reference in the proper referencing environment, which is that of the subprogram that passed the actual parameter.

8.10.5. Parameter Transmission Examples

Consider the following C function:

```
Void Swap (int x, int y)
{
    int temp = x;
    x = y;
    y = temp;
}
```

we call this with statement

```
Swap (a, b);
```

C uses pass-by value, so when this fuction is called *x* and *y* interchanged but value of *a* and *b* are not changed.

In Pascal swap function written with the same in mode semantics as:

```
Procedure swap (x, y : integer)
    temp : integer;
    begin
    temp : = x;
    x : = y;
    y : = temp;
    end;
```

Swap operation is successful by used C++ reference parameter as

```
Void Swap (int & x, int & y)
{   int temp = x;
    x = y;
    y = temp;
}
```

This simple operation is not possible in Java.

The semantics of pass-by value result is identical to those of pass-by reference, except when aliasing is involved. To explore pass-by value result consider the following function swap, which we assume uses pass-by value result parameters. It is written in a syntax similar to that of Ada.

```
Procedure swap (a : integer, b : integer) is
    temp : integer;
begin
```

```
        temp : = a;
        a : = b;
        b : = temp;
        end swal;
    It is called with
        Swap (x, y);
```

This swap subprogram operates correctly.

8.10.6. Aliases and Parameters

There are possibility of multiple names for the same data object in a single referencing environment. This term is known as aliasing. An alias may be created during parameter transmission in one of two ways:

1. **Formal parameter and non-local variable:** A data object transmitted as an actual parameter by reference may be directly accessible in the subprogram through a non-local name. The formal parameter name and the non-local name then become aliases because each refers to the same data object.
2. **Two formal parameters:** The same data object may be transmitted as an actual parameter by reference in two positions in the same actual parameter list. The two formal parameter names then become aliases because the data object may be referenced through either name.

8.11. EXPLICIT COMMON ENVIRONMENTS

A common environment set up explicitly for the sharing of data objects is the most simple method for data sharing. A set of such data object that are shared among a set of subprograms is allocated storage in a separate named block. Each subprogram contains a declaration that explicitly names the shared block. Such a shared block is known by various names line common block of FORTRAN and packages in Ada.

Specification part: A common environment is identical to a local environment for a subprogram, except that it is not a part of any single subprogram. It may contain definitions of variables, constants and types, but no subprograms or formal parameters. Consider the specification of a package in Ada.

```
Package XYZ is
    X : constant integer : = 50;
    type table is array (1 ... X) of real;
    Table A, Table b; Table
end.
```

The package specification defines a type, a constant two tables. The package definition is given outside of any subprograms that use the variable.

Implementation part: The declarations for the common environment are added to the compiler symbol table as an additional set of local names that may be referenced in the subprogram. In FORTRAN and C, each subprogram using the common environment must also include declarations for each shared variable so that the compiler knows the relevant declarations even through the common environment is also declared elsewhere.

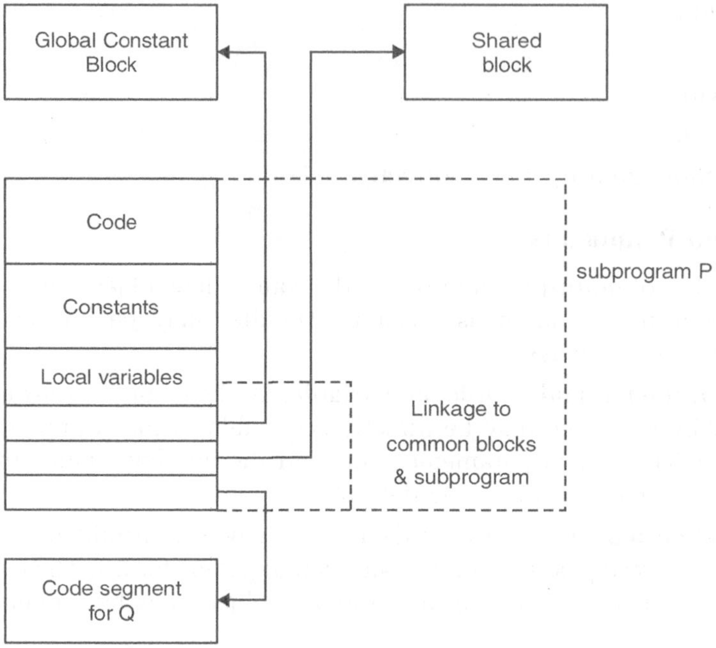

Fig 8.14. Linking to Common Blocks in Subprogram.

A subprogram that references a data object in a common block must know the base address of the block. A simple implementation is to allocate a location in the code segment for the subprogram to contain a pointer to the block. These pointer linkages between a subprogram and the common blocks that it uses are similar to linkages between a subprograms that it calls. One of the primary task of the link editor that assembles a collection of subprograms and common blocks in memory prior to one start of execution is the storing of the actual linkage pointers in each code segment as required for execution. Figure 8.14 illustrate this structure.

8.12. NON-LOCAL ENVIRONMENT

Most languages provide some other method of accessing variables from external environment. An alternative to the use of explicit common environments for shared data is the association of a non-local environment with each executing subprogram. The non-local variables of a subprogram are those that are visible within the subprogram but are not locally declared. Global variables are those that are visible in all program units.

The non-local environment for a subprogram S consists of a set of local environments of other subprogram activations that are made accessible to S during its execution. If a variable is reference in S and has no local declaration then the non-local environment is used to determine the association for variable. There are two methods for accessing non-local variables: static scoping and dynamic scoping.

The problem with static scoping is sharing of non-local variables. A program structure may be dictated by the accessibility of subprograms and non-local variables to other subprograms.

With dynamic scoping two problem arises; first, during the time span beginning when execution of a subprogram begins and ending when that execution ends, the local variables of the subprogram are visible to any other executing subprogram regardless of its textual proximity. There is no way to protect local variables from this accessibility. A second problem with dynamic scoping is the inability to statically type check references to non-locals, because it is not possible to statically determine the declaration for a variable referenced as a non-local.

8.12.1. Most Recent Association Rule

According to most recent association rule, non-local environment is determined during program execution. No static scope rules are used *i.e.*, no attempt is made during program translation to determine the definition associated with a reference to an identifier that is not defined locally in the subprogram. The most troublesome aspect of this non-local environment is that it may change between activations of subprogram. During program execution, when a data object X is created as part of the activation of subprogram S, the dynamic scope of the association for X becomes all the activations of subprogram called by S or by those subprograms and so on.

Implementation of most recent association rule: Implementation of most recent association rule for nonlocal reference is straight forward. The central stack implemantation is used for storing subprogram activation records. Suppose that a subprogram S1 calls subprogram S2 which calls S3. When S3 is executing, the central stack might looks as.

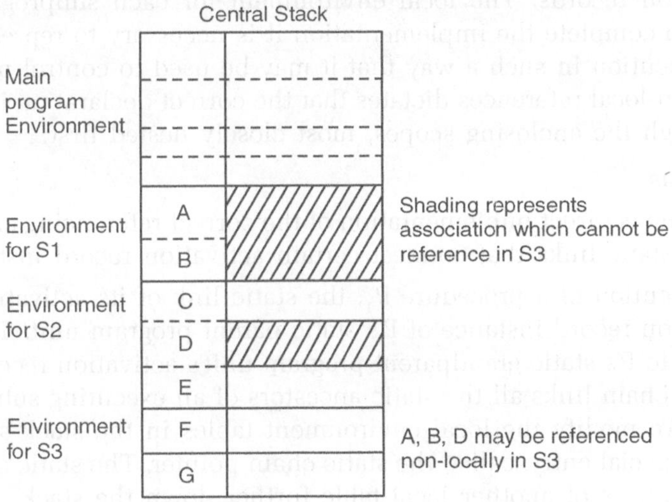

Fig 8.15. Active Referencing Environment of S3 during Execution.

To resolve a non-local reference to A, the stack is searched beginning with the local environment for S3 and working back through the association in the stack until the most recent association for A is found.

Some of the associations in the stack will be hidden by later associations for the same identifier. This implementation of the most recent association rule is costly. The alternative implementation uses a central table common to all subprograms, the central referencing environment table. The central table is set up to contain at all times during program execution all the currently active identifier associations, regardless of whether they are local or non-local.

8.12.2 Implementation Mechanism for Non-local References

Handling of non-local references to shared data is more complex. The non-local referencing environment of each subprogram during execution is already determined by the static scope rule used during translation. The implementation problem is to retain consistency between the static and dynamic scope rule so that a non-local reference during program execution is correctly related to the data object corresponding to the definition for that identifier in the program text.

The static scope rules are straightforward to implement in the compiler. Each subprogram definition is processed during compilation, a local table of declaration is created and attached to a chain of such local tables that represent the local environments of the main program and other subprograms within which this subprogram is nested.

There are two major implementation techniques for creating accesses to nonlocal variables in a static scoped language. Static chains and displays. A reference to a nonlocal variable requires a two step access process. All variables that can be nonlocally accessed are in existing activation record instances and therefore are somewhere in the stack. The first step of the access process is to find the instance of the activation record in the stack in which the variable was allocated. The second part is to use the local offset of the variable to access it.

During program execution in a block structured language, a central stack is used for subprogram activation records. The local environment for each subprogram is stored in its activation record. To complete the implementation it is necessary to represent the static block structure during execution in such a way that it may be used to control nonlocal referencing. The semantics of non-local references dictates that the correct declaration is the first one found when looking through the enclosing scopes, most closely nested first.

8.12.2.1 Static chains

Static chain technique is direct implementation of the correct referencing environment. A static chain is a chain of static links that connect certain activation record instances in the stack.

During the execution of a procedure P_1, the static link of its activation record instances points to an activation record instance of P's static parent program unit. That instance's static link points, in turn, to P's static grandparent program unit's activation record instance, if there is one. So the static chain links all the static ancestors of an executing subprogram in order of static parent first. We modify the local environment tables in the stack slightly so that each table begins with a special entry, called the static chain pointer. The static chain pointer always contains the base address of another local table further down the stack.

An integer is associated with a static scope that indicate how deeply it is nested in the outermost scope. This is called static depth. If main program calls a procedure X and procedure X calls a procedure Y. Then the static depth of main program is 0 and procedure X contains the static depth 1 and procedure Y contains the static depth 2.

The length of the static chain needed to reach the correct activation record instance for a non-local reference to a variable A is exactly the difference between the static depth of the procedure containing the reference to A and the static depth of the procedure containing the declaration for A. This difference is called the chain offset or nesting depth.

Consider the following program.

Program P_1;
Procedure P_2;
Procedure P_3;
...
end; {P_3}
...
end; {P_2}
...
end; {P_1}

The static depths of P_1, P_2 and P_3 are 0, 1, and 2, respectively. If procedure P_3 references a variable declared in P_1, the chain offset of that reference would be 2. If procedure P_3 references a variable declared in P_2, the chain offset of that reference would be 1.

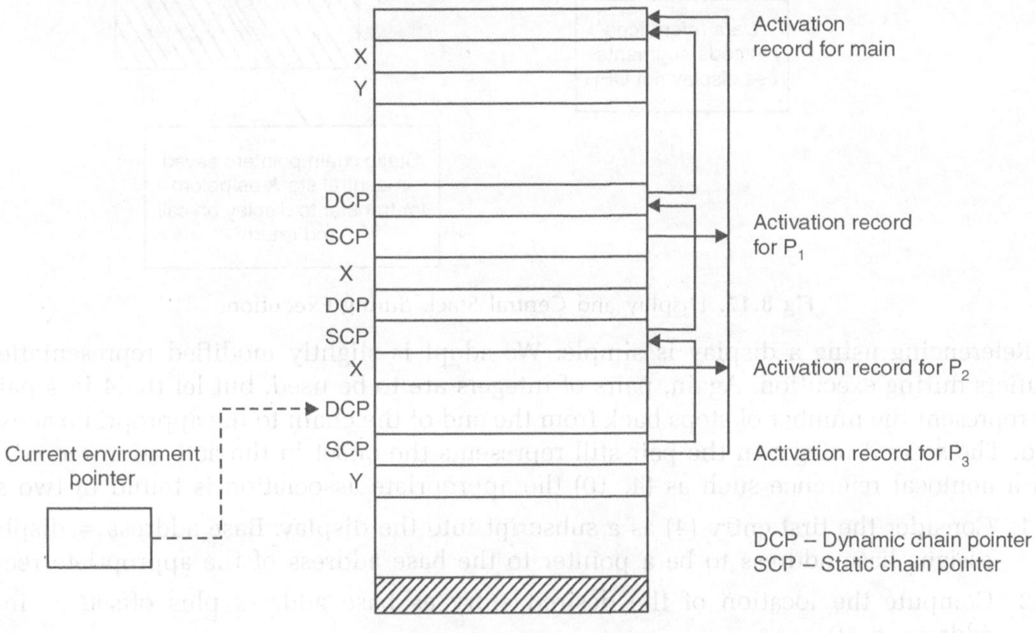

Fig 8.16. Use of Static Chain and Dynamic Chain Pointers.

The static chain pointer form the basic for a simple referencing scheme. To satisfy a reference to X we follow the CEP pointer to the current local environment on top of the stack. If no association for X is found in the local environment, then we follow the static chain pointer in that local table down the stack to a second table.

8.12.2.2 Displays

The alternative of static chain method is a display. In this approach, we can collect the static links in a single array called a display. The contents of the display at any specific time is a list of addresses of the accessible activation record instances in the stack one for each active scope- in the order in which they are nested.

The display is separate from the central stack and is after represented in a set of high speed registers. At any given point during execution, the display contains the same sequence of pointers that occur in the static chain of the subprogram currently being executed.

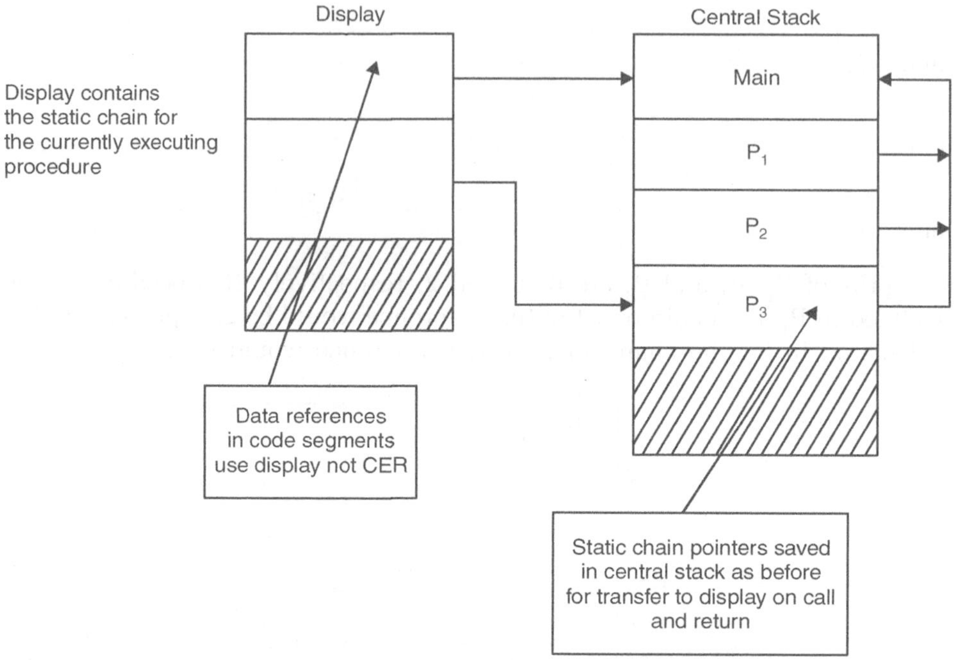

Fig 8.17. Display and Central Stack during Execution.

Referencing using a display is simple. We adopt is slightly modified representation for identifiers during execution. Again, pairs of integers are to be used, but let the 4 in a pair like (4, 3) represent the number of steps back from the end of the chain to the appropriate activation record. The second integer in the pair still represents the offset in the activation record. Now, given a nonlocal reference such as (4, 10) the appropriate association is found in two steps:

1. Consider the first entry (4) as a subscript into the display. Base address = display [4] assigns base address to be a pointer to the base address of the appropriate record.
2. Compute the location of the desired entry as base address plus offset, as in base address + 10.

These two steps combine into one using indirect addressing through the display entry. If the display is represented in high speed registers during execution, then only one memory access per identifier reference is required. Overall, displays are better if there are many references to distant non-local variables Static chaining is better if there are few references to distant non-local variables, which is the more common situation.

8.13. IMPLEMENTING DYNAMIC SCOPING IN NON-LOCAL REFERENCES

There are two ways in which non-local references in a dynamic scoped language can be implemented: deep access and shallow access. The difference between binding and access here is that deep and shallow bindings results in different semantics; deep and shallow accesses do not.

8.13.1. Deep Access

When a program in a language uses dynamic scoping refers to a non-local variable, the reference can be resolved by searching through the declaration in the other subprograms that are currently active, beginning with the one most recently activated.

It is similar to accessing non-local variables in a static scoped language, except that the dynamic chain is used instead of static chain. The dynamic chain links together all subprogram activation record instances in the reverse of the order in which they are activated. The dynamic chain is exactly what is needed to reference non-local variables in a dynamic scoped language. This method is called deep access because it searches deep in the stack.

Consider the following example program:

```
    Procedure P;
    integer A, B;
    begin
    A = D + E
    ...
    end;
Procedure Q;
    integer C, A;
    begin
    ...
    end;
Procedure R;
    integer D, C
    begin
    ...
    end;
Program     Main_1;
    integer u, v;
    begin
    ...
    end;
```

Suppose the following sequence of procedure calls occurs:

Main_1 calls R

R calls R

R calls Q

Q calls P

Figure 8.18. shows the stack during the execution of procedure P after this calling sequence. Activation record instances do not have static links, which would serve no purpose in a dynamic scoped language.

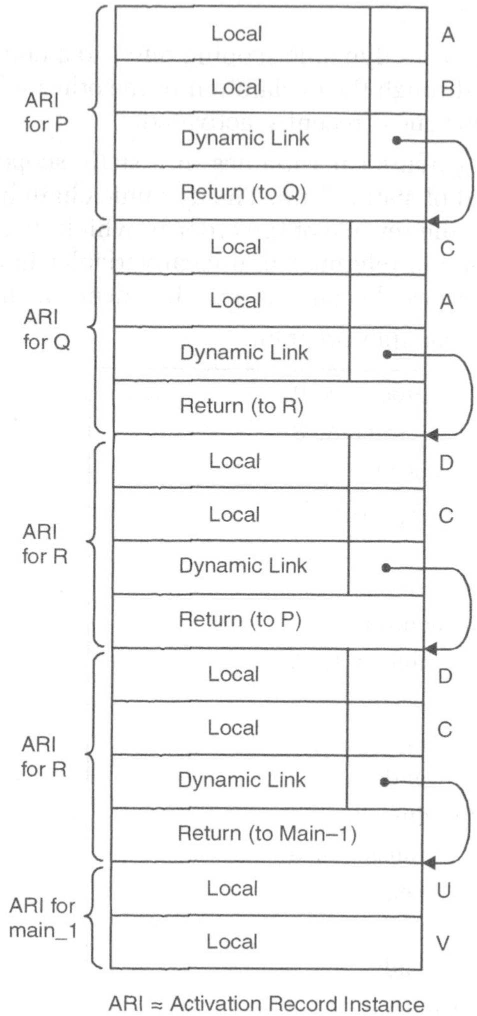

Fig 8.18. Stack Content for a Dynamic Scoped Program.

Consider the reference to the variable A, D and E in procedure P. The reference to A is found in the activation record instance for P. The reference to D is found by searching all of the activation record instances on the stack, because the only existing variable with that name is in Main_1.

8.13.2. Shallow Access

An alternative implementation method for dynamic scoping is shallow access. In this method, variables declared in subprograms are not stored in the activation records of those subprograms. Because with dynamic scoping there is at most one visible version of a variable of any specific name at a given time, a very different approach can be taken. A separate stack is created for each variable name in a complete program. When a new variable with a particular name is created by a declaration, then the variable is given a cell on the stack for its name. Every reference to the name is to the variable on top of the stack associated with that name, because the top one is the most recently created. When the sub-program terminates, the lifetime of its variables completes and the stacks for those variable names are popped. This allow very fast references to variable.

Fig. 8.19. Shows the example program that shows the variable stacks.

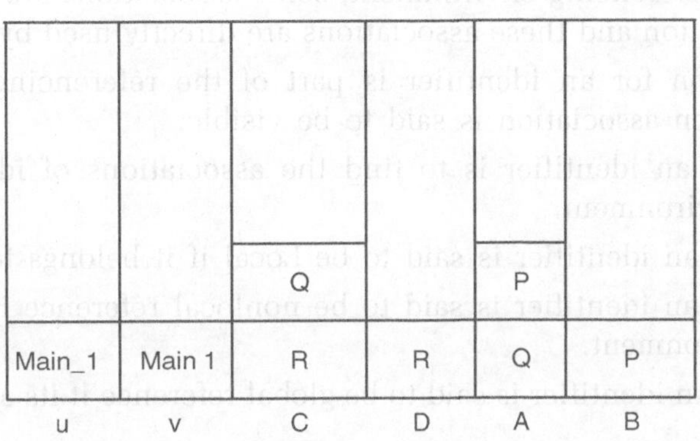

The name in the stack cells indicates the program units of the variable declaration.

Fig 8.19. One Method of Using Shallow Access to Implement Dynamic Scoping.

Another approach for implementing shallow access is to use a central table that a location of each variable name in the program. A bit called active is maintained that tells the curent binding or variable associated with that name. Any access to any variable can then be to an offset into the central table. Maintenance of a central table is straightforward. That have been several variations in the design of the central table. The choice between shallow and deep access to non-local variables depends on the relative frequencies of subprogram calls and non-local references.

The shallow access method provides much faster references to nonlocals, especially distant non-locals, but its lost of subprogram linkage is high. Deep access method provides fast subprogram linkage.

Some Important Terms

- Data control manages the passing of data among the sub-programs.
- Data control is concerned with the binding of identifiers to particular data objects and subprograms.
- In direct transmission, the result of an operation may be directly passed to another operation as an operand.
- Naming of program element means what kinds of names are given to data object during program.
- An association is a binding between identifiers and particular data object and sub-program.
- A referencing environment of a sub-program contains a set of identifier association of subprograms that are available for use in referencing during its execution.
- The local referencing environment contains the association that are created on beginning of sub-program.

- In the global referencing environment association are created at the beginning of the main program.
- In Non-local environment the association are created at the start of execution.
- In predefined referencing environment, some associations are defined directly by the language definition and these associations are directly used by different subprograms.
- If an association for an identifier is part of the referencing environment for that subprogram then association is said to be visible.
- A reference to an identifier is to find the associations of identifier in a particular referencing environment.
- A reference to an identifier is said to be Local if it belongs to a local environment.
- A reference to an identifier is said to be nonlocal reference if its association is in a non-local environment.
- A reference to an identifier is said to be global reference if its association is in a global reference.
- A referencing operation is an operation with the signature:

  Referencing operation: id $\times$ referencing environment $\rightarrow$ data object or subprogram.
- If a data object have several associations in different referencing environment by a different name then it is called aliasing.
- The scope of a variable is the range of statements during which the variable is visible.
- Static scoping can be performed at compile time and is independent of the execution history of the program.
- In static scoping, some variable declaration can be hidden from some subprograms.
- A dynamic scope rule defines the dynamic scope of each association in terms of the dynamic course of program execution.
- By dynamic scoping, there is no need to determine scope at compile time.
- Dynamic scoping makes program much more difficult to read.
- A block is a section of code having its own local variables and whose scope is limited to a set of statements.
- The concept of block structure is found in block structured languages such as Pascal, PL/I and Ada.
- A local environment table consists of pairs, each containing an identifier and the associated data object.
- The retention approach provide the capability of history sensitive in the result on each call that determine the inputs.
- The Deletion approach cannot carry the data from one call to the another call.
- An expression which appears in a function or procedure call is termed an argument.
- An identifier which appears in a function or procedure is termed a parameter.
- A formal parameter is a particular kind of local data object within a subprogram.
- An actual parameter is a data object that is shared with the caller subprogram.
- An actual parameter is represented at the point of call of the sub-program by an expression, termed as an actual parameter expression.

- In positional correspondence, pairing of actual and formal parameters are based on their respective positions in the actual and formal parameter list.
- Parameter passing mechanisms or methods are the ways by which parameters are transmitted to and/or from called subprogram.
- There are three distinct semantic models by which formal parameters are characterized.
  - IN Mode
  - OUT Mode
  - IN OUT Mode
- By IN Mode, formal parameter can receive data from the corresponding actual parameter.
- By OUT Mode, the formal parameter can transmit data to the actual parameter.
- By an IN OUT mode, formal parameter can receive/transmit data from the corresponding actual parameter.
- There are five principal way to pass an argument to a function:
  - Pass-by value
  - Pass-by reference
  - Pass-by value-result
  - Pass-by result
  - Pass-by name
- There are possibility of multiple names for the same data object in a single referencing environment. This term is known as aliasing.
- A common environment set up explicity for the sharing of data objects is the most simple method for data sharing.
- According to most recent association rule, non-local environment is determined during program execution.
- The central stack implementation is used for storing sub-program activation records.
- Handling of non-local references to shared data is more complex.
- Implementation of non-local references is done by
  - Static chains
  - displays
- A static chain is a chain of static links that connect certain activation record instances in the stack.
- In display method, we can collect the static links in a single array called a display.
- There are two ways in which non-local references in a dynamic scoped language can be implemented.
  - Deep Access
  - Shallow Access

Review Questions

1. Define the term Data control and also explain attributes of Data control.
2. Write a short-note on Names and Referencing environment,
3. What do you mean by a Referencing environment? Explain different components of the referencing environment of a subprogram.
4. Write short notes on:
   (*a*) Visibility of Associations
   (*b*) Referencing Operations
   (*c*) Concept of Aliasing.
5. Define the term scope of a variable. Explain static and dynamic scope.
6. Explain local data and local referencing environment.
7. Explain importance of static and dynamic scoping.
8. Explain Evaluation of static and Dynamic scoping.
9. Explain the concept of block structure in detail.
10. Explain static scope rule associated with block structured languages.
11. Explain static and dynamic scope rule for local referencing environment.
12. What do you mean by a parameter? Explain correspondence between parameters.
13. What do you mean by parameter? Explain the different parameter transmission schemes.
14. Write short notes on:
    (*a*) Semantic Models of parameter passing
    (*b*) Call by value and call by reference
    (*c*) Formal and actual parameters
    (*d*) Implementation of parameter transmission methods.
15. Explain parameter passing methods in different languages.
16. Explain specification and implementation of Explicit Common Environments.
17. What do you mean by non-local environment? Explain implementation mechanism for non-local references.
18. Write short notes on:
    (*a*) Static Chains
    (*b*) Displays.
19. Explain how non-local references in a dynamic scoped language can be implemented?
20. Define Most recent association rule. Explain how most recent association rule is implemented?

❑❑❑

Chapter 9 STORAGE MANAGEMENT

Storage Management is a key area in the study of programming language, since it is tightly intertwined with the meaning of programs. Memory or storage is the area where data and instructions are stored. Storage management for data and instructions is one of the central concerns of the programmer, language implementor and language designer. There are various storage management techniques with the help of these techniques data is stored in memory. In this chapter we are dealing with these storage management techniques and different terms related with storage management. We also discuss the various problems associated with storage management. Programmer is also deeply concerned with storage management and must design programs that use storage efficiently, the programmer is likely to have little direct control over storage. Runtime stack helps to clarify our understanding of how memory is organized to implement functions, a different memory area, called the heap, helps us to understand the runtime behaviour of dynamic objects.

The storage management is the art and the process of coordinating and controlling the use of memory by different data objects. In this chapter we are dealing the runtime management or dynamic memory allocation, which is a necessary activity for modern programming languages. For a long time, the automation of this activity has been a key element in the implementation of functional and logical programming languages. We are discuss major runtime elements requiring storage, different storage management techniques like Static Storage Management, Stack Based Storage Management, Heap Storage Management etc. We also discuss programmer or system controlled memory management techniques C and C++ have allowed the runtime management of dynamic memory to be assumed by either the programmer or the system. While there are several automatic memory management routines available for C and C++, their use by the programmer is entirely optional. Java on the other hand, insists that memory management is too tricky and error prone to be left to the programmer; only the system can be responsible for memory management. While each language design ordinarily permits the use of certain storage management techniques, the details of the mechanisms and their representation is hardware and software, are the task of the implementer.

9.1. MAJOR RUNTIME ELEMENTS REQUIRING STORAGE

During runtime or executing the data objects, there are various elements that are requiring storage. The storage management is viewed as a place where data and translated programs are stored. In case of runtime storage management encompasses many other areas like subprograms return points are also considered. The major runtime elements that are requiring storage are as follows:

1. **Storage for code segments for translated programs:** A large block of memory is reserved for translated user programs. Here programs will be the blocks of executable machine language code. Space is reserved for these translate code.
2. **Run-time system programs:** Another large block of memory is reserved for system programs. These system programs provide support to the executive of user programs. These system programs will be software interpreter, translators, linker, loader etc. Another system programs are print string functions, library routines such as sine, cosine functions etc. A large block of memory is reserved for these type of system programs.
3. **Temporaries in parameter transmission:** During the execution of programs, when a subprogram is called, then a list of actual parameters must be evaluated and temporary results are stored because the evaluation of the list is not yet to be completed. For these type of temporary storage, a large block of memory is required. So for temporaries in parameter transmission a large block is reserved.
4. **Subprogram return points and coroutines resume points:** A subprogram may be invoked from different points in a program. For coroutines also the resume points provides the sequence control between coroutines. So space is reserved for subprogram return points and coroutines resume points. Central stack or some other storage management methods are used to provide storage.
5. **Different referencing environments:** There are different referencing environments like local referencing environment, Non-local referencing environment, Explicit Common environment etc. These environment requires storage during execution. So a substantial block of storage is reserved for these environments.
6. **Temporaries storage during expression evaluation:** When a expression is evaluated, then system defined temporary storage is provided for intermediate results of evaluation. For example, in evaluation of expression (A + B) + (C * D), the result of addition of A and B is temporary stored and result of multiplication of C and D is also stored temporary. These stored result are again used for further results. So a large block of memory is provided for this temporaries storage.

7. **Miscellaneous system data:** Various type of system data is used during program execution. These system data contains information in the form of symbol table, status information for input-output and various miscellaneous piece of state information. So a large block of storage is required for these system data.
8. **Input-output buffer:** In every programming languages, various input-output operations are performed and for these operations buffers are used. These buffers provides the temporary storage between program initiated input-output operations and transfer of data between files and system.
9. **User defined data structures and constants:** A large space is also reserved for all the data structures and constant defined by user. These data structures and constant are declared in user programs.
10. **Subprogram call and return operations:** When a subprogram is called then subprogram activation record is created. So storage is provided to these activation record, the local referencing environment and other data which are created during call of subprogram. Similarly, the execution of a subprogram return operations usually requiring freeing of the storage allocated during the call. So a large space is reserved for this subprogram call and return operation.
11. **Data structure creation and destruction operation:** In some languages, new data strucutures are created at arbitray points during program execution. These operations requiring storage that is separate from storage at the subprogram entry and when these data structures performs their task then explicit destruction operation are provided to free the space. So these operation requiring storage at runtime. Example of these operations are 'C' language malloc and free function and C++ new and delete functions.
12. **Component insertion and deletion operations:** Some language provides operations like insertion and deletion of components of data structures. So storage may be provided to insert the new components to the existing data structure and freeing when the deletion takes place.

So these are the major runtime elements that are requiring storage. These are the major elements that requires storage during runtime.

9.2. PROGRAMMER AND SYSTEM CONTROLLED STORAGE MANAGEMENT

Storage management is generally controlled by system. The question arises if storage management is controlled by programmer then what are the advantages and disadvantages of this technique. In 'C' language, programmer control over storage via malloc and free functions, which allocate and free storage for programmer- defined data structure. The syntax for malloc function in 'C' language is

```
int * ptr;
    ptr = (int *) malloc (n * size of (int));
```

After the execution of this statement, a consecutive memory block is created equal to the number *n* and size of each block is 2 byte.

But some other language does not allow the direct control of programmer. In that case storage management is affected only implicitly through the use of various language features.

There are difficulties with programmer control of storage management. First, it may place extra burden on the programmer and it may also interfere with the necessary controlled storage management. It is not baneficial to allow the programmer to handle this burden. The programmer can hardly be expected to concern himself with storage for subprogram return points, system data or tempoaries used in programs. He also control the storage management for local data. There are also some problem like garbage collection and dangling references when storage is provided to data structures. So it is dangerous to provide storage to programmer, because it may lead to errors or loss of access to a variable storage. Programmer controlled storage management also may interfere with system controlled, in that case some special storage areas or routines may be required for programmer controlled storage, allowing less efficient use of storage overall.

There are some advantages also for programmer controlled storage management. First one is, it is extremely difficult for the system to determine when storage may be most effectively provided and when to free the storage. Programmer knows better when a particular data structure is needed storage and when is no longer needed and may be free.

This shows that programmer controlled storage management have some advantages and some disadvantages. Advantages shows that programmer controlled storage management is beneficial because programmer knows better when the storage is required and when to free the storage. Disadvantages shows that it create extra burden to programmer and it creates errors and fails during the execution. So our discussion does not solve this problem. This is a debate topic in the software engineering community.

9.3. STORAGE MANAGEMENT PHASES

Storage management phases shows how the storage is provided to the data structures, how the storage spaces is recovered for again use. Storage management phases are basically of three types:

1. **Initial allocation:** Initial allocation means how storage is provided initially. At the start of execution each piece of storage may be either free or allocated for some use. If it is free, then it is available for allocation dynamically as execution proceeds. Every storage management may use some techniques for keeping track of free storage as well as mechanisms for allocation of these free storage when it is needed during allocation. There are various allocation strategies like static, stack based and heap storage management schems. These techniques are discussed later in this chapter.

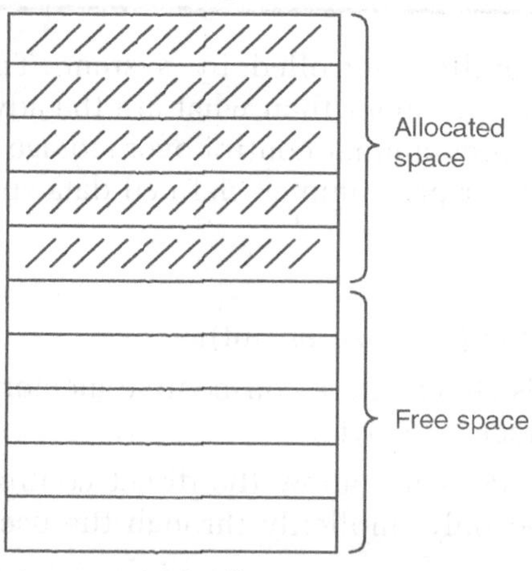

Fig 9.1. Allocated Space (Initial Allocation) and Free Space List Structure.

2. **Recovery:** When some blocks and memory spaces are free after initial allocation then storage manager recovered these spaces or blocks. These recovered space is used by other data objects. So it is task of storage manager to recover the free space to the further use. There are different methods for determining whether a block is free or not. Recovery is done by stack pointer which points to the free spaces or some other methods like garbage collection. If a space or block is freed then it is returned to the free space list.
3. **Compaction and reuse:** Compaction is process by which we construct large blocks of free storage from small pieces. It is a technique by which we can collect the free spaces. Compaction is done to reuse the free spaces. Reuse of storage also involve the same mechanism or techniques that are used for initial allocation. Compaction is done because small pieces of memories are not sufficient for a request of larger memory block. So if the compaction is not done then these small blocks of memories are not assigned to different processes because they are not sufficient for a bigger request.

Compaction can be of two types:

(*a*) **Partial Compaction:** Partial compaction is done when active block of memory cannot be shifted, then only adjacent free blocks are shifted and free space list may be compacted. It is expensive to shift active blocks to one end.

(*b*) **Full compaction:** Full compaction is done when active block can be shifted. In that case all active blocks may be shifted at one end while free spaces are shifted at another end. By full compaction, all the free blocks are placed one end. In this case, these large blocks can be assigned to the request of larger block size.

After compaction reuse of storage is done like the initial allocation case means these free spaces are again used by different processes and some methods used as we use in initial allocation methods.

These are the three storage management phases.

9.4. STATIC STORAGE MANAGEMENT TECHNIQUE

The simplest form of storage allocation is static allocation. In this allocation scheme, storage

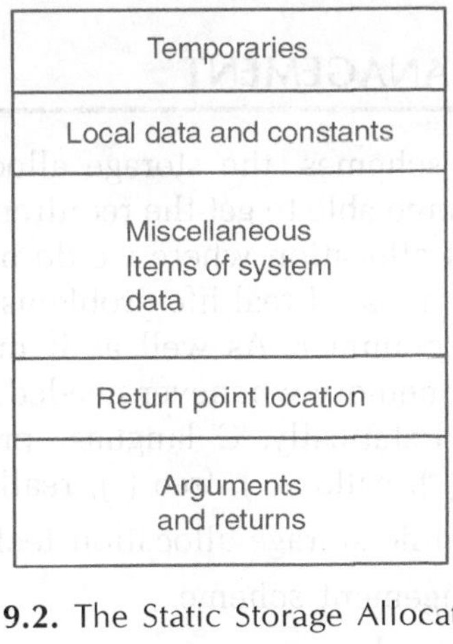

Fig 9.2. The Static Storage Allocation.

for code segments of user and system programs is allocated statically. It means allocation is done at translation or compile time and it remains fixed during execution. Static allocation includes storage for temporaries, local data and constant, miscellaneous items of system data, return point location etc.

The space for all programs and data can be allocated at compile time. In static allocation no runtime storage management software, so there is no concern for recovery and reuse.

Example of static storage management shows in language FORTRAN. In FORTRAN, all storage is allocated statically. Each subprogram is compiled separately with the compiler setting up the code segment containing the compiled program, its data areas, return point location, temporaries etc. During program execution no storage management needs take place.

Static storage allocation is efficient scheme because no space or time is required for storage management during runtime. The translator can generate the direct address for all data items because all allocation is done during compile time. It is not efficient for recursive subprogram calls and data structure whose size is not determined at compile time.

9.4.1. Advantages of Static Storage Management

There are various advantages of static storage management scheme:

1. It is easy to implement static allocation scheme.
2. All allocation is done at compile time. So it requires no runtime support.
3. Static storage allocation eliminates the possibility of running out memory or out of bounds.
4. The translator can generate the direct l-value addresses for all data items.
5. FORTRAN and COBOL language uses static storage management schemes.
6. Type checking is done at compile time.

9.4.2. Disadvantages of Static Storage Allocation Scheme

1. It does not support data structures whose size is not determined at compile time.
2. It is incompatible with recursive subprogram calls.
3. It does not support runtime storage management.

9.5. DYNAMIC STORAGE MANAGEMENT

In dynamic storage management schemes, the storage allocation is done at execution time. Dynamic storage management scheme able to get the requirement chunk of memory at runtime. This scheme is best suited type of allocation where we do not know the memory requirement in advance, which is the case with most of real life problems. In other words dynamic memory allocation gives flexibility for programmer. As well as it makes efficient use of memory, by allocating the required amount of memory whenever needed, unlike static allocation where we declare the amount to be allocated statically. 'C' language provide dynamic allocation and de-allocation functions: like malloc ( ), calloc ( ), free ( ), realloc ( ).

There are two kinds of dynamic storage allocation techniques.

(*i*) Stack based storage management scheme.

(*ii*) Heap storage management scheme.

9.5.1. Stack Based Storage Management Scheme

The simplest runtime storage management scheme is the stack based storage management. Storage is treated a large free sequential block of memory at the start of execution. When storage is allocated then it is taken from sequential location in the stack beginning at one end. When storage is freed is placed in reverse order and placed always on the stack top.

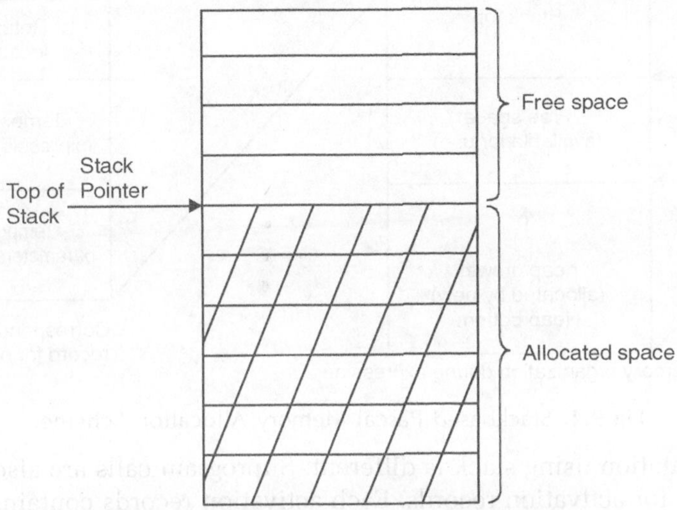

Fig 9.3. Stack Based Memory Management.

Stack based memory management is shown in figure 9.3. stack pointer always point to top of stack when storage is allocated. Stack pointer moves upward and when storage is freed then pointer moves downward. All free storage lies above the pointer and all allocated spaces are lies below the pointer. Freeing a block of storage automatically recovers the freed storage and makes it available for reuse. Because many of the program and data elements requiring storage are tied to subprogram activations, it is the strictly nested last in first out structure (LIFO) of subprogram calls and return in most languages. It stack storage management an appealing technique.

When a subprogram is called, a new activation record is created on the top of the stack, termination causes its deletion from the stack. Most pascal implementation uses single central stack of activation records of subprograms together with a statically allocated area containing system programs and subprogram code segment. The structure of pascal subprogram is shown in Fig. 9.4.

The activation record contains all the variable items of information associated with a given subprogram activation.

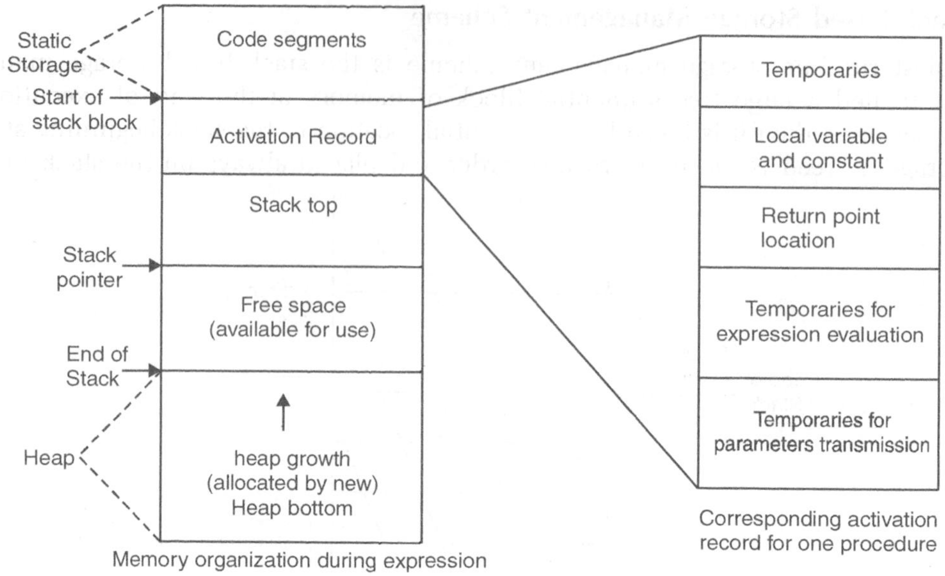

Fig 9.4. Stackbased Pascal Memory Allocation Scheme.

LISP implementation using stack is different. Suprogram calls are also strictly nested and a stack may be used for activation records. Each activation records contains a return point and temporaries for expression evaluation and parameter transmission. Local referencing environments might also be allocated in the same stack, except that the programmer is allowed to directly manipulate these association. A typical LISP memory organization is shown in Fig. 9.5.

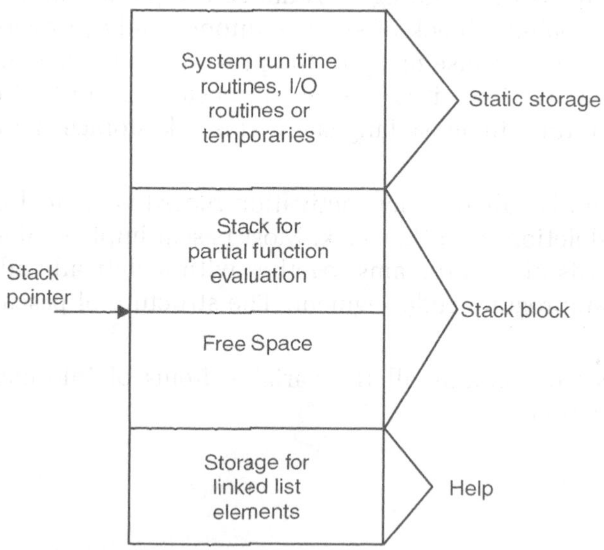

Fig 9.5. LISP Stack Based Memory Organization.

LISP implementation requires also a heap storage area, which is managed through a free space list and garbage collection, with a special area and storage manager for full word data items such as numbers.

Stack-based storage management is the most widely used technique for runtime storage management. It provides clean and efficient support for nested subprogram and recursion. Stack follows order of activation last in first out (LIFO) rule in that subprogram call pushes stack frame and sub-program exit pop out stack frame. The use of a stack of subprogram activation records in characteristic of implementation of every language. How stack storage is divided into an area allocated statically, area allocated as stack and an area allocated to heap is different in different languages. So stack based implementation scheme is the most widely used technique for runtime storage management.

9.5.2. Heap Storage Management Scheme

Heap management can be a very complex runtime process. Heap contains values that are dynamically allocated and structured while the program is running, such as strings, dynamic arrays, object and various dynamic data structure like linked lists. The heap becames fragmented as it is used for the dynamic allocation and deallocation of storage blocks of different sizes. So many languages use garbage collection algorithms to manage heap memory so that the available space is efficiently utilized.

A heap is a block of storage within which pieces are allocated and freed in some relatively unstructured manner. Here the problems of storage allocation, recovering, compaction and reuse may be severe.

The need for heap storage arises because every languages requires storage to be allocated and freed at arbitrary points during program execution. A language allows creation, destruction or extension of programmer data structures at arbitrary program points. For example, In LISP a new element may be added to an existing list structure at any point, again requiring storage to be allocated.

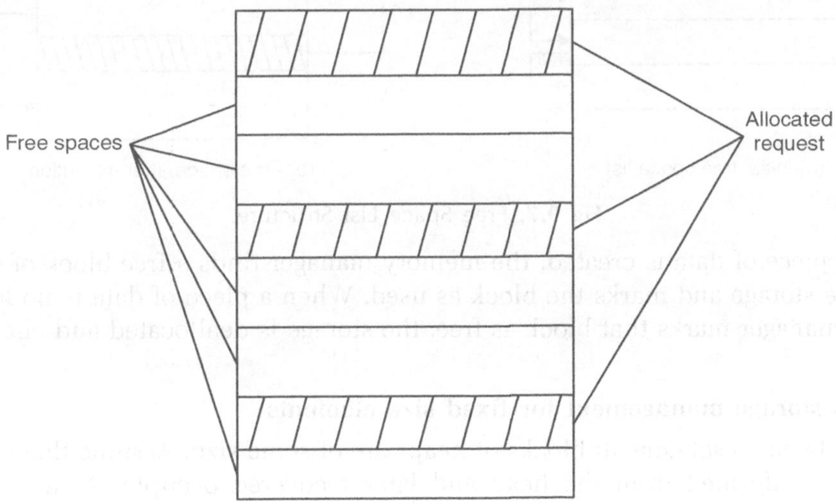

Fig 9.6. Heap Storage Management.

We can examine the process in two separate situations: one in which all heap storage is allocated and deallocated in units of a single size, and one in which variable size segments are allocated and deallocated.

There are two categories of heap storage management technique depended on size:

1. Fixed Size Elements
2. Variable Size Elements.

These categories are made according to the size of block whether block of heaps are fixed sizes or variable sizes. The heap storage management is required in the following situation.

1. The data whose size is vary as program is running.
2. The storage is allocated and freed at arbitrary points during program execution.
3. Allocation and deallocation is in a non-nested fashion.
4. We can not determine the size of data structure at runtime.

Initially all blocks of heap are free means there is no block is filled. The heap is maintained as a list of free space called free space list. The first word of each item on the free list points to the first word of the next item on the free list as shown below.

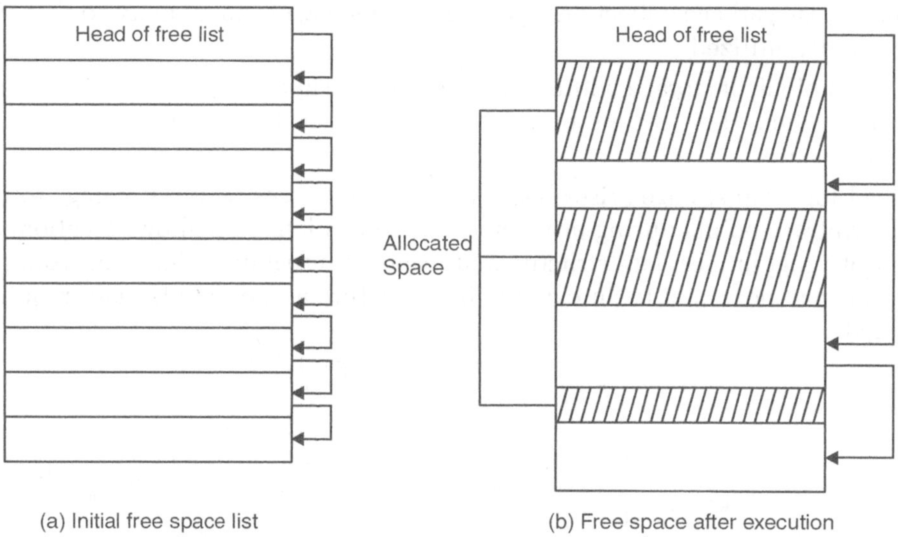

Fig 9.7. Free Space List Structure.

When a piece of data is created, the memory manager finds a free block of sufficient size to allocate the storage and marks the block as used. When a piece of data is no longer needed, the memory manager marks that block as free, the storage is deallocated and changing the free space list.

9.5.2.1. Heap storage management for fixed size elements

In fixed size elements scheme all blocks of heaps are of some size. Assume that each fixed size element that is allocated from the heap and later recovered occupies N words of memory. Where N might be any number. Assuming the heap occupies a contiguous block of memory.

We divide the heap block into a sequence of K elements and each of them having N words long, such that K × N is the size of heap. Whenever an element requires storage, one of these block is allocated from the heap and whenever an element is freed, it must return back to free space list.

In fixed size allocation, all available blocks are linked together using the pointers in the blocks, forming a list of available space. Allocation is a simple matter of taking the required number of blocks from this list when they are needed. Deallocation is much more complex process.

Recovery: Recovery means collect the free space and return to free space list. Return of newly freed storage to the free space list is simple, provided such storage may be identified and recovered. But identification and recovery may be quite difficult. The problem is to determine which elements in the heap are available for reuse and therefore may be returned to the free space list. There are three solution for identifications:

(*i*) Explicit return by programmer or system.

(*ii*) Reference counter or Reference counting.

(*iii*) Garbage collection method.

(*i*) **Explicit return by programmer or system:** It is one of the simplest scheme that are used for recovery. According to this scheme when an element has been is use become available for reuse, it must be identified explicitly as free and returned to free space list. System routine is responsible for returning space as it become available for reuse. Different languages use different functions for this like Dispose used in Pascal; free used in 'C' and delete used in C++. Explicit return by programmer or system is a simplest method because system identifies the free spaces and system recovers the free spaces for reuse.

It is a simple recovery technique for heap storage, but there are some problems with explicit return by programmer or system.

(*a*) **Garbage collection:** Garbage collection is a problem in memory management. It occurs when all access paths to a data object are destroyed but the data object continues to exist, the data object is said to be garbage. A garbage element is one that is available for reuse but not on the free space list and thus it has become in accessible. Garbage in any block of heap memory that cannot be accessed by the program. There is no pointer accessible to the program whose value reference that block. If garbage accumulates, available storage is gradually reduced until the program may be unable to continue for lack of known free space. The explicit return of heap storage facilitates creating garbage.

(*b*) **Dangling references:** A dangling reference is an access path that continues to exist after the life time of the associated data object. In this case structure of object is destroyed and remaining access paths becomes dangling references.

In the context of storage management, a dangling reference is a pointer to an element that has been returned to the free space list. If a program attempt to modify through a dangling reference a structure that has already been freed, the content of an element on the free-space list may be modified in advertently. It may be difficult for the runtime system to avoid creating garbage or dangling references. Dangling reference may compromise the integrity of the entire runtime structure during execution.

These problem with explict return some other approaches are there. One is called reference counts requires explicit return but provides a way of checking the number of pointers to a given element so that no dangling reference are created. Another approach, garbage collection is to allow garbage to be created but no dangling references.

(*ii*) **Reference counter:** The reference counter method of storage reclamation accomplishes its goal by maintaining a counter in every cell, which stores the number of pointers that are currently pointing to the cell. Embedded in the decrement operation for the reference counters, which occurs when a pointer is disconnected from the cell, is a check for a zero value. If the reference counter reaches to zero, it means that no program pointers are pointing at the cell, and it has thus become garbage and can be returned to the list of available space. Consider the following example heap in which each node is reference count (RC) is shown as an integer inside a dotted line. At this moment there are four nodes and three are active and the free-list contains all other nodes in the heap that are available for future use. Thus, three nodes are directly or indirectly accessible from p or q.

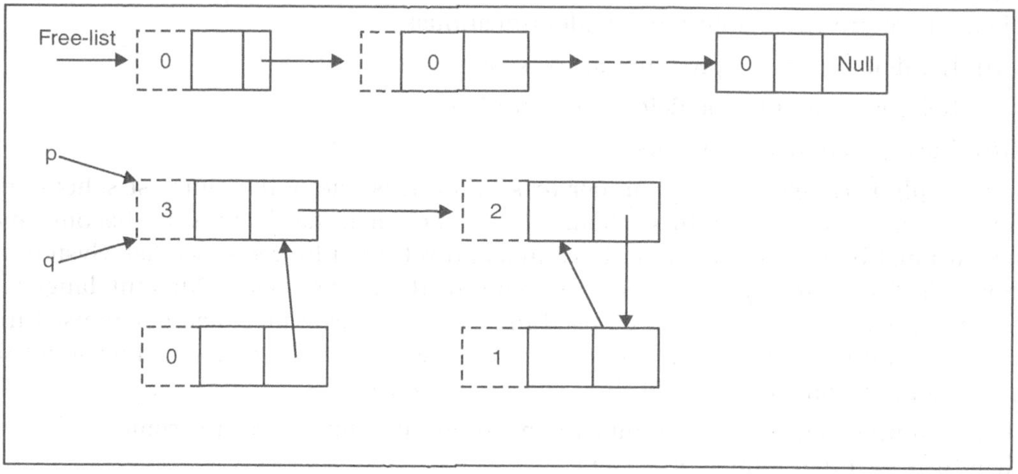

Fig 9.8. Example Heap for Reference Counting.

The reference counting algorithm is applied dynamically, that is whenever a new or delete operation occurs on a pointer, the algorithm is activated and as many orphans as possible are returned to the free-list. In this scheme, an orphan is simply a node whose reference count become zero, or any of its descendents whose reference count become zero as a result of a delete operation.

When a new operation occurs in the program, the algorithm allocates a heap node from the free-list are initializes its reference count to 1. Whenever a pointer assignment occurs in the program such as

$q = p;$

Some book-keeping on the reference counts must be done:

1. The reference count for p's node is increased by 1.
2. The reference count for q's node is decremented by 1.
3. If the reference count for q's node becomes 0, the reference count for each of its descendents is decreased by 1, q's node is returned to the free-list and this step is repeated for each of q's node's is descendents.
4. The pointer q is assigned the value of p.

When a delete q operation occurs, step 3 in the above algoritm is applied and q's node returned to the free-list.

The advantage of reference counter method is that it occurs dynamically, whenever pointer assignment or other heap action is triggered by the program.

There are three distinct problems with the reference counter method. First, if storage cells are relatively small, the space required for the counter is significant. Second, some execution time is obviously required to maintain the counter values. Every time a pointer value is changed, the cell to which it was pointed must have its counter decremented and the cell to which it is now pointing is incremented. Third, complication arise when a collection of cells is connected circularly.

(*iii*) **Garbage collection:** The primary alternative to reference counter is called garbage collection. With this method, the runtime system allocates storage cells as requested and disconnects pointers from cells as necessary, without regards for storage reclamation, until it has allocated all available cells. At this point a garbage collection process is begun to gather all the garbage left floating around in the heap. To facilitate the garbage collection process, every heap cell has an extra indicator bit or field that is used by the collection algorithm.

The term garbage collection refers to any strategy for reclamation of unused heap blocks for later use by the program. Several garbage collection algorithm have been used more or less successfully over the last 40 years. The first language that needed garbage collection were the functional languages, since their runtime activities were dominated by the need to dynamically create, destroy and change the structure of linked lists. The main garbage collection algorithms in use today are derived from those of the functional languages. The basic philiosphy behind garbage collection is simply to allow garbage to be generated in order to avoid dangling references. When the free space list is entirely exhausted and more storage is needed, the computation is suspended temporarily and an extraordinary procedure instituted, a garbage collection, which identifier garbage elements in the heap and returns them to the free space list.

Two stages are involved in garbage collection:

1. **Mark:** In this stage each element in the heap which is active, *i.e.*, which is part of an accessible data structure, must be marked. Every element must contain a garbage collection bit set initially to "on". The marking algorithm sets the garbage collection bit of each active element "off".
2. **Sweep:** When the marking algorithm has marked active elements, all those remaining whose garbage collection bit are "on" are garbage and they must be returned to the free space list. Then a simple scan procedure applies. This procedure checked the bit of each element during scan procedure. If "off" it leaves the element and if it is "on" then it is sent to free space list. All garbage collection bits are reset to 'on' during the scan. The marking part of the garbage collection is most difficult process. The free space list is exhausted when garbage collection is initiated, each element in the heap is either active on garbage. Inspection of an element can not indicate its status because there is nothing intrinsic to a garbage element to indicate that it is no longer accessible from other active element.

The mark and sweep algorithms makes two passes on the heap. It is invoked whenever a new node is requested by the program and heap is full. Thus, when the assignment on the left is executed, the meaning on the right is implied.

```
P = new node ( );
    If (free list = = Null)
Call Mark ( ) & sweep ( );
If (Free list ! = Null)
   { P = free list;
Free List = Free list. Next;
}
Else abort ('Heap full')
```

Here, the final else class reflect the event that garbage collection fails to find any block for free list which abort the program.

During pass 1, the 'mark' pass, every heap block that can be reached by following a chain of pointers originating in the runtime stack is marked as accessible. That is all references R in the runtime stack to heap addresses causes the following function to be invoked:

```
Mark (R):  If (R. MB = = 0)
           R.MB = 1
           If (R.next ! = Null)
           Mark (R. next);
```

If all blocks are remain unmarked *i.e.*, (MB = 0) in this are identified as orphans.

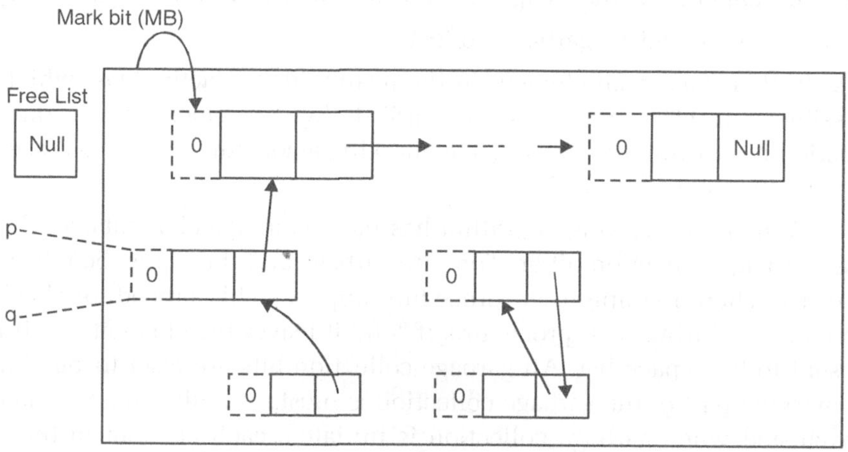

Fig 9.9. Example for Mark & Sweep Algorithm.

After Mark Algorithm, Pass 1 would leave the heap in the configuration shown in Fig. 9.10.

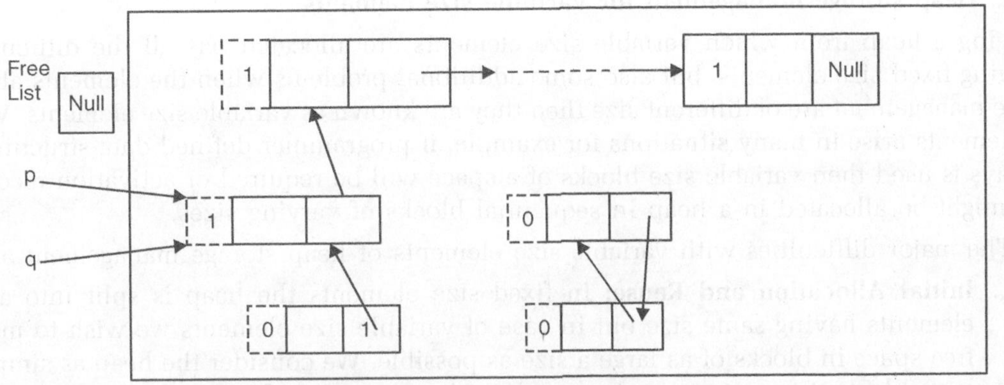

Fig 9.10. After Pass 1 of Mark.

After this sweep algorithm traverses the entire heap, returning all unmarked nodes to the free list and unmarking all blocks that had been marked in Pass 1.

```
Sweep ( ); i = j;
        While (i < = n) {
            if (i.MB = = 0)
            free (i)
        else i.MB = 0;
        i = i + 1
        }
```

The function free (N) restore the node referenced by N to the free list.

Free (N) :   N. Next = Free List;

Free List = N

The result of sweep process is shown in Fig. 9.11.

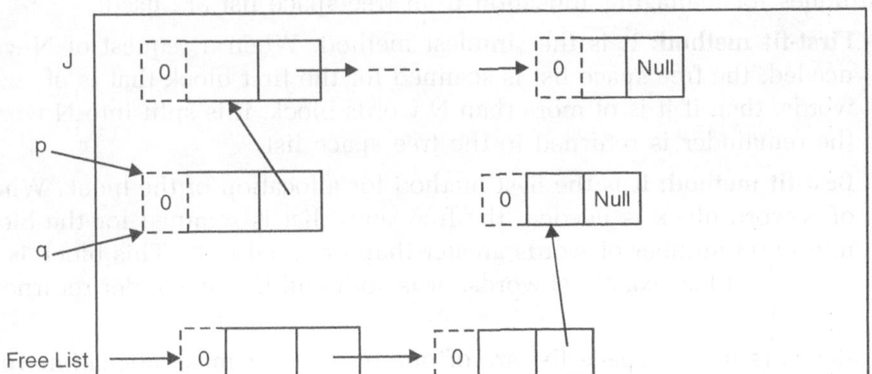

Fig 9.11. Heap After Sweep Process.

So by mark and sweep process we can identified the free block and returned them to free space list.

9.5.2.2. Heap storage management for variable size elements

Managing a heap from which variable size elements are allocated has all the difficulties of managing fixed size elements, but also some additional problems when the elements allocated storage management are of different size then they are known as variable size elements. Variable size elements arise in many situations for example, if programmer defined data structure such as arrays is used then variable size blocks of a space will be required or activation records for tasks might be allocated in a heap in sequential blocks of varying sizes.

The major difficulties with variable size elements of heap storage management are:

1. **Initial Allocation and Reuse:** In fixed size elements the heap is split into a set of elements having same size but in case of variable size elements we wish to maintain free space in blocks of as large a size as possible. We consider the heap as simply one large block of free storage a heap pointer is appropriate for initial allocation. When a block of N words is requested, the heap pointer is advanced by N and the original heap pointer value returned as a pointer to the newly allocated element. As storage is freed behind the advancing heap pointer, it may be collected into a free space list. When the heap pointer reaches to the end of the heap block. Some of the free space block in the heap must now be reused. There are two possibilities for reuse.
   - (*i*) When a block is requested for memory. Then search the free space list for an appropriate size block and returning any left over space to the free list after the allocation.
   - (*ii*) Then we collect the free spaces by compacting the space by moving all the active elements to one end of the heap, leaving the free space as a single block at the end and resetting the heap pointer to the beginning of this block.
2. **Reuse of Spaces from a free space List:** It is the simplest approach, when a request for an N-Word element is received. Then scan five free space list for a block of N or more elements. A block of N words can be allocated directly. A block of more than N words must be split into two blocks of an N word block, which is immediately allocated, and the remainder block, which is returned to the free space list. A number of particular techniques for managing allocation from free space list are used:
   - (*i*) **First-fit method:** It is the simplest method. When a request of N-word block is needed, the free space list is scanned for the first block that is of size N or more words, then if it is of more than N words block, it is split into N word block and the remainder is returned to the free space list.
   - (*ii*) **Best-fit method:** It is the best method for allocation of the block. When a request of N-word block is needed, the free space list is scanned for the block with the minimum number of words greater than or equal to N. This block is allocated as a unit. If it has exactly N words, or is split and the remainder returned to the free space list.

   If elements in free space list are of ordered size, it make allocation very easy and efficient because to find the appropriate size is very easy by scanning.
3. **Recovery with variable size blocks:** There are different techniques for recovery when variable size blocks are involved. Explicit return is one of the simplest method but there are problems of dangling references and garbage. Reference count may be used in the ordinary manner. Here garbage collection is a feasible technique. But some additional problems arise with variable size blocks. Garbage collection proceeds as

with fixed size elements. It contains a marking phase followed by a collecting phase. Marking must be based on the same pointer chain technique. The difficulty here is collecting the free spaces. There will be a simple sequential scan of memory that check the garbage collection bit. If the bit was 'on' it returned to free space list and if it was 'off', it was still active and leave it.

The simple method added to garbage collection bit is length indicator, it specify the length of the block. So by length indicates length of each block is maintained. This makes, a sequential scan of memory possible, looking only at the first word of each block. During this scan, adjacent free blocks may also be compacted into a single block before returning to the free space list. This eliminates the partial compaction problem that will be discussed next.

4. **Memory fragmentation problem:** The main problem with heap storage management system using variable size elements faces is that of memory fragmentation. We have a large block of free space when a request comes then this block is fragmented into smaller pieces through allocation, recovery and reuse. If only the simple first-fit or best-fit allocation technique is used, it is apparent that free space blocks continue to split into ever smaller pieces. So a storage reaches when a block of N words comes and there is no sufficiently large block exist. There are two types of fragmentations:

External fragmentation: When processes are loaded and removed from memory, the free memory space is broken into little pieces. External fragmentation exists when enough total memory space exists to satisfy a request, but it is not contiguous; storage is fragmented into a large number of small holes.

Consider there are two block of memory having size 260 K and 300 K, a total of 560 K. and a request comes for a block of 500 k. These two blocks does not satisfy this request because these two blocks are fragmented. If they are combined then this satisfy the need. So it is of no use. This problem is known as External fragmentation. One solution to this problem is compaction.

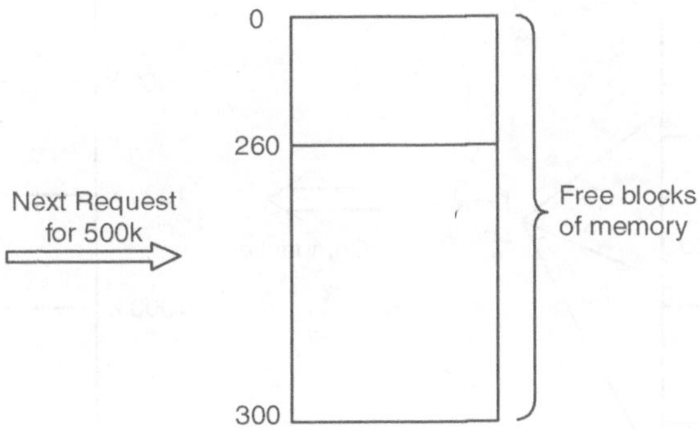

Fig 9.12. Memory Allocation.

Internal fragmentation: Another problem that arises with the multiple partition allocation scheme as shown in Fig. 9.13. Consider the hole of 18464 bytes. Suppose that the next process request 18462 bytes. If we allocate request block, we are left with a hole of 2 bytes. The overhead is keep track of this hole will be substantially larger than the hole itself. Then general approach is to allocate very small holes as part of the larger request. Thus, the allocated memory may be slighty larger than the requested memory. The difference between these two numbers is internal fragmentation memory that is internal to a partition, but is not being used.

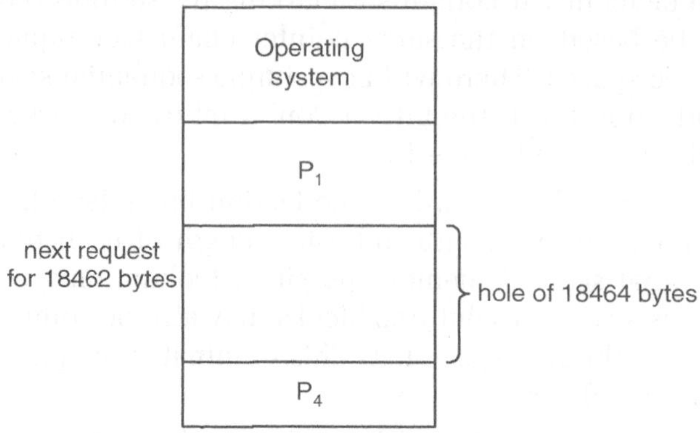

Fig 9.13. Internal Fragmentation Problem.

5. **Compaction:** Solution to fragmentation problem is campaction. The process of compaction refers to construct large blocks of the free storage from the small blocks by merging them together. Depending on whether active blocks within the heap may be shifted in position, one of two approaches to compaction is possible:
   (*i*) **Partial compaction:** If active blocks cannot be shifted then only adjacent free block on the free space list may be compacted. It is too expansive to shift the active block.
   (*ii*) **Full compaction:** If active blocks can be shifted, then all active blocks may be shifted to one end of the heap, leaving all free space at the other in a contiguous block. It requires that when an active is shifted, all pointer to that block will be modified to point the new location.

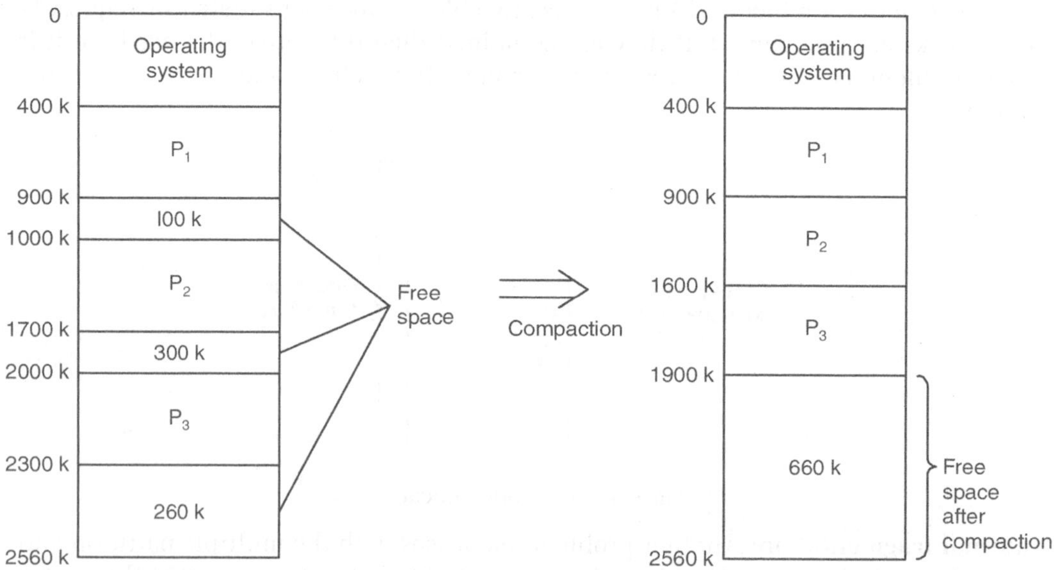

Fig 9.14. Compaction.

When compaction is possible, we must determine its cost. Swapping can also be combined with compaction.

Some Important Terms

- Storage management is a key area in the study of programming languages.
- The storage management is the art and the process of coordinating and controlling the use of memory by different data objects.
- Major runtime elements are those elements that requires storage during execution time.
- There are different type of elements that requiring storage during runtime:
  - Storage for code segments for translated programs.
  - Runtime system programs.
  - Temporaries in parameter transmission.
  - Subprogram return points and coroutines resume points.
  - Different referencing environments.
  - Temporaries storage during expression evaluation.
  - Miscellaneous system data.
  - Input-output buffers.
  - User defined data structures and constants.
  - Subprogram call and return operations.
  - Data structure creation and destruction operation.
  - Component insertion and deletion operation.
- Storage management is either controlled by programmer or system controlled.
- Storage management phases are:
  - Initial Allocation
  - Recovery
  - Compaction and Reuse
- In static storage management, storage for code segments of user and system programs is allocated statically.
- In dynamic storage management schemes, the storage allocation is done at execution time.
- Two kinds of dynamic storage allocation techniques.
  - Stack based storage management scheme.
  - Heap storage management scheme.
- Stack based memory management scheme is based on last in first out strategy of allocation and free of blocks.
- Heap contains values that are dynamically allocated and structured while the program is running, such as strings, dynamic arrays, object and various dynamic data structure like linked lists.
- A Heap is a block of storage with in which pieces are allocated and freed in some relatively unstructured manner.

- In heap management, problems of storage allocation, recovery, compaction and reuse may be severe.
- There are two categories of heap storage management technique depended on size:
  - Fixed size elements.
  - Variable size elements.
- If the size of block of heaps are of fixed size then it is called fixed size elements heap.
- If the size of block of heap are of variable size then it is called variable size element heap.
- Recovery means collect the free space and return to free space list.
- Free space list is a list of free elements after recovery the element is returned to free space list.
- Reference counter maintaining a counter in every cell, which stores the number of pointers that are currently pointing to the cell.
- The term garbage collection refers to any strategy for reclamation of unused heap blocks for later use by the program.
- Two stages are involved in garbage collection
  - Mark
  - Sweep
- The major difficulties with variable size elements of heap storage management are:
  - Initial allocation and Reuse.
  - Reuse of spaces from a free space list.
  - Recovery with variable size blocks.
  - Memory fragmentation problem.
  - Compaction.
- Memory fragmentations are of two types:
  - External fragmentation
  - Internal fragmentation
- Compaction refers to construct large block of the free storage from the small blocks by merging them together.
- Compaction is of two types:
  - Partial compaction
  - Full compaction.

Review Questions

1. What are the merits and demerits of programmer and system controlled storage management?
2. List the different data elements requiring storage during the program execution.
3. Explain the stack based storage management technique.

4. Explain the storage management phases in detail.
5. Explain the static storage management technique.
6. Define the term heap storage management. Explain the concept of heap storage management for fixed size and variable size elements in detail.
7. Write short notes on:
   (a) Garbage and dangling references.
   (b) Mark and sweep algorithm.
   (c) Fixed size and variable size elements.
   (d) Reference count.
8. What do you mean by fragmentation problem? Explain external and internal fragmentation problems.

❑❑❑

Chapter **10** # PROGRAMMING LANGUAGES

Like our natural languages, programming languages facilitate the expression and communication between people. However, programming languages differ from natural languages in two ways. First, programming languages also enables communication of ideas between people and computing machines. Second, programming languages have a narrower expressive domain than our natural languages. That is, they facilitate only the communication of computational ideas. Thus, a programming language must meet different requirements than a natural language. In the study of programming languages, we identify many similarities between programming languages and natural languages.

Programming languages are notations or symbols that are used for specifying, organizing and reasoning about computations. It is tool for instructing machines. It is a tool for controlling computerized devices. Programming language increases our capacity to use different constructs in writing programs, enables us to choose languages for projects were intelligently and makes learning new languages easier.

In chapter 1, we have studied language paradigm that consist of different type of programming languages like imperative, declarative, procedural, non-procedural, object-based languages, block structured, logic, functional and data-base languages. Now, we discussed different types of programming languages in this chapter in detail. In chapter 1, we just give an overview of different programming languages. Now we discuss is detail the different type of programming languages. We discuss, a paradigm as a collection of abstract features that categorize a group of languages which are accepted and used by a group of professionals. Now, we discuss different type of programming languages.

10.1. IMPERATIVE PROGRAMMING

Imperative programming is the oldest and well developed programming paradigm. It emerged with the first computers in the 1940s, and its elements directly mirror the architectural characteristics of modern computers as well. In the mid 1940s, John Von Neumann and other recognized that both a program and its data could reside in the main memory of a computer, an idea implicit in Turing's earlier work. Early computers had stored their programs outside the computer's memory, typically using a wire plug board. The idea of storing a program in the computer's memory led to an enormous increase in the potential power and versatility of computers.

The architecture of the so-called Von Neuman-Eckert model is the basis for the imperative programming paradigm. The machine's memory contains both program instructions and data values. At the heart of this architecture is the idea of assignment changing the value of a memory location and destroying its previous value. All imperative languages include assignment as a central element. In addition, they support variable declarations, expressions, conditional statements, loops and procedural abstraction.

Declaration assign names to memory locations and associate types with stored values. Expressions are interpreted by retrieving the current values of the named variables from their respective memory locations and computing a result from those values. Given any reference to a variable *x*, the memory returning the current value in the location associated with *x*. Commands are normally executed in the order they appear in the memory, while conditional and unconditional branching statements can interrupt this normal flow executions.

An imperative language is said to be Turing complete is it provides an effective basis for implementing any algorithm that can be designed. Imperative languages containing integer variables and values, basic arithmetic operations, assignment statements, memory-based statement sequencing, conditionals and branching statements are turing complete.

An imperative programming language is thus one which is turing complete and also supports certain common features that have emerged with the evolution of the imperative programming paradigm:

- Control structures
- Exception and error handling
- Input/output
- Procedural abstraction
- Assignment and Expressions.
- Library support for data structures.

The first three of these features have been discussed in earlier chapters. The remaining three we will discussed below.

Procedural abstraction: The process of procedural abstraction allows the programmer to be concerned mainly with the interface between the function and what it computes ignoring the details of how the computation is accomplished.

A systematic way of producing a program is called stepwise refinement. The programmer starts with a description of the function computed by a program, together with its input and output and then systematically breaks the function down into a collection of more primitive functions using sequencing iteration and selection.

The process of stepwise refinement utilizes procedural abstraction by developing an algorithm from its most general form into a specific implementation.

Assignment and expression: Assignment statement is the fundamental concept of all imperative languages. It has general form

Target = expression.

There are variety of assignment operator symbols; the most popular of these are '=' used in Fortran and ":=" used in Algol. The semantics of an assignment are simple. The expression is evaluated a value which is then copied to the target. That is, most imperative language use copy semantics. In addition, imperative languages provide libraries of standard functions that can perform various computations during the evaluation of an expression. It is also important to examine language dependent libraries that facilitate the organization of data into flexible arrays, stacks, queues, graphs, hash tables and other useful forms.

Library support for data structures: The fundamental data structures in imperative languages are arrays and record structures. Modern languages have extensive libraries of functions that facilitate the development of complex applications. Programmers rely on these libraries to avoid reinventing the wheel every time a common function or data structure is needed by an application. Library has the following major parts:

1. A collection of I/o functions,
2. A collection of function for defining and manipulating data structures,
3. A string class,

4. A framework for fitting the program to an execution environment.
5. A complex number class,
6. Exception handling functions,
7. Memory allocation and deallocation functions,
8. A class optimized for matrix arithmetic.

Programmers who prefer an imperative style over an object-oriented style can easily exploit the functionality provided by the standard C++ Library.

The following list summarizes the main elements provided by the standard C++ library:

- Iterators.
- Vectors
- Stack, queques and priority queues.
- Lists
- Sets and multisets.
- Maps
- Graphs
- Strings
- Generics
- Overloading

The following list summarizes some of the major functions that can be used to manipulate these data structures:

- Inserting and Removing elements from vectors, lists and maps.
- Subscripting a vector.
- Change the size of vectors and lists.
- Vector, list, set, map, graph and string searching.
- Vector and list sorting.
- Stack and Queue operations.
- Graph functions like shortest paths etc.
- String functions like substring, insertion etc.
- Arithmetic, comparison, and I/o functions for complex numbers.

10.2. PROCEDURAL LANGUAGES

Procedure-oriented programming basically consists of writing a list of instructions or actions for the computer to follow and organizing these instructions into groups known as function. Procedural languages are command driven or statement-oriented language. Conventional programming, using high-level languages such as COBOL, FORTRAN and C, is commonly known as procedure-oriented programming (POP). In the procedure-oriented approach, the problems is viewed as a sequence of things to be done such as reading, calculating and printing. A number of functions are written to accomplish these tasks. The primary focus is on functions. A typical program structure for procedural programming is shown in Fig. 10.1.

The technique of hierarchical decomposition has been used to specify the tasks to be completed for solving a problem.

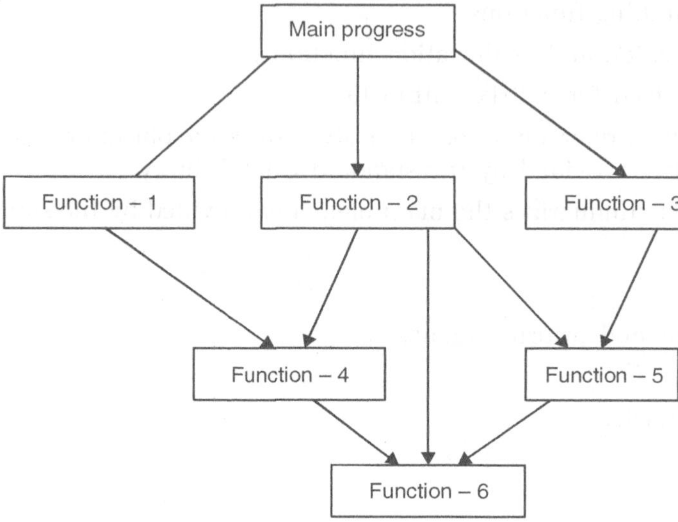

Fig 10.1. Typical Structure of Procedure-Oriented Programs.

We normally use a flow chart to organize these actions and represent the flow of control from one action to another. In a multi-function program, many important data items are placed as global so that they may be accessed by all functions. Each functions may have its own local data. Figure 10.2 shows the relationship of data and functions in a procedure-oriented program.

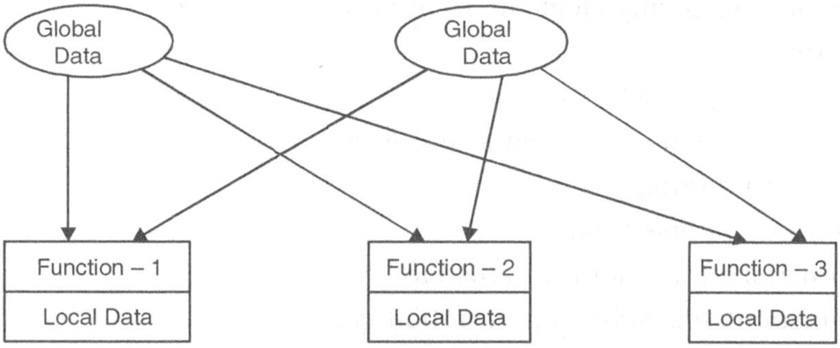

Fig 10.2. Relationship of Global Data and Functions in Procedural Programming.

Global data are more vulnerable to an inadvertent change by a function. In a large program it is very difficult to identify what data is used by which function. In case we need to revise an external data structure, we also need to revise all functions that access the data. This provides an opportunity for bugs to creep in.

The process of procedural abstraction allows the programmer to be concerned mainly with the interface between the function and what it computes, ignoring the details of how the computation is accomplished. C, FORTRAN and COBOL are the procedural languages. It is very difficult to define user-defined data types. It only supports built in data types. It has limited set of control structures of data is not supported well. User defined data types are created in object-oriented programming like C++. Some important characteristics of procedural languages are:

1. Emphasis is on-doing thing *i.e.*, building algorithm.
2. Large programs are divided into smaller program known as functions.
3. Most of the functions share global data.
4. Data move freely from one function to another.
5. Function changes the data from one form to another.
6. It employs top-down approach in program design.

10.3. NON-PROCEDURAL LANGUAGES

The non-procedural languages are fact oriented. Programs in such languages do not state exactly how a result is to be computed but rather describe the form of the result. The difference is that we assume the computer system can some how determine how the result is to be gotten. What is needed to provide this capability for logic programming languages is a concise means of supplying the computer with both the relevant information and a method of inference for computing desirable results.

Non-procedural languages are basically declarative programming languages. These are used in RDBMS, Expert Systems, natural language processing and education. Example of non-procedural languages are prolog, Sql etc. It is simpler than procedural languages. In non-procedural languages there is no procedure is defined which specifies what is to be done and how a result is to be computed.

An example commonly used to illustrate the difference between procedural and non-procedural systems is the process of rearraying a list of data into some particular order, otherwise known as sorting. In a language like C++, sorting is done by explaining in C++ program all of the details of some sorting algorithm to a computer that has a C++ compiler. The computer, after translating the C++ program into machine code or some interpretive intermediate code, follows the instructions and produces the sorted list.

In a non-procedural languages, it is necessary only to describe the characteristics of the sorted list. It is some permutation of the given list such that for each pair of adjacent elements, a given relationship holds between the two elements. To state this formally: Suppose the list to be sorted is in an array named list that has a subscript range 1 ... n. The concept of sorting the element of the given list, named old_list, and placing them in a separate array, named new list, can then be expressed as follows: Sort (Old-list, new-list) $\subset$ permute (old_list, new_list) $\cap$ sorted (new-list) sorted (list) $\subset \forall$; such that $1 \leq j < n$, list $(j) \leq$ list $(j + 1)$.

Where permute is a predicate that returns true if its second parameter array is a permutation of its first parameter array. From this description, the non-procedural language system could produce the sorted list. That makes non-procedural programming sound like the mere production of concise software requirements specifications, which is a fair assessment. Unfortunately, however, it is not that simple.

10.4. STRUCTURED PROGRAMMING LANGUAGES

The goto statement controversy began with a letter to the editor of the communications of the ACM from Edsger Dijkstra, entitled "Go To considered Harmful" with that letter, the structured programming revolution was launched.

In general structured programming was all about designing programs from first principles, using only three basic control structures the sequence, the conditional, and the while loop. In particular, structured programming advocated a ban on the use of any form of goto statement, since it was unnecessary and it encouraged writing incomprehensible code.

A program is structured is the flow of control through the program is evident from the syntactic structure of the program text. This term is used for program design that enphasizes:

1. Hierarchical design of program structures using only the simple control forms of composition, alternation and iteration.
2. Single-entry-single exit program structure.
3. Representation of the hierarchical design directly in the program text, using the structured control statements.
4. Avoiding the use of goto statement.
5. In program text, the textual sequence of statements corresponds to the execution sequence.
6. Use of single purpose groups of statement, even if it must be copied.
7. When a program is written according to structured programming design then it usually is much easier to understand, debug, verify to be correct and later modify and reverify.

Older languages such as COBOL and FORTRAN contain. Some one-in, one-out control statements but still rely on goto statements and statement labels. Both languages have been difficult to adopt to modern language concepts. The example of structured programming languages includes pascal, C and Ada etc. Structured languages is designed for programmer flexibility than absolute runtime performance. These structured languages are much more complex than procedural languages.

Overall the structured programming revolution was a success. Programmers abandoned the unrestricted goto statement in favour of explicit looping and conditional constructs. It is extremely rare today to see an unconditional goto statement, although it use if still occasionally defended. While structured programming as a design methodology lies firmly within the imperative programming paradigm, its utility is less obvious in the object oriented world.

10.5. OBJECT-ORIENTED PROGRAMMING LANGUAGES

The concept of object-oriented programming has its roots in SIMULA 67 but was not fully developed until the evolution of smalltalk resulted in producing smalltalk 80. Some consider smalltalk to be the only purely object-oriented programming language. A language that is object oriented must provide support for three key language features: abstract data types, inheritance and a particular kind of dynamic binding.

The major motivating factor in the invention of object-oriented approach is to remove some of the flaws that are encountered in the procedural approach. Object-oriented programming treats data as a critical element in the program development and does not allow it to move freely around the system. It ties data more closely to the functions that operate on it , and protects it from accidental modifications from outside function. Object-oriented programming allow decomposition of a problem into a number of entities called objects and then builds data and functions around these objects. The organization of data and functions in object-oriented programing is shown in Fig 10.3. The data of an object can be accessed only by the functions associated with that object. However, functions of one object can access the functions of other objects.

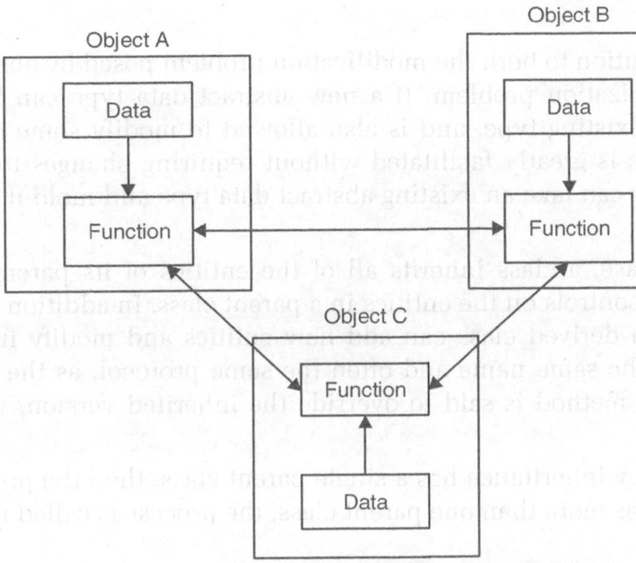

Fig 10.3. Organization of Data and Functions in OOP.

Some of main features of object-oriented programming are:

- Emphasis is on data rather than procedure.
- Programs are divided into what are known as objects.
- Data structures are designed such that they characterize the objects.
- Functions that operate on the data of an object are tied together in the data structure.
- Data is hidden and cannot be accessed by external functions.
- Objects may communicate with each other through functions.
- New data and functions can be easily added when ever necessary.
- It follows bottom up approach in program design.

We define object-oriented programming as an approach that provides a way of modularizing programs by creating partitioned memory area for both data and functions that can be used as templates for creating copies of such modules on demand.

10.5.1. Abstract Data Types

Data abstraction extends the notion of type by providing the programmer with an encapsulation mechanism for defining new data types that are close to the application at hand.

Encapsulation is a mechanism which allows logically related constants, types, variables, methods and so on, to be grouped into a new entity. Example include procedures, packages and classes.

By utilizing this mechanism, the program can limit the scope and visibility of the data values and encapsulated functions for this newly defined data type. Thus, we have the notion of an abstract data type. The key goal of data abstraction is to package the data type and its functions together in a single module so that the functions provide a public interface to the type.

10.5.2. Inheritance

Inheritance offers a solution to both the modification problem posed by abstract data type reuse and the program organization problem. If a new abstract data type can inherit the data and functionality of some existing type, and is also allowed to modify some of those entities and add new entities, reuse is greatly facilitated without requiring changes to the reused abstract data type. Programmers can take an existing abstract data type and mold it to fit a new problem requirement.

In the simplest case, a class inherits all of the entities of its parent class. This can be complicated by access controls on the entities in a parent class. In addition to inheriting entities from its parent class, a derived class can add new entities and modify inherited methods. A modified method has the same name and often the same protocol, as the one of which it is a modification. The new method is said to override the inherited version, which is then called an overriden method.

If a class created by inheritance has a single parent class, then the process is called single inheritance. If a class has more than one parent class, the process is called multiple inheritance.

10.5.3. Polymorphism and Dynamic Binding

Another characteristic of object-oriented programming language is a kind of polymorphism provided by the dynamic binding of messages to method definitions. The term polymorphic means "having many forms".

In object-oriented languages polymorphism refers to the late binding of a call to one of several different implementations of a method in an inheritance hierarchy such methods must be instance methods.

Polymorphism provided by dynamic binding is supported by allowing one to define polymorphic variables of the type of the parent class that are also able to reference objects to any of the subclasses of that class. The parent class can define a method that is overriden by its subclasses. The operations defined by these methods are similar, but must be customized for each class in the hierarchy. When such a method is called through the polymorphic variable, that call is bound to the method in the proper class dynamically. One purpose of this dynamic binding is to allow software system to be more easily extended during both development and maintenance. Such programs can be written to perform operations on generic class objects. These operations are generic in that they can apply to objects of any class related through derivation from the same base class. The essence of object-oriented programming is solving problems by identifying the real world objects of the problem and the processing required of those objects, and then creating simulations of those objects, their processes and the required communication between the objects.

10.5.4. Design Issues for Object-oriented Languages

There are various design issues that must be considered when designing the programming language feature to support inheritance and dynamic binding. These issues are discussed below:

1. **The concept of objects:** In object-oriented language, everything is based on object. From the smallest integer to a complete software system all is based on objects. The

concept of objects provides the pure uniformity of the language and its use. This has some disadvantage that simple operations must be done through the message passing process. This can slower the processing of operations as compared to imperative model, where simple and fast machine instructions implement such simple operations.

In this model there are user defined and predefined classes. All classes are treated the same way and all computation is accomplished through message passing. One alternative to the exclusive use of objects that is common in imperative language to which support for object-oriented programming has been added is to retain a complete imperative typing model and simply add the object model. Another alternative to the exclusive use of objects is to have an imperative style structure for the primitive scalar types.

2. **Allocation and Deallocation of Objects:** In the allocation and deallocation of objects, there are two things, first is related from the place from where objects are allocated. They are allocated by the compiler, allocated as stack-dynamic objects from the runtime stack or explicitly created from the runtime stack or explicitly creating by heap with the operator or function such as new and delete use in C++. Second is related with the allocation of objects from heap. The question is whether deallocation is implicit or explicit. If it is implicit, some implicit method of storage reuse is required, such as reference counter or garbage collection that are discussed in chapter 9 under the heap storage management technique. If allocation is explicit then issues such as dangling reference on dangling pointer can be raised.

3. **Single and Multiple Inheritance:** The object-oriented paradigm supports code reuse through inheritance. Classes exist in an object-oriented language in a class hierarchy. A class can be declared as a subclass of another class, which is called the parent class or superclass.

   Inheritance comes into two varieties: single inheritance and multiple inheritance. C++ Python and Eiffel support mutiple inheritance whereas Java and smalltalk support only single inheritance.

   In single inheritance, the class hierarchy from a tree rooted in the most general class, for example, Object. A class D is a subclass of another class C when it extends or specializes the meaning of class C by adding new instance variables or methods, or by modifying the definitions of C's public and protected methods. A Java class definition uses the extends keyword to identify its superclass; if this keyword is omitted, the class is implicitly a subclass of the most general class object.

   In contrast to single inheritance languages, some object-oriented languages support multiple inheritance which allows a class to be a subclass of one or more superclasses. Under multiple inheritance, a class may inherit instance variables and methods from several distinct classes. Multiple inheritance has advantages and disadvantages. It facilitates code reuse by allowing a subclass to inherit features from several parent classes one disadvantage of multiple inheritance is that its semantics becomes very complicated in certain circumstances.

4. **Polymorphism and Type Checking:** In object-oriented languages polymorphism refers to the late binding of a call to one of several different implementations of a method in an inheritance hierarchy. Such methods must be instance methods. Polymorphism in the object-oriented realm is defined to be the use of a polymorphic pointer or reference to access a method whose name is overridden in the class hierarchy that

defines the object to which the pointer or reference is pointing. The polymorphic variable is the type of the parent class and the parent class defines at least the protocol of a method that is overridden by the derived classes. The polymorphic variable can reference objects of the parent class and derived classes, so the class of the object to which it points cannot always be statically determined. The binding of messages to methods that are sent through polymorphic variables must be dynamic. The issue here is when the type checking of this binding takes place.

There are two types of type checking that must be done between a message and a method in a strongly typed language: the message's parameter types must be checked against the method's formal parameter and the return type of the method must be checked against the message's expected type.

5. **Visibility and Information Hiding:** Information hiding is made explicit by requiring that every method and instance variable in a class have a particular level of visibility—Public, Protected or Private—with regard to its subclasses and client classes.

   A public variable or method is visible to any client and subclass of the class. The public methods of a class define the interface of the class to the outside world.

   A protected variable or method is visible only to a subclass of the class. This provides subclasses with direct access to the class is protected instance variables and methods.

   A private variable or method is visible to the current class, but not to its subclasses or its clients.

6. **Interfaces:** An interface encapsulates a collection of constants and abstract method signatures. An interface may not include either variable, constructors or non abstract methods.

   Syntactically an interface declaration looks like an abstract class definition, except that the word interface replaces the word class. The main difference between an interface and an abstract class is that all the methods in an interface must be abstract; only constants may be concretely declared there. However, in an abstract class, object can be declared and some methods may be fully implemented. Because it is not a class, an interface does not have a constructor, but an abstract class does.

7. **Static and Dynamic Binding:** Dynamic binding of messages to methods in an inheritance hierarchy is an essential part of object-oriented programming. It is a question whether all binding of messages to methods is dynamic. The alternative is to allow the user to specify whether a specific binding is to be dynamic of static. The static binding are faster than dynamic. So static binding has advantage over dynamic binding.

10.5.5. Role of Object-oriented Programming in C+ +

C++ supports for object-oriented programming. C++ classes, as they are used to support abstract data type. The whole collection of details of C++ classes, inheritance and dynamic binding is large and complex. We discuss only some important issues among them.

(*i*) **Basic characteristics:** C++ is designed from 'C'. It retains the type system of C and adds classes to it. Therefore, C++ has both traditional imperative language types and the class structure of an object-oriented language. This makes it a hybrid language, supporting both procedural and object-oriented programming.

The objects of C++ can be statically allocated by the compiler, stack dynamically allocated or head allocated using the new operator and deallocation is done through delete operator. All C++ classes include one constructor method to initialize the data members of the new object. C++ supports constructor that calls implicitly when an object is created and a destructor method, which is also implicitly called to destruct a object.

(*ii*) **Inheritance:** A C++ class can derive the features from its parent class. By inheritance a derived class can access the features of there parent class. The data and functions defined in the classes are known as data member and member functions. Some or all of the data members and member functions of the base class may be inherited by the derived class, which can modify or reuse the data. Class members may be private, protected or public. Private members are accessible only by member functions and friends of the class. Public members are accessible by any functions. Protected members are like private members, except in derived classes, whose access is described below. The syntactic form of a derived class is

```
Class derived : Visibility mode    Base class
{
    || data members and member function declarations
};
```

Visibility mode can be either public or private. Private members of a base class are inherited by a derived class, but they are not visible to the members of that derived class and are therefore of no use there C++ supports single, multiple, multilevel, hybrid inheritance. C++ provides multiple inheritance by allowing more than one class to be named as the parent of a new class. For example,

```
Class X
    {
    // ... declaration ...
    };
Class Y
    {
    // ... declaration ...
    };
Class 2 : Public C, Public Y
    {
    // statements
    };
```

Here class Z inherits all of the members of both X and Y. If both X and Y happen to include members with the same name, they can be unambiguously referenced in objects of class Z by using the scope resolution operation.

(*iii*) **Dynamic binding:** C++ supports dynamic binding. In C++, a pointer or reference variable that has the type of a base class can be used to point to objects of any class derived from that base class, making it a polymorphic variables. Dynamic binding is one of the powerful features of C++. This requires the use of pointers to objects. Member functions that must be dynamically bound must be declared to the virtual function by preceding their headers with the reserved word virtual, which can only appear in a class body. When we use the same function name is both the base and derived classes, the function in a base class is declared as virtual using the keyword virtual preceding its normal declaration. When a function is made virtual, C++ determines which function to use at runtime based on the type of object pointed to by the base pointer, rather than the type of the pointer. Thus, by making the base pointer to point to different object, we can execute different versions of the virtual function.

Program given below illustrate the use of virtual function in C++.

```
# include <iostream .h>
Class Base
    { Public:
        void display( )
    {
        cont << "Display base class";
    }
Virtual void show( )
    {
    cont << "Show Base class";
    }
};
Class Derived : Public Base
{
Public:
    Void display( )
    {
        cont << "Display Derived class";
    void show( )
    {
        cont << "Show Derived class";
    }
};
void main ( )
{
    Base      B;
    Derived   D;
    Base      *bptr;
cont << "bptr point to Base";
bptr = &B;
bptr → display ( );
bptr → Show ( );
cont << "bptr points to derived";
    bptr = & D
    bptr → display ( );
    bptr → show ( );
}
```

The output of the program would be

bptr points to Base
Display Base class
Show Base class
bptr points to derived
Display Base class
Show Derived class

Here when bptr is made to point to the object D. The statement

bptr → display ( );]

calls only the function associated with the Base whereas the statement

bptr → Show ( );

calls the derived version of show ( ). This is because the function display ( ) has not been made virtual in the Base class.

Dynamic binding allows the code that uses members to be written before all or even any of the version of member function are written. New derived classes could be added years later, without requiring any change to the code that uses such dynamically bound members. This is a powerful features of object-oriented languages.

10.5.6. Role of Object-oriented Programming in Java

Java is a mixed language containing both primitive data types, such as int and objects. Java user copy semantics for primitive data types and reference semantics for objects. All methods must exist as part of some class and are virtual by defualt. Java benefit by not trying to remain totally backward compatible with C, unlike C++, Java uses automatic garbage collection, which greatly simplifies the task of memory management for the programmer.

(*i*) **Basic Characteristics:** Java does not use objects exclusively. However, in Java only values of the primitive scaler types (Boolean character and numeric types) are not objects.

Java has no enumeration or record types, and its arrays are objects. The reason to have non-objects is efficiency. Java is a statically typed, single inheritance object-oriented language. Java has direct support for:

- Inner classes
- Public, protected and private visibility of both variables and methods.
- Abstract classes
- Interfaces
- Templates
- Run-time type identification
- Reflection

All Java objects are explicit heap dynamic. Most are allocated with the new operator, but there is no explicit deallocation operator. Garbage collection is used for storage reclamation.

(*ii*) **Inheritance:** C++ supports several type of Inheritance. But Java suports only single inheritance. However, it includes a kind of virtual class, called an interface, which provides a version of multiple inheritance. An interface definition is similar to a class definition, except it can contain only named constant and method declaration. It has no definitions. Therefore, an interface is no more than its names indicates—it defines only the specification of a class. The interface is used to define a class that inherits both some of the methods and variables from its parent class, and also implements a parent interface. Inheritance involves Java applets. Applets are programs that are interpreted by a world-wide web browser after being downloaded from a web server. When applet is used to implement animation, it is after defined to run in its own thread of control. This concurrency is supported by a predefined class named thread. However, an applet class being designed to use concurrency cannot inherit from both Applet and Thread. Java includes a predefined interface named Runnable that supplies the interface to one of the methods of thread.

In Java, a method can be defined to be final, which means that it cannot be overriden in any descendant class. When the final reserved word is specified on a class definition, it means the class cannot be the parent of any subclass.

(*iii*) **Encapsulation and dynamic binding:** There are two types of encapsulation constructs, classes and packages. A package is a logical, rather than a physical, encapsulation. Any class definition can specify that it belongs in a particular package. A package creates a new name space. Any method or variable that does not include an access modifier called package scope. The methods and variable that are not declared private are visible throughout the package in which they are declared. Package scope is an alternative to the friends of C++, which are meant to provide access to private methods and instance variables in a class to other specified methods or classes. In Java, when there are non-public methods or variables that we want to make visible to other classes, we define them to be protected. All non-private variables and methods of all of the classes in a package are friends.

In C++, a method is defined to be virtual to allow dynamic binding. In java, all method calls are dynamically bound unless the called method has been defined to be final, in which case it cannot be overridden and all bindings are static.

The design of Java is similar to C++ but differs from several significiant ways. Both support object-oriented programming but differs as. In keeping with its consistent adherence to object-oriented principles, as in its lack of functions, Java does not allow parentless classes. It also use dynamic binding to bind method calls to method definitions. Access control for the contents of a class definitions are rather simple than access controls of C++.

10.6. FUNCTIONAL PROGRAMMING LANGUAGES

Functional programming emerged as a distinct paradigm in the early 1960s. The functional programming paradigm, which is based on mathematical functions, is the design basic for one of the most important nonimperative styles of languages. This style of programming is supported by functional, or applicative, programming languages.

Its creation was motivated by the needs of researchers in artificial intelligence and its subfields symbolic computation, theorem proving, rule—based systems and natural language processing.

The original functional language was LISP, but it soon acquired some important imperative features that increased its execution efficiency. Scheme is a small, static scoped dialect of LISP. COMMON LISP is an amalgam of several early 1980s dialects of LISP. The LISP language is primarily for symbolic data processing. It has been used for symbolic calculations in differential and integral calculus, game playing, mathematical logic and other fields of artificial intelligence. The essential feature of functional programming is that a computation is viewed as a mathematical-function mapping inputs to outputs. Unlike imperative programming, there is no notion of state and therefore no need for an assignment statement. Thus, the effect of a loop is achieved via recursion, since there is no way to increment or decrement the value of a variable in the state, since there are no variables. Functional programming is viewed as a more reliable paradigm for software design.

10.6.1. Mathematical Functions and the Lambda Calculus

A mathematical function is a mapping of members of one set, called the domain set, to another set, called the range set. A function definition specifies the domain and range set, either explicitly or implicitly, along with the mapping.

Consider a typical mathematical function such as the square of a number is defined as:

Square $(n) = n * n$.

This definition gives the name of the function, followed by its arguments in parentleses, followed by an expression that defines the meaning of the function. Square is a function that maps from the set of real numbers R (its domain) to the set of real numbers R (its range), or more formally

Square : $R \rightarrow R$.

A function is said to be total if it is defined for all elements in the domain, and partial otherwise. The square function is total over the set of real numbers. Function application are specified by pairing the function name with a particular element of the domain set. The range element is obtained by evaluating the function mapping expression with the domain element substituted for the occurrences of the parameter. For example, square (2.0) yield the value 4.0. A functional language is pure if there is no concept of an assignment operator or a memory cell; otherwise, it is said to be impure.

However, most functional programming languages retain some form of assignment operator and are, thus, impure. The value of a function such as square depends only on the values of its arguments and not on any previous computation or even the order of the evaluation of its arguments. This property of a functional language is known as referential transparency. A function has referential transparency if its value depends only on the values of its arguments.

The foundation of functional programming is the Lambda Calculus, developed by Alonzo Church (Church, 1941). A lambda expression specifies the parameters and definition of a function, but not its name. For example, consider a lambda expression that defines the function square.

$(\lambda x \,.\, x * x)$

The identifier x is a paremeter used in the function body $x.* x$. Application of a lambda expression to a value is dnoted by:

$((\lambda x \,.\, x * x)2)$ which evaluates to 4.

This example is an illustration of an applied lambda calculus. A pure or uninterpreted lambda calculus, in the following way:

1. Any identifier is a lambda expression.
2. If M and N are lambda expression, then the application of M to N, written (MN), is a lambda expression.

3. An abstraction, written (λ x.M), where x is an identifier and M is a lambda expression, is also a lambda expression.

A simple set of BNF grammar rules for the syntax of the pure lambda calculus can be written as:

Lambda Expression → Variable |(MN)| (λvariable.M)

M → Lambda Expression

N → Lambda Expression

Examples of Lambda expressions are:

x

(λx.x)

((λx.x) (λy.y))

An evaluation of a lambda expression is a sequence P ⇒ Q ⇒ R ⇒ ... in which each expression in the sequence is obtained by the application of a beta-reduction to the previous expression. If P is a lambda expression, then a redux of P is any subexpression obtained by a beta reduction. A lambda expression that does not contain a function application is called a normal form.

An example of an evaluation is:

((λy.((λx.xyz) a))b) ⇒ ((λy.ayz) b) ⇒ abz

In this example, we evaluated the innermost λ expression first; we could have just as easily done the outermost reduction first:

((λy.((λx.xyz) a))b) = ((λx.abz) a) = abz

A functional programming language is essentially an applied lambda calculus with constant values and functions built in. The pure lambda expression (xyx) can just as easily be written (x×x) or (x * x).

Eager evaluation in functional languages refers to the strategy of evaluating all arguments to a function at the time of the call. With eager evaluation, function such as if and cannot be defined without potential runtime errors, as in the scheme function:

(if (= x 0) 1 (/ 1x))

which defines the value of the function to be 1 when x is zero and 1/x otherwise. If all arguments to a function is not evaluated until it is needed.

10.6.2. Different Functional Form or Higher Order Function

A functional form is one that either takes functions as parameters or yields a function as its result, or both. There are three type of functional forms:

(i) Function composition

(ii) Construction

(iii) Apply to all

(i) **Function composition:** A function compositions has two functional parameter and value of the first actual parameter function applied to the result of the second. It means value of first parameter is depends on other parameter. Function compostion is written as an expression, using ° as an operator, as

$h \equiv f \circ g$

for example, if

$f(x) \equiv x * 2$

$g(x) \equiv 5 + x$

then h is defined as

$h(x) \equiv f(g(x))$, or $h(x) \equiv (5 + x) * 2.$

(*ii*) **Construction:** Construction is a functional form that takes a list of parameters. The parameter is passed to each of the functions and collects the results in a list of sequence. A construction is syntactically denoted by placing the functions in brackets, as in $[f, g]$. Consider the following example:

Let $f(x) = x * x * x$

$g(x) = 4 * x$

$h(x) = x/2$

then

$[f, g, h]$ (2) yields (8, 8, 1)

(*iii*) **Apply to all:** Apply to all is functional form that takes a single function as a parameter. If a list of arguments is applied, apply to all applies its functional parameter to each of the values in the list argument and collects the result in a list or sequence.

Let $f(x) = x * x * x$

then

$\alpha(f, (2, 3, 4))$ fields (8, 27, 64)

There are many other functional forms also.

10.6.3 Basics of Functional Programming Languages

The main issues of a functional programming language is to use of mathematical functions to the greatest extent possible. This approach is different from the imperative language, in which expression is evaluated and their result is stored in a memory location which is represented as a variable in program. This will result low level programming methodology. In an assembly language, we will store the temporary results.

For example

$(a + b) * (c - d)$

The value of $(a + b)$ is computed first. This value must be stored while $(c - d)$ is evaluated. The compiler handles the storage of tempory results of expression evaluation in high level languages.

A purely functional programming language does not use variables or assignment statements., This frees the programmer from concerns about the memory cells of the computer on which the program is executed. Repetition must be done by recussion rather than by repetition. Without variables, iterative construct are not possible and the execution of purely functional program has no state in the sense of operational and denotational semantics (operational & denotational semantics are discussed in chapter-3). The execution of a function always produces the same result when given the same parameters. It is called referential transparency. A functional language provides a set of primitive functions, a set of functional forms to construct complex functions from those primitive functions. The functional languages are often implemented with interpreters and they can also be compiled. A well defined functional languages requires only a small number of primitive functions.

10.6.4. Overview of Functional Programming Language LISP

LISP was the first functional programming language and most widely used. There are other functional programming languages also. LISP no longer represents the latest design concept for functional language in last 30 years. In addition, all LISP dialect include imperative language features, such as imperative-style variables assignment statement and iteration. In this section, we will study the fundamental concepts of functional programming language LISP.

10.6.4.1. LISP data type and structures

There are two types of data objects in the original LISP

(*i*) Atoms

(*ii*) LISTS

(*i*) **Atoms:** Atoms are like identifiers used in imperative languages. Atoms are the symbols of LISP. Numeric constants are also considered atoms.

(*ii*) **LISTS:** LISP used lists as its data structure because they were thought to be an essential part of list processing. However, use rarely requires the operations like insertion and deletion. Lists are specified by delimiting their elements with in parentheses. The elements of simple lists are restricted to atoms, as in

(X Y Z)

Nested list structures are also specified by parentheses like

((XYZ) (ZE) (cd))

is a list of the elements.

Lists are usually stored as single linked list structures in which each node has two pointers and represents an element. A node for an atom has its first pointer pointing to some representation of the atom, such as its symbol or numeric value. The internal representation of (XYZ) is shown as in Fig. 10.4.

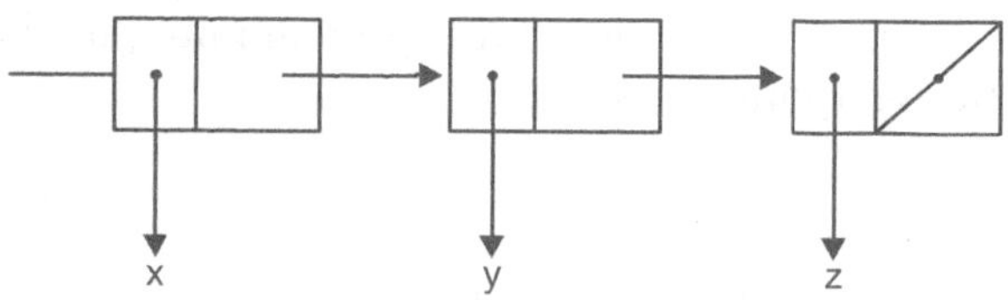

Fig 10.4. Internal Representation of (x y z).

10.6.4.2. The LISP interpreter

The notation for LISP programs that would be close to FORTRAN with additions when necessary. This notation was called meta notation or M-notation. McCarthy thought that the processing of symbolic lists was a more natural model of computation than Turing machines. One of the common requirements of the study of computation is that one must be able to prove certain computability characteristics of the whole class of whatever model of computation is being used.

The requirement for the universal function of LISP was a rotation that allowed functions to be expressed in the some way data was expressed. Functions calls were specified in a prefix list form called cambridge Polish, as shown below:

(Function_Name argument 1 argument 2 .... argument n)

For example, if * is a function that takes no numeric parameters,

(* 64) evaluates to 24.

Binding of function to names could be referenced by other functions and by themselves. This name binding was specified by a list consisting of the function name and a list containing the lambda expression, as in

(function-name (LAMBDA (arg 1 ... arg n) expression))

Nameless functions are sometimes useful in functional programming. LISP functions specified in this new rotation were called S-expression, for symbolic expression. Eventually, all LISP structures, both data and code, were called S-expressions. An S-expression can be either a list or an atom. A universal function that could evaluate any other functions. This function was named EVAL and was itself in the form of an expression. There were several important results of this quick, easy and unexpected implementation. First, all early LISP systems copied EVAL and were therefore interpretive. Second, the definition of M-notation, which was the planned programming notation for LISP, was never completed or implemented, so s-expression became LISP's only notation. Another feature of early LISP systems that was apparently accidental was the use of dynamic scoping. Functions were evaluated in the environments of their callers. Dynamic scoping was used for most dialects of LISP before 1975.

10.6.5. Overview of Scheme

Over the years a number of variants of LISP were developed, today only two major variants remain in widespread use: Common LISP and scheme. Scheme is discussed in this section and common LISP will be discussed in 10.6.6.

When viewed as a pure functional language, our scheme subset has no assignment statement. Instead programs are written as (recursive) functions on input values which produce output values; the input values themselves are not changed. In this sense scheme notation is much closer to mathematics than are the imperative and object-oriented programming languages like C and Java.

Without an assignment statement, our scheme subset makes heavy use of recursive functions for repetiton, Instead of the while statement that we find in imperative language. As a small language with simple syntax and semantics, scheme is well-suited to educational application, such as courses in functional programming and also general introductions to programming.

10.6.5.1. Expressions

Expression in scheme are constructed in cambridge prefix notation, in which expressions are surrounded by parentheses and the operator or function precedes its operands, as in the example:

Expression	**Value**
54	54
(* 5, 4)	20
(+ 5, 7, 9)	21

(– 6, 7)	–1
(– 15, 7, 2)	6
(– 24 (* 4 3))	12
(+ (* 5 4) (–6 2))	24

Suppose we have a function that has two parameters, an atom and a list, whose purpose is to determine whether the given atom is in the given list. Neither the atom nor the list should be evaluated, they are literal data to be examined. To avoid evaluating a parameter, it is first given as a parameter to the primitive function QUOTE, which simply returns it without change. The following example illustrate QUOTE.

(QUOTE A) returns A

(QUOTE (XYZ)) returns (xyz)

10.6.5.2. LISTS

There are two primitive list selectors in scheme:

(*i*) CAR

(*ii*) CDR

The CAR function returns the first element of a given list the following example illustrate CAR:

(CAR' (ABC)) returns A

(CAR evens) returns 2

(CAR' (6, 8)) returns 6

(CAR' (8)) returns 8

(CAR' ( )) is an error

The CDR function returns the remainder of a given list after its CAR is removed:

(CDR' (ABC)) returns (BC)

(CDR evens) returns (2, 4, 6, 8)

(CDR' (6, 8)) returns (8)

(CDR' (CDR'A)) is an error

The names of the CAR and CDR functions are peculiar at best. The 704 also included two machine instructions, named CAR (Contents of address register) and CDR (contents of decrement register), that extracted the associated fields.

CONS is the primitive list constructor. It builds a list from its two agruments, the first of which can be either an atom or a list; the second is usually a list.

(CONS 'A' ( )) returns (A)

(CONS 8 ( )) return (8)

(CONS 4 (CONS 6(CONS 8 ( )))) returns (4 6 8)

(CONS 4 (CONS 6 ((CONS 8 9))) returns (4 6 8 9)

Notice that the last example created a dotted list, since the second argument of the innermost CONS is not a List.

The result of several CONS operations are:

(CONS 'A' ())

(A)

(CONS 'A' (B C))

(ABC)

(CONS '()' (AB))

(() AB)

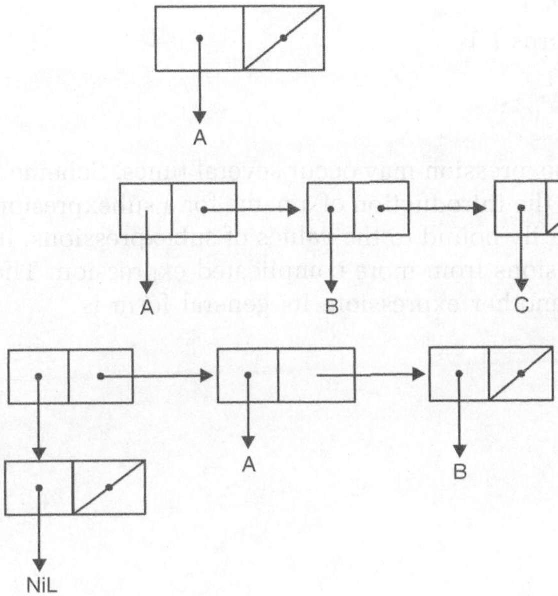

Fig 10.5. The Result of Several CONS Operations.

Three important predicate functions among scheme's primitive function are EQ? Null? and LIST?

The EQ? functions takes two symbolic parameters. It returns # T if both parameters are atoms and the two are the same; otherwise, it returns ( ).

Consider the following example

(EQ? 5 5) returns # T

(EQ? 5 1) returns ( )

(EQ? 'A' (AB)) returns ( )

(EQ? '(1 2 3)' (1 (2 3))); returns ( )

(EQ? '( )' ( )) returns # T

(EQ? '(AB)' (AB)) returns ( ) or # T

The Last case indicates, the result of comparing lists with EQ? is implementation dependent-some field # T and some yield ( ).

The LIST? predicate function returns # T is its single argument is a list and ( ) otherwise, as in the following examples:

(LIST? ′ (1 2)) returns # T

(LIST? ′ (A B)) returns # T

(LIST? ′ ()) returns # T

(LIST? ′ (A)) returns ( )

The Null? function tests its parameter to determine whether it is the empty list and returns # T if it is consider the following examples:

(NULL? ' (A B)) returns ( )

(NULL? ' ()) returns # T

(NULL? ' (1 2 3)) returns ( )

(NULL? 5) returns ( )

10.6.5.3. Let expressions

In defining a function a subexpression may occur several times. Scheme follows the convention in mathematics of allowing the introduction of a name for a subexpresion. Let is a function that allows names to be temporarily bound to the values of subexpressions. It is often used to factor out the common subexpressions from more complicated expression. These names can then be used in the evaluation of another expression. Its general form is

```
( Let
    (
        ( var 1 expr 1)
        (var 2  expr 2)
          ⋮
        (var n  expr n)
    )
    body
)
```

An example of the use of a let function follows:

(Let ((*x* 2) (*y* 3) (+ x y))   ; returns 5

(Let ((Plus +) (*x* 2) (Plus *x* 3))   ; returns 5

A more interesting use of a let function occurs when it appears inside the definition of a function:

```
(define (subset y x alist))
    ( if (null? alist) ' ( )
        (let ( ( head ( car alist )) ( tail (cdr alist)))
            (if ( equal? x head)
                (cons y (subst y x tail))
                    (cons head (subset y x tail))
) ) ) )
```

As in mathematics, a let function merely introduces a set of names for common expression. The name are bound to their values only in the body of the let function.

10.6.5.4. LAMBDA and DEFINE functions

Lambda: LISP languages use lambda notation in the list form to define functions. For example, the lambda expression list.

(LAMBDA (L) (CAR (CDR L)))

is a function that returns the second element of its given parameter, which must be a list. This function can be applied in the same way that named functions are by placing it in the beginning of a list that contains the actual parameters. For example, we could have

```
((LAMBDA (L) (CAR (CDR L)))' (A B C))
```

which yields B. The scheme functions that are defined as parameters of the lambda expression are not quoted; an example is the parameter L is the call to CDR in the expression above. L is called a bound variable within the lambda expression. A bound variable never changes in the expression after being bound to an actual parameter value at the time the lambda expression is first called for evaluation.

DEFINE FUNCTION: Scheme function are defined using define. Scheme is an applied lambda calculus with the ability to give names to specific lambda definitions. DEFINE serves two fundamental needs of scheme programming, to bind a name to a value and to bind a name to a lambda expression. The former use may sound like DEFINE can be used to create imperative language style variables. However, these name bindings create named constants, not variables.

DEFINE FUNCTION can be used in two different forms.

The simplest form of DEFINE is one used to bind a symbol to the value of an expression.This form is (DEFINE SYMBOL expression).

For example,

```
(DEFINE Pi 3.14159)
(DEFINE two Pi (* 2 Pi))
```

If these two expresions have been typed to the scheme interpreter and then P*i* is typed, the number 3.14159 will be displayed; when two P*i* is typed, 6.28318 will be displayed.

```
(DEFINE x 20)
```

Assigns the value 20 to the variable x and when x is used in expression its value will be considered as 20.

Second form of DEFINE function, is used to bind with a lambda expression to a name. In this case, the lambda expression is abbreviated to remove the word lambda. In this form, DEFINE takes two lists of parameters. The general form of such a DEFINE is

```
( DEFINE (Function_name Parameters)
  body
)
```

Where the parameters are separated by spaces and the body is a sequence of expressions in the form of lists.

When we call to DEFINE binds the name square to the expression that follows it:

```
(DEFINE (square number) (* number number))
```

When the expression used as

```
(Square 5)
```

which displays 25.

Another example consider the Factorial function, which can be defined in scheme as follows:

```
(define (factorial n)
(if (< n 1) 1 (* n ( factorial (–n 1)))
```

For example the function application (factorial 4) evaluates to 24 using the above definition in the following way:

```
(factorial 4)  = (* 4 (factorial 3))
               = (* 4 (* 3 (factorial 2)))
               = (* 4 (* 3 (* 2 (factorial 1))))
               = (* 4 (* 3 (* 2 (* 1(factorial 0)))))
               = (* 4 (* 3 (* 2 (* 1 1))))
               = (* 4 (* 3 (* 2 1)))
               = (* 4 (* 3 2))
               = (* 4 6)
               = 24
```

10.6.5.5. Semantics of COND

The scheme used multiple selector using COND. COND is a slightly generalized version of the mathematical conditional expression; it allows more than one predicate to be true at the same time. Because different mathematical conditional expression have different number of parameters, COND does not require a fixed number of actual parameters. Each parameter to COND is a pair of expression in which the first is a predicate.

The general form of COND is

```
( COND
    (Predicate 1 expression {expression})
    (Predicate 2 expression {expression})
    ...
    (Predicate n expression {expression})
    (ELSE expression {expression})
)
```

In some implementations, ELSE is optional.

The predicates of the parameters are evaluated one at a time, in order from the first, until one evaluates to #T. The expression that follow the first predicate that is found to be # T are then evaluated, and the value of the cost is returned as the value of COND. The atom # *T* could be used as a constant predicate in a COND, in which case # T's expressions are always evaluated and the value of the Last is returned as COND's value.

If no parameter to COND has a predicate that evaluates to # T, COND returns ( ).

10.6.6 COMMON LISP

COMMON LISP combine the features of several early dialects of LISP, including scheme, into a single language. It is quite large and complex language. Its syntax, primitive functions and fundamental nature comes from the LISP. It supports both dynamic and static scoping. By default scoping for variable is static, but by declaring a variable to be "Special", that variable becomes dynamically scoped.

The main features of COMMON LISP are:

1. A large number of data type and structures including records, arrays, complex numbers and strings.
2. Its input and output operations are powerful.
3. It uses a form of packages for modularizing collections of functions and data.
4. Providing access control.
5. It uses SET!, SET-CAR! and SET CDR! functions of scheme.
6. It uses function named PROG that allows sequence of statements, commonly found in imperative languages.

   ```
   ( PROG (Local variables)
   expression - 1
   ...
   expression - 4
   )
   ```
7. USES go to transfer control to a label within the scope of PROG.
8. USES RETURN to exit from PROG.
9. SETQ is a common LISP function that corresponds to Scheme's SET ! and DEFUN is its version of DEFINE.

Scheme and COMMON LISP are opposites. Scheme is for smaller and somewhat cleaner, in part because of its exclusive use of static scoping. COMMON LISP on the other hand is a commercial language and has succeeded in being a widely used language for AI applications. Scheme is used in college courses on functional programming. It is mostly studied as a functional language because of its relatively small size. An important design consideration of COMMON LISP that caused it to be a very large language is the desire to make it compatible with several earlier dialects of LISP.

10.7. LOGICAL PROGRAMMING LANGUAGE

Logic programming or declarative programming emerged as a distinct paradigm in the 1970s. It is different from other paradigms because it requires the programmer to declare the goals of the computation, rather than the detailed algorithm by which these goals can be achieved. The goals are expressed as a collection of assertions, or rules about the outcomes and constraints of the computation. For this reason, logic programming is sometimes called rule-based programming. The approach is to express programs in a form of symbolic logic and use a logical interference process to produce result. Logic programs are declarative rather than procedural, which mean that only the specifications of the desired results are stated rather than detailed procedures for producing them.

The syntax of logic programming languages is different from that of the imperative and functional language. The semantics of logic programs also bears little resemblance to that of imperative language. Programming that uses a form of symbolic logic as a programming language is often called logic programming and language based on symbolic logic are called logic programming language.

Applications of declarative programming fall into two major domains artificial intelligence and database information retrieval. Across the artificial intelligence area, Prolog has been influential. Some subfields of artificial intelligence enjoy the use of other declarative languages, as in the use of MYCIN for modelling expert systems.

In the data base area, the Structured Query Language (SQL) has been very popular.

Two interesting and distinguishing features of logic programs are non-determinism and backtracking. A nondeterministic logic program may find several solutions to a problem rather than just one, as would be the norm in other programming domains. Further, the backtracking mechanism which enables nondeterminism is built into prolog interpreter, and therefore is implicit in all prolog programs.

10.7.1. LOGIC and Predicate Calculus

A logic program expresses the specifications for problem solutions using expressions in mathematical logic. This style enolved out of the needs of researches in natural language processing and automatic theorem proving. Conventional programming languages are not particularly well suited to these researcher's needs. However, writing down the specification of a theorem or a grammar as a formal logical expression provides an effective vechicle to study the process of theorem proving and natural language analysis in an experimental laboratory setting.

Proposition: A proposition can be thought of as a logical statement that may or may not be true. It consists of objects and the relationships of objects to each other. Formal logic was developed to provide a method for describing propositions, with the goal of allowing those formally stated propositions to be checked for validity.

Symbolic logic: Symbolic logic can be used for the three basic needs of formal logic to express propositions, to express the relationships between propositions and to describe how new propositions can be inferred from other proposition that are assumed to be true.

Predicate Calculus: The particular form of symbolic logic that is used for logic programming is called predicate calculus.

10.7.2. Horn Clauses

A Horn Clause has a head *h*, which is a predicate, and a body, which is a list of predicates $P_1, P_2,...P_n$.

Horn clause are written in the following style:

$$h \leftarrow P_1, P_2,...P_n$$

This means that *h* is true only if P_1, P_2 ... and P_n are simultaneously true.

Consider the following example:

Suppose we want to capture the idea that it is showing in some city C only if there is precipitation in city C and the temperature in city C is freezing. We can write this as the following Horn Clause:

Snowing (C) $\leftarrow$ Precipitation (C), freezing (C)

The above Horn Clause can be written equivalently as the predicate:

Precipitation (C) $\wedge$ freezing (C) $\supset$ Snowing (C)

Any Horn Clause can be written equivalently as a predicate. Unfortunately, the converse is not true; not all predicate can be translated into Horn Clauses.

A six step procedure translates a predicate P into a Horn Clause.

1. Eliminate implication from P, using the implication property.
2. Move negation inward in P, using the deMorgan and quantification properties, so that only individual terms are negated.
3. Eliminate existential quantifiers from P, using a technique called Skolemization.
4. Move all universal quantifiers to the beginning of P; as long as there are no naming conflicts, this step does not change the meaning of P.
5. Use the distributive, associative, and commutative properties to convert P to conjunctive normal form.
6. Convert the embedded disjunctions to implications, using the implication property. If each of these implication has a single term on its right, then each can be rewritten as a series of Horn clauses equivalent to P.

10.7.3. Propositions

The objects in logic programming propositions are represented by simple terms, which are either constants or variables. A constant is a symbol that represents an object. A variable is a symbol that can represent different objects at different times, although in a sense that is far closer to mathematics than the variables in an imperative programming language.

The simplest propositions, which are called atomic propositions, consists of compound terms. A compound term is one element of a mathematical relation, written in a form that has the appearance of mathematical function notation. A compound term is composed of two parts: a functor, which is the function symbol that names the relation and an ordered list of parameters. A compound term with a single parameter is a 1-tuple; one with two parameters is a 2-tuple, and so forth.

Propositions can be stated in two modes: One in which the propositions is defined to be true, and one in which the truth of the proposition is something that is to be determined. In other words, propositions can be stated to be facts or queries. Compound propositions have two or more atomic propositions, which are connected by logical connectors, or operator, in the same way compound logic expressions are constructed in imperative languages. The name, symbols and meaning of the predicate calculus logical connectors are as follows:

Name	Symbol	Example	Meaning
Negation	$\neg$	$\neg$ a	not a
Conjunction	$\cap$	$a \cap b$	a and b
disjunction	$\cup$	$a \cup b$	a or b
equivalence	$\equiv$	$a \equiv b$	a is equivalent to b
implication	$\supset$	$a \supset b$	a implies b
	$\subset$	$a \subset b$	b implies a

The operation $\neg$ has the highest precedence. The operator $\cap$, $\cup$, and $\equiv$ all have precedence higher than $\supset$ and $\subset$.

10.7.4. Clausal Form

The problem with the predicate calculus is that there are too many different ways of stating proposition that have the same meaning. It provides redundancy. In a computerized system, it is a serious problem clausal form is a standard and simple form of propositions. A proposition in claused form has the following general syntax:

$$X_1 \cup X_2 \cup \ldots \cup X_n < Y_1 \cap Y_2 \ldots \cap Y_m$$

in which the X_s and Y_s are terms. The meaning of this clausal form proposition is as follows: If all of the X_s are true, then at least one y is true. The main characterstics of clausal form are:

- Existential quantifier are not required.
- Universal quantifier are implicit in the use of variables in the atomic propositions.
- No operator other than conjunction and disjunction are required.

The right side of a clausal form proposition is called the antecedent. The left side is called the consequent because it is the consequence of the truth of the antecedent.

10.7.5. Resolution and Unification

Making a single inference form a pair of Horn clauses is called resolution. It allows inferred proposition to be computed from given propositions, thus providing a method with potential application to automatic theorem proving.

When applied to Horn clauses, resolution says that if h is the head of a Horn clause and it matches with one of the terms of another Horn clause, then that term can be replaced by h.

In other words, if we have the clauses

$h \leftarrow$ terms

$t \leftarrow t_1, h, t_2$

then we can resolve the second clause to $t \leftarrow t_1$, terms, t_2. For instance, consider the following clauses:

Speaks (Mary, English)

talks with (X, Y) $\leftarrow$ speaks (X, L), speaks (Y, L), X $\neq$ Y.

The first of these is a Horn clause with an empty list of terms, so it is unconditionally true, thus, resolution allows us to reduce the following:

talks with (Mary, Y) $\leftarrow$ speaks (Mary, English), speaks (y, English), Mary $\neq$ Y.

with the assumption that the variables X and L are assigned the values "Mary" and "English" in the second rule. Resolutions thus helps to arrive at conclusions.

The assignment of variables to values during resolution is called instantiation. Unification is a pattern matching process that determines what particular instantiations can be made to variables while making a series of simultaneous resolutions. Unification is recursive, so it eventually finds all possiple instantiations for which resolutions can be made.

10.7.6. Overview of Logic Programming in PROLOG

The development of prolog and other research efforts in logic programming received limited attention outside of Edinburgh and Marseille until the announcement in 1981 that the Japanese government was launching a large research project called the fifth generation computing systems. One of the primary objectives of the project was to develop intelligent machines, and prolog was chosen as the basic for this effort.

Prolog is the principal language used in logic programming. The development of Prolog is based on two powerful principles called resolution and Unification. Applications of logic programming are widespread in the areas of natural language processing, automatic reasoning and theorem proving, database search and expert systems. There are now a number of diferent dialects of Prolog. These can be grouped into several categories. The syntactic forms of these are some-what different.

10.7.7. Different Prolog Program Elements

There are different types of prolog programming elements.

Term: Prolog programs are made from terms, which can be constants, variables, or structures. A constant is either an atom or an integer. Atoms are the symbolic values of Prolog and are similar to their counter parts in LISP. A variable is a series of letters (A - Z, a - z,...) that must begin with a capital letter (Like Bob). Variables are not bound types by declaration. The binding of a value, and thus a type, to a variable is called an instantiation. Instantiation occurs only in the resolution process. A variable that has not been assigned a value is called Uninstantiated.

A structure is a predicate with zero or more arguments, written in functional notation. For example, the following are Prolog structures.

n (Lion)

Speaks (Who, Indian)

*n*P (A, B)

The number of arguments is called the structure's arity.

The general form of structure is

Functor (Parameter List).

The functor is any atom and is used to identify the structure.

Facts and Rules: Prolog facts and rules are realization of the formal idea of Horn Clauses. A fact is a term followed by a period (.) and is similar to a Horn Clause without a right hand side; a variable cannot be a fact. A rule is a term followed by:- and a series of terms separated by commas and ended by a period (.). A rule has the following form :

term:- $term_1$, $term_2$, ..., $term_n$

This is equivalent to the Horn Clause:

term $\leftarrow$ $term_1$, $term_2$, ..., $term_n$.

Rules are ineterpreted as only if assertions with the comma playing the role of the logical and operator. The above form asserts that term is true only if $term_1$, $term_2$, ... $term_n$ are simultanously true. A Prolog program is a series of facts and rules.

A Prolog rule succeeds when there are instantiations of its variables for which all of the terms on the right of the :– operator simultaneously succeed for those assignments. Otherwise, the rule is said to fail. A fact always succeeds; that is, it is universally true.

Goal Statements or Queries: Logical propositions are used to describe both known facts and rules that describe logical relationships among facts. These statements are the basic for the theorem proving model. The theorem is in the form of a proposition that we want the system to either prove or disprove. In Prolog, these propositions are called Goals or Queries. The syntactic form of Prolog goal statements is identical to that of headless Horn Clauses. For example, we could have

man (fred).

To which the system will respond either Yes or No. The answer yes means that the system has proved the goal was true under the given database of facts and relationships. The answer no means that either the goal was proved false or the system was simply unable to error or disprove it.

When variables are present, the system not only asserts the validity of the goal but also identifies the instantiations of the variables that make the goal true. For example,

father (X, ANIL);

can be asked. The system will then attempt, through unification, to find an instantiaitons of *x* that results in a true value for the goal. Efficient use of Prolog requires that the programmer know precisely what the Prolog system does with his or her program.

When a goal is a compound proposition, each of the facts is called a subgoal. To prove that a goal is true, the inferencing process must find a chain of inference rules and/or facts in the data-base that connect the goal to one or more facts in the database. For example, if X is the goal, either X must be found as a fact in the database or the inferencing process must find a fact P_1 and a sequence of propositions P_2, P_3, P_4, ... P_n such that P.

P_2 :– P_1

P_3 :– P_2

...

Q :– P_n

In some cases, proving a subgoal is called satisfying that subgoal. Consider the following avery:

man (bob).

This goal statement is the simplest kind. It is relatively easy for resolution to determine whether it is true or false. If the database includes the fact

man (bob)

the proof is trivial. If, however, the database contains the following fact and inference rule,

father (bob).

man (X) :– father (X).

Prolog would be required to find these two statements and use them to infer the truth of the goal.

These are two approaches to attempting to match a given goal to a fact in the database. The system can begin with facts and rules of the database and attempt to find a sequence of matches that lead to the goal. This approach is called bottom-up resolution, or forward chaining. The alternative is to begin with the goal and attempt to find a sequence of matching propositions that lead to some set of original facts in the database. This approach is called top-down resolution, or backward chaining.

LISTS: The basic data structure in Prolog Programming is the list, which is written as a series of terms separated by commas and enclosed in brackets [and]. Sentences are usually represented as lists of atoms, as in the following example:

[apple, grape, Mango, Orange]

The empty list is denoted by [], while a don't care entry in a list is represented by an underscore (-). The following denote lists of one, two, and three elements, respectively.

[_, _, Z]

The head (first) element of a list is distinguished from its remaining elements by a vertical bar. Thus,

[Head / Tail]

denotes a list whose first element is Head and whose remainig elements from the list [Tail], often termed the tail of the list.

Here is a simple prolog function that defines the concatenation of two lists together to form one. The first two arguments for this function represent the two lists being concatenated, and the third represents the result.

```
append ([], A, A)
append ([Head / Tail], Y, [Head / Z]):– append (Tail, Y, Z).
```

This rather odd looking recursive definition has two parts. The "base case" is defined by the first line, which simply offirms that the empty list concatenated with any other list returns that other list as the result. The recursive case, defined by the second line, says that if Z is the result of concatenating list Tail and Y, then concatenating any new list [Head / Tail] with *y* gives the result [Head / Z].

Here are three more functions with lists that are very useful in Prolog programming. The first two, called prefix and suffix, mean exactly what their names suggest. X is a prefix of Z if there's a *y* which we can append to X to make Z.

The definition of y as a suffix of Z is similar.

```
Prefix (X, Z):– append (X, Y, Z).
Suffix (Y, Z):– append (X, Y, Z)
```

The third useful function defines recursively the notion of membership in a list. X is a member of a list if it is identical to the first element or a member of the list's fail.

```
member (X, [X /_]).
member (X, [–/y]):– member (x, y)
```

10.7.8. Practical Aspects of Prolog

Prolog is not, in practice, an altogether 'Pure' logic programming language. It has some features designed to make programming more efficient and practical. The several prominent features are given below:

Tracing: Prolog has a built-in structure named trace that displays the instantiations of values to variables at each step during the attempt to satisfy a given goal. Trace is used to understand and debug prolog programs. To understand trace, it is best to introduce a different model of the execution of prolog programs, called the tracing model.

For example, consider the predicate factorial defined as follows:

```
factorial (0, 1).
Factorial (N, Result):– n > 0, M is N – 1,
Factorial (M, SubRes), Result is N * SubRes.
```

This predicate defines the factorial function recursively, with the first line defining the base case (0! = 1) and the second the third lines defining the recursive case ($n! = n$ (n – 1)!). We need to introduce the intermediate variable M to force the evaluation of N – 1 before the recursive call.

To trace this function, we can do this:

```
? – trace (factorial / 2)
factorial / 2: Call redo exit fail
Yes
? – factorial (4, X).
call: (7) factorial (4, – G173)
call: (8) factorial (3, – L131)
call: (9) factorial (2, – L144)
call: (10) factorial (1, – L157)
call: (11) factorial (0, – L170)
Exit: (11) factorial (0, 1)
Exit: (10) factorial (1, 1)
Exit: (9) factorial (2, 2)
Exit: (8) factorial (3, 6)
Exit: (7) factorial (4, 24)
X = 24
```

In the first call, the first argument is bound to 4, and the second is bound to an anonymous variable (–G173). This same pattern is repeated for each of the next four recursive calls, until the base case occurs and the second argument –L170 is finally assigned to value 1. Now the recursion unwinds, assigning intermediate values to the anonymous variables and doing the multiplications.

The Cut and Negation: To allow the user to control database and subgoal ordering, prolog, in another concession of efficiency, allows some explicit control of backtracking. This is done with the cut operator. It is a special function, which forces the evaluation of a series of subgoals on the right hand side of a rule not to be retried if the right hand side succeeds once. Cut is specified by an exclamation point (!). The cut operator is actually a goal, not an operator. As a goal, it always succeeds immediately, but it cannot be resatisfied through backtracking. Thus, a side effect of the cut is that subgoals to the left in a compound goal also cannot be resatisfied through backtracking.

For example, in the goal.

x, *y*, !, W, Z.

If both *x* and *y* succeed but W fails, the whole goal fails. This goal would be used if it were known that whenever W fails, it is a waste of time to resatisfy *b* or *a*. The purpose of the cut then is to allow the user to make programs more efficient by telling the system when it should not attempt to resatisfy subgoals that presumably could not result in a complete proof. Cut is particularly useful in a programming strategy in Prolog called generate and test.

One problem with Prolog is its difficulty with negation. Consider the following database of two facts and a relationship:

Parent (A, B).

Parent (A, C).

Sibling (X, Y):– (Parent (M, x), Parent (M, y)).

Now, supposed we typed the query

Sibling (X, Y).

Prolog will respond with

X = B

Y = B

Thus prolog "thinks" B is a sibling of himself. This happens because system first instantiates M with A and X with B to make the first subgoal, Parent (M, X), true. If then starts at the beginning of the database again to match the second subgoal, Parent (M, Y) and arrives at the instantiation of M with A and Y with B. Because the two subgoal satisfied independents, with both matching starting at the database's beginning, the response above appears. To avoid this, X must be specified to be a sibling of Y only if they have the same parents and they are not the same. The most exacting method would require adding a fact for every pair of atoms, stating that they were not the same.

Arithmetic operators: The arithmetic operators were functors, so that the sum of 5 and the variable A was formed with

+ (5, A).

The infix operator is can be used to force instantiation of a variable. This operator takes an arithmetic expression as its right operand and a varaible as its left operand. All variables in the expression must already be instantiated, but the left side variable cannot be previously instantiated.

X is Y / 15 + z.

If Y and Z are instantiated but X is not, then this clause will cause X to be instantiated with the value of the expression. When this happens, the clause is satisfied. If either Y and Z is not instantiated or X is instantiated, the clause is not satisfied and no instantiation of X can take place. The semantics of is proposition is considerably different from that of an assignment statement in an imperative language.

The operator not is implemented in Prolog in terms of goal failure. That is, the clause not (P) succeeds when resolution of P fails. Thus, not can be used to define a function in place of the cut. It is important to point out that the not operator does not always act like logical negation.

The assert function: Prolog applications often encounter situations where the program must "update" itself in response to the most recent query. For instance, in a database application, one might want to add a new member to the family tree and let that member play a role in the program is response to later queries. This can be done using the assert function, which essentially allows the program to dynamically after itself by adding new facts and rules to the existing one. Suppose A is the father of B. We would do this by the statement:

? – assert (father (A, B)).

Moreover, the assert function can be added to the body of a function definition add new facts and rules to the database. This kind of activity is important for program that simulate learning in the sense that they can store new knowledge as they interact with the user.

10.7.9. Applications of Logic Programming

There are different applications of logic programming.

1. **Natural Language Processing:** Prolog programs that are effectively BNF grammars which, when executed, will parse sentences in a natural language. Certain kinds of natural language processing can be done with logic programming. In particular, natural language interfaces to computer software system, such as intelligent databases, and other intelligent knowledge-based system can be conveniently done with logic programming. For describing language syntax, forms of logic programming have been found to be equivalent to context free grammars. Using prolog to encode complex grammars in this way is often more cumbersome than helpful. For that reason, Prolog provides a very compact notation that directly mimics the notation of context free grammar rules themselves. This notation is called as definite clause grammar (DCG).
2. **Expert systems:** Expert systems are computer systems designed to emulate human expertise in some particular domain. They consist of a database of facts, an inferencing process, some heuristics about the domain, and some human interface that makes the system learn from the process of being used, so their databases must be capable of growing dynamically. Prolog can and has been used to construct expert systems. It can easily fulfill the basic needs of expert systems, using resolution as the basis for query processing, using its ability to add facts and rules to provide the learning capability, and using its trace facility to inform the user of the reasoning behind a given result. Prolog has the ability to query the user for additions information to the system when it is needed one of the most widely known use of logic programming in expert systems is the expert system construction system known as APES. One of the central problem for the designer of an expert system is dealing with the inevitable inconsistencies and incompleteness of the database.
3. **RDBMS and EDUCATION:** Relational database management systems (RDBMSs) store data in the form of tables. Queries on such database are often stated in relational calculus, which is a from of symbolic logic. The connection between logic programming and RDBMSs should be obvious. Simple tables of information can be described by prolog structures, and relationship between tables can be conveniently and easily described by prolog rules. The retrieval process is inherent in the resolution operation. The goal statements of prolog provide the queries for the RDBMS. Logic programming is thus a natural match to the needs of implementing an RDBMS.

One advantage of using logic programming to implement an RDBMS is that only a single language is required. In a typical RDBMS, a database language includes statements for data definitions, data manipulations and queries, all of which are embedded in a general-purpose programing language, such as COBOL. Another advantage of using logic programming to implement an RDBMS is that deductive capability is built in. Conventional RDBMS cannot deduce anything from a database other than what is explicitly stored in them. The general purpose language like COBOL is used for processing the data and input and output functions. All of these functions can be done in a logic programming language.

In the area of education, there are extensive experiments in teaching children as young as seven how to use the logic programming language micro prolog. Researches claim a number of advantages in teaching prolog to young people. This can help students in learning a variety of subjects, such as solving equation in mathematics and grammars for natural languages.

10.8. COMPARISON BETWEEN PROCEDURAL AND NON-PROCEDURAL LANGUAGES

The difference between Procedural and Non-procedural languages are:

Procedural languages	*Non-procedural Languages*
1. Procedural languages are statement oriented or command driven	1. The nonprocedural languages are fact oriented.
2. In procedural languages we know what is to be done by a program and how the computation is performed means there is a procedure for doing computation.	2. In nonprocedural languages we are only know what is to be done but there is no procedure to tell how these computation are performed.
3. It consists of a series of procedures that executes when called.	3. The non-procedural languages, are based on symbolic logics.
4. These are generally imperative programming language.	4. These are generally declarative programming languages.
5. FORTRAN, PASCAL, C are the examples of procedural languages.	5. Prolog, USP, SQL are examples of non procedural languages.
6. It is more complex than non-procedural languages.	6. It is simpler than procedural languages.
7. It have large no of potential connections between functions and data, if there are may functions and may global data items.	7. There are no such connections present in non-procedural paradigm.
8. It contains textual context or execution sequence.	8. It contains mathematical Logics and propositions.

10.9. DIFFERENCE BETWEEN PROCEDURAL LANGUAGES AND OBJECT ORIENTED PROGRAMMING

The difference between a procedural and Object-Oriented Language is as under:

Procedural Language	*Object-Oriented Languages*
1. Emphasis is on doing things (algorithms).	1. Emphasis is on data rather than procedures.
2. Large programs are divided into smaller programs known as functions.	2. Programs are divided into what are known as objects.
3. Most of the functions share global data.	3. All functions share local data means functions and other data are tied together in the data structure.
4. Data move openly around the system.	4. Data is hidden and cannot be accessed by external functions.
5. Functions transform data from one form to another.	5. Object may communicate with each other through functions.
6. It employs top-down approach in program design.	6. It employs bottom up approach in program design.
7. C, Pascal, FORTRAN and procedural languages.	7. C++ is object oriented language.
8. It is very difficult to define user defined data types.	8. It support user defined data types. For example: Classes used in C++.

10.10. DIFFERENCE BETWEEN 'C' AND 'C++' PROGRAMMING LANGUAGES

C is procedural language that is each statement in the language tells the computer to do somthing C++ is derived from C language. It is a superset of C. C++ known as C with classes C++ is object-oriented language. There are some common facts. Primitive data in C++ are same as in C and C++ expressions are also as C. The difference between C and C++ languages are:

C Language	*C++ Language*
1. C is a procedural language.	**1.** C++ is an object-oriented language.
2. It supports built-in and primitive data types.	**2.** It supports both built in and user defined data types.
3. There are no clases in C.	**3.** It supports classes.
4. No inheritance possible in C.	**4.** Inheritance is possible in C++.
5. In C, Declaration of variable is done at the starting of program.	**5.** In C++, Declaration of variable is done at any point within a block not just at the beginnig.
6. No name spaces are present in C.	**6.** Name spaces are present in C++.
7. The function malloc () and calloc () are used for dynamic memory allocation.	**7.** The function new and delete are used for dyanmic memory allocation.
8. In C, Polymorphism is not possible.	**8.** C++ uses the concept of polymorphism.
9. Operator overloading is not possible in C.	**9.** Operator overloading is possible in C++.
10. Virtual function are not present in C.	**10.** Virtual functions are present in C++.

10.11. COMPARISON OF FUNCTIONAL AND IMPERATIVE LANGUAGES

The Difference between imperative and functional languages are:

Imperative Languages	*Functional Languages*
1. Imperative languages are based directly on the Von Neumann architecture.	**1.** The functional languages are not based on Von Neumann architecture.
2. In imperative languages, programmer is concerned with the management of variables and assignment of values to them.	**2.** In a functional language, the programmer need not be concerned with variables, because memory cells need not be abstracted into the language.
3. Management of variables in imperative language increased the efficiency of execution.	**3.** It decreases the efficiency of execution.
4. The syntax of imperative languages are more complex.	**4.** Functional languages can have a very simple syntactic structure.
5. Concurent execution in the imperative language is difficult to design and use.	**5.** Concurrent execution is easy to design and use.
6. The semantics are difficult to understand.	**6.** The semantics are simple as compared with imperative languages.
7. In imperative language, the programmer must make a static division of the program into its concurrent parts which are them written as tasks.	**7.** Programs in functional languages can be divided into concurrent parts dynamically by the execution system.
8. The example of Imperative languages are C, C++, Ada, Pascal etc.	**8.** The examples of functional languages includes LISP, ML, Scheme etc.

Some Important Terms

- Natural languages faci litate the expression and communication between people.
- Programming languages are notations or symbols that are used for specifying, organizing and reasoning about computations.
- Different type of programming languages are:
  - Imperative Languages
  - Declarative Languages
  - Procedural Languages
  - Non procedural Languages
  - Object-based Languages
  - Block-structured Languages
  - Logical Programming Languages
  - Functional programming Languages
  - Database Languages
- All imperative language include assignment as the central elements.
- Common features of Imperative programming paradign are:
  - Control structures
  - Exception and error handling
  - Input / Output
  - Procedural abstraction
  - Assignment and Expression
  - Library support for data structures
- Procedure-oriented programming basically consists of writing a list of instructions or actions for the computer to follow and organizing these instructions into group known as functions.
- In procedural languages emphasis is on algorithms.
- Data move freely from one function to another in procedural languages.
- Procedural languages follows top-down approach in program design.
- Non-procedural languages are fact oriented.
- Non-procedural languages are also called declarative programming languages.
- Non-procedural languages used in RDBMS, Expert systems, Natural language processing and education.
- The basic control structures in structured programming are:
  - The sequence control
  - The conditional statement
  - While Loop
- A program is structured if the flow of control through the program is evident from the syntactic structure of the program text.

- Hierarchical design of program structures using only the simple control forms of composition, alternation and iteration.
- Structured programming have single-entry single-exit program structure.
- Structure programming avoids the use of goto statements.
- Object-oriented languages must provide support for three key language feature: abstract data types, inheritance and a kind of dynamic binding.
- OOP allows decomposition of a problem into a number of entities called objects.
- Main features of object-oriented programming are:
  - Emphasis is on data rather than procedure.
  - Functions that operate on the data of an object are tied together in the data structures.
  - Programs are divided into what are known as objects.
  - Data is hidden and cannot be accessed by external functions.
  - It follows bottom up approach in program design.
- The term polymorphic means "having many forms".
- Design issues for object-oriented languages:
  - The concept of objects
  - Allocation and Deallocation of objects.
  - Single and Multiple Inheritance.
  - Polymorphism and Type checking.
  - Visibility and Information Hiding.
  - Interfaces
  - Static and Dynamic Binding.
- Dynamic binding is one of the powerful features of C++.
- Java has direct support for:
  - Inner classes
  - Public, Protected and private visibity modes.
  - Abstract classes
  - Interfaces
  - Templates
  - Runtime type identification
  - Reflection
- Functional programming paradigm is based on mathematical functions.
- Functional programming languages are LISP, Scheme and common LISP.
- The LISP language is primarily for symbolic data processing.
- A mathematical function is a mapping of members of one set, called the domain set, to another set, called the range set.
- A function is said to be total if it is defined for all elements in the domain and partial otherwise.
- A functional language is pure if there is no concept of an assignment operator or a memory cell; otherwise it is said to be impure.

- A Lambda expression specifies the parameter and definition of a function, but not its name.
- The foundation of functional programming is the Lambda Calculus, developed by Alorzo Church.
- A functional form is one that either takes functions as parameters or fields a function as its result, or both.
- Three type of functional form are:
  - Function composition
  - Construction
  - Apply to all
- There are two types of data objects in the original LISP.
  - Atoms
  - LISTS
- Two major variants of LISP are
  - Scheme
  - Common LISP
- Expression in scheme are constructed in cambridge prefix notation.
- There are two primitive list selectors in scheme
  - CAR
  - CDR
- Let is a function that allows names to be temporarily bound to the values of subexpression.
- LISP languages use lambda notations in list form to define functions.
- Scheme function are defined using define
- The simplest form of DEFINE is one used to bind a symbol to the value of an expression.
- Second form of DEFINE function is used to bind with a lambda expression to a name.
- COND is a generalized version of the mathematical conditional expressions.
- COMMON LISP combine the features of several early dialects of LISP, including scheme into a single language.
- Logical paradigm requires the programmer to declare the goals of the computation rather than the detailed algorithm by which these goals can be achieved.
- The syntax of logic programming languages is different from that of the imperative and functional language.
- Programming that uses a form of symbolic logic as a programming language is often called logic programming.
- Language based on symbolic logic are called logic programming language.
- A propositon can be throught of as a logical statement that may or may not be true.
- Symbolic logic can be used for the three basic needs of formal logic to express propositions, to express the relationship between propositions.

- The particular form of symbolic logic that is used for logic programming is called predicate calculus.
- Clausal form is a standard and simple form of propositions.
- Making a single inference form a pair of Horn clauses is called resolution.
- Prolog is the principle language used in logic programming.
- Different Prolog program Elements are:
  - Term
  - Facts
  - Rules
  - Goal statements or Queries
  - LISTS
- Practical aspects of prolog are:
  - Tracing
  - The Cut and Negation
  - Arithmetic operators
  - The assert function
- Different application of logic programming are:
  - In Natural language processing
  - In Expert systems
  - In Relational database management systems
  - In Education
- Examples of procedural languages are FORTRAN, PASCAL, and C languages.
- Non-procedural languages are Prolog, USP, SQL.
- Objects-oriented programming like C++ supports user defined data types.
- C is a procedural and C++ is an object-oriented language.
- Main feature of object-oriented programming includes operator overloading, Virtual functions polymorphism, name spaces etc.
- Imperative languages are C, C++, Ada and Pascal.
- Functional language includes LISP, ML, Scheme etc.
- C language supports built in and primitive data types.
- C++ is a superset of 'C' language.

Review Questions

1. Compare 'C' and 'C++' programming languages.
2. Explain the following:
   (*i*) Functional programming language
   (*ii*) Non procedural programming language.

3. What are imperative and non-imperative languages? Explain in detail.
4. Explain structured programming languages in detail?
5. What are object-oriented languages? What are the features of object-oriented programming?
6. Explain design issues for object-oriented languages.
7. Explain Role of object-oriented programming in C++.
8. Explain Role of object-oriented programming in JAVA.
9. Explain mathematical functions and LAMBDA calculus in functional programming.
10. What are the two forms of DEFINE?
11. Describe the semantics of COND and LET.
12. What are the three primary uses of symbolic logic in formal logic?
13. What do you understand by LAMBDA function in LISP? Explain.
14. Using suitable examples explain the use of cut (!) and fail predicates of PROLOG in managing the flow of control.
15. List the difference between a procedural language and object-based language.
16. What do you mean by logical programming languages?
17. What do you mean by procedural language?
18. What are the different sections in a PROLOG program? Discuss their purposes.
19. Write short-note on functional and objects-oriented programming language.
20. Explain Different functional form or higher order function.
21. Explain LISP Data types and structures in detail?
22. Write short notes on:
    (*a*) Scheme
    (*b*) Common LISP
23. Explain semantics of COND statement.
24. Explain following terms:
    (*a*) HORN CLAUSES
    (*b*) LOGIC and PREDICATE CALCULUS
    (*c*) Propositions
    (*d*) Clausal form
    (*e*) Resolution and Unification
25. Explain different prolog program elements.
26. Write short notes on following:
    (*a*) Tracing
    (*b*) LISTS
    (*c*) Goal statements or Queries
    (*d*) Cut and Negation
    (*e*) Assert function.
27. Explain applications of logic programming?
28. Differentiate the following:
    (*a*) Procedural language and Non-procedural languages.
    (*b*) Functional and imperative languages.

❑❑❑

INDEX

D

E

F

G

H

I

J

L

M

N

O

P

R

S

T

U

V

❑❑❑